THE FISH
THAT
CHANGED
AMERICA

THE FISH THAT CHANGED AMERICA

True Stories about the People Who Made
Largemouth Bass Fishing an All-American Sport

By Steve Price

Preface by Kevin VanDam

Skyhorse Publishing

Skyhorse Publishing books may be purchased in bulk at special discounts for sales promotion, corporate gifts, fund-raising, or educational purposes. Special editions can also be created to specifications. For details, contact the Special Sales Department, Skyhorse Publishing, 307 West 36th Street, 11th Floor, New York, NY 10018 or info@skyhorsepublishing.com.

Skyhorse® and Skyhorse Publishing® are registered trademarks of Skyhorse Publishing, Inc.®, a Delaware corporation.

Visit our website at www.skyhorsepublishing.com.

10 9 8 7 6 5 4 3 2 1

Library of Congress Cataloging-in-Publication Data is available on file.

Cover design by: Brian Peterson
Cover photo credit: Steve Price

Print ISBN: 978-1-62914-558-7
Ebook ISBN: 978-1-62914-950-9

Printed in China

For Ann,
who kept me on course
even when the fish were biting

Contents

Foreword

By Slaton L. White

America's fish? No question, it's the largemouth bass. Found from multi-armed impoundments to farm ponds small enough to spit across, the bass is as American as, well, apple pie. The ready availability of this democratic fish is one reason it has become the country's number-one gamefish, but that in itself doesn't fully explain the cult of bass fishing.

There's something else. It's the nature of the largemouth bass. A friend of mine once wrote, "The fish is a brawler, a potbellied thug with no respect for decency or refinement. Ain't that great?" You bet.

When *Field & Stream* was coming to terms with professional bass fishing—slowly, belatedly, reluctantly—I hitched a ride with Steve Price on a bass boat following competitors at the 1999 B.A.S.S. Masters Classic in the Louisiana Delta. On the morning of the second day, we crept behind eventual winner Davey Hite as he worked a series of long weed-beds. For hours, he cast tight against the beds, and I watched in wonder as cast after cast landed exactly where Hite wanted. The show reminded me of legendary pitcher Bob Gibson, who was famous for a ferocious competitive fire as well as murderous control.

That's when I realized those at the top of this game were athletes of the first order. And when you talked to these select few, you realized they were playing a far different game than you were, but if you paid attention, you would come away a better angler.

As an editor at *Field & Stream* I commissioned many bass fishing articles from Steve. He rose above the rest because of his erudition, clarity of expression, and an obvious command of the subject at hand. But most of all, he became a go-to guy because of his great fishing sense. I always felt that if a reader took his tips and techniques to the lake over the weekend he would end up catching more fish. And unlike many self-professed experts of that time, who relied on themselves for their expertise, Steve was willing to talk to a wide range of participants, including tournament pros, lure and line manufacturers, and guides to supplement that knowledge.

As a writer, Steve was at the top of his game, but he wanted more, as I found out over a long meal at, of all places, the Las Vegas Hilton, after a trade show. We were talking about bass fishing articles when he said, "I've done plenty of how-to, and I know it's the bread-and-butter of this business, but I want to do something more."

"What?" I asked.

"The why," he said.

Steve wanted to explore the last frontier of bass fishing—why the fish did what it did, why it hit certain lures at certain times, and why it sometimes swam imperiously away when offered what seemed to be an irresistible morsel.

I wish I could remember more of the conversation; it was one of the most fascinating evenings of my professional life. During our talk he revealed himself to be a true student of the fish and the people who pursued it for a living.

Steve is that rarity in our business; he's an observer. He wants to know what that fish is thinking. When he looks at a watershed he wants to break through that divine divide between water and air to make a connection with the creature that swims beneath the surface.

He looks at the people who populate the special world of bass fishing in the same way. What makes them tick? Why do they cast the way they do, why do they select the lures that they do?

Again, the why. For why we do something is, in the end, infinitely more interesting than the how or where. This inveterate curiosity has led him to this book, an appraisal of the fish that truly changed America. Steve looks at the tackle, the lakes, the boats, and the business of bass fishing. But most of all, he looks at the people, and the fish, that are the heart of this world. And what a world it is.

Slaton L. White
Deputy Editor, *Field & Stream*

Preface

Readers of this book will quickly notice one characteristic common to the majority of personalities described here: catching their first largemouth bass, at whatever age it happened, became a defining moment in their lives. It's something we can all be thankful for today, for, collectively, they turned their defining moments into creating the sport and business of bass fishing we enjoy today.

I understand the passion that drove them, because I caught my first bass at around the age of three, and now, more than forty years later, the fish continues to be the focus of my career. Bass, both largemouth and smallmouth, do that to people. Maybe it's the way they hit a lure, or the way they jump and fight after being hooked. To be sure, there are larger fish in many of our nation's lakes, and they will strike the same artificial lures bass do; often, they live in the very same waters. But none of them act quite the way a bass does.

I can also understand the influences the sport's pioneers have had on following generations, because one of the biggest influences in my fishing career was Virgil Ward, among those profiled here. My very first spinnerbait was Virgil's Bass Buster Lures Beetle Spin, and his television show, *Championship Fishing*, taught me how to use them; today, thanks to those early experiences, spinnerbaits are a major part of my professional bass tournament fishing arsenal.

When I was seven years old, my father took me along on his annual Memorial Day weekend fishing trip to Lake Leelanau in northern Michigan. I caught my first smallmouth on that trip, a 10 ½-inch fish that hit my live nightcrawler. We were just drifting our baits along the bottom because we didn't have a trolling motor to control our boat, nor did we have any type of electronic depth finder, items commonly found on all bass boats today. For us, a trolling motor didn't come until several years later. Then we added a flasher-type depth finder, and still later we finally bought our first real bass boat, a 16 ½-foot Pro Craft.

I fished my first bass tournament with my older brother Randy when I was fourteen. Now, as I write this, I'm preparing for my twenty-fourth season as a full-time bass tournament pro, and even on my days off between events I still want to go bass fishing. Bass do that to people.

Kevin VanDam
Four-Time Bassmaster Classic Champion
Seven-Time Bassmaster Angler of the Year

Introduction

For the past four decades I have enjoyed a front row seat in the evolution of bass fishing as it changed from a quiet pastime into a worldwide, multi-billion dollar sport and industry. As a writer, photographer, and angler I have shared countless hours and days on the water with the best bass fishermen in the world, and been lucky enough to have witnessed and participated in this dramatic change.

Like many of my generation, I had been introduced to bass fishing at an early age, walking the shorelines of small, rural ponds with my grandfather and casting plugs I had swiped from his tackle box. My father had made me a four-foot steel rod and attached a Pflueger reel spooled with black Dacron line, and the first two lures I had swiped were a green Arbogast Jitterbug and a green/yellow Hawaiian Wiggler.

I never caught a lot of bass, but I did catch enough to keep casting for more of them. I was lucky enough, too, to have decided by age 15 to become an outdoor writer and photographer specializing in fishing, hunting, camping, and wildlife stories. As it happened, my subsequent career in this field began just as bass fishing started its rocket ship rise in popularity, and living in southeast Texas not far from lakes like Toledo Bend, Sam Rayburn, and Livingston, and later in Birmingham within easy driving distance of the famous Tennessee River impoundments, I was perfectly located to watch it happen.

Bass fishing changed from pastime to business in part because of competitive tournaments, and the publicity they generated. That publicity, in turn, sparked a demand for more and more information from the tournament fishermen themselves—how they caught bass—so in essence, the sport fed upon itself during those years. Bass fishing also grew because it is a participatory sport, too, unlike practically every other professional sport. Very few baseball fans will ever get to stand on the pitcher's mound in Yankee Stadium and throw a baseball, nor will racing fans drive their family car around Indianapolis or Daytona. Virtually every bass fisherman, however, can purchase the very same rods, reels, and lures today's best-known professionals use, and cast those lures to the very same places in a lake. That's why bass fishing became what it is today.

This book, however, is not simply about tournament bass fishing, although some of the stories I have included do involve competitive anglers. Rather, I have tried to embrace a wider view of the entire sport, and show how different facets of bass fishing meshed so perfectly at the same time. I have let the participants themselves—those who laid the foundation for what all bass anglers today enjoy—tell their own stories of what happened during those not-so-long-ago years. Thus, many of the stories I have included, such as the standing room–only funeral for a bass, which I attended, do not specifically pertain to actually catching a fish.

I began collecting these specific interviews years ago, long before the idea for this project was born, but many interruptions along the way delayed and pushed completion of this book further back than I ever imagined. A number of people I would have liked to have interviewed are no longer alive, and others have died since I interviewed them. One individual, long-time friend Jim Bagley of the Bagley Bait Company, died between our first and planned second interview for this book. I am certain, also, that I obtained the very last interviews Virgil Ward, Don Butler, and Tom Mann ever gave, as all three died within days after graciously giving time to me.

My interviews with Billy Westmorland and Charlie Brewer are among the oldest, and with Billy took place at his home and on Dale Hollow Reservoir not long after he lost the world record smallmouth that was still haunting him at every step; he and I fished for it again at the very same spot and with the same lures. Charlie Brewer and I, after first fishing together in August 1979, spent literally hundreds of hours together fishing all over Alabama during the next decade. The same is also true with Bill Huntley of T-H Marine, with whom I first fished in 1976.

Some may question why certain individuals have been included here, while others have not. A primary reason is the lack of editorial space in the book. There are dozens of others I would have liked to have included, all of whom left some mark on the sport. In some cases, however, that mark was also a repetition of a previous mark made by another; what I have tried to do is present a variety of stories, which, when taken together, show a more complete picture of the sport and how it has evolved.

Historically, the decades between 1970 and 1990, when so much of the growth of bass fishing occurred, have often been described as the Golden Age of Bass Fishing. It was a very special time during which the encyclopedia of bass fishing was being written, as my former editor Bob Cobb describes those years, and it will never happen again. Perhaps that's what evolution is all about, and I am thankful for the opportunity I've had to watch it happen.

Steve Price
Dubois, Wyoming

THE FISH

Chapter One

The Gamest Fish That Swims

"He is plucky, game, brave and unyielding to the last when hooked.
He has the arrowy rush and vigor of the trout, the untiring strength and
bold leap of the salmon, while he has a system of fighting tactics peculiarly
his own. I consider him, inch for inch and pound for pound, the gamest
fish that swims."

Quite possibly no more famous words have ever been penned than these by Dr. James A. Henshall, of Cincinnati, Ohio, which first appeared in his *The Book of the Black Bass,* in 1881. Today, more than a century later, they continue to serve as the rallying cry of anglers everywhere whenever called upon to defend the honor of *Micropterus salmoides*, the largemouth bass.

In recent decades, however, as the largemouth has transitioned into the most popular gamefish in America, little defense has been required. No species has ever received as much public attention, created such a nationwide economic impact, or changed the American lifestyle as dramatically as has this individual species.

Indeed, the economic impact the largemouth generates is staggering. The fish is the centerpiece of its own industry variously estimated to be worth $40 billion or possibly more. Cities, counties, and entire states depend on the revenue the largemouth brings in license sales and fishing-based recreation. In Texas, for example, where bass fishing is extremely popular, sport fishermen spend more than $3 billion annually

Dr. James A. Henshall, a Cincinnati physician, was also an avid bass fisherman, and his book, The Book of the Black Bass, *published in 1881, was the first publication detailing the life history of the species that would become America's favorite game fish a century later.*

on fishing trips and equipment, much of it for chasing largemouth bass. Some 80,000 jobs in the state relate directly to fishing, which alone generates well over $150 million in state revenues annually. Just one bass lake, Lake Fork, has in some years brought in more than $20 million to the surrounding counties.

In California, where the overall fishing industry is also worth more than $3 billion annually, revenue from bass fishing in the small lakes in and around San Diego alone totals more than $30 million each year. Guides on some of the more popular lakes there have had visiting clients from South America, Mexico, Japan, Malaysia, and France. Of the approximately 30 million licensed freshwater anglers over the age of 16 in the United States, a minimum of 12 million concentrate on largemouth bass, according to the US Fish and Wildlife Service.

Surprisingly, the fish is not a true bass, but it's not an import, either. Largemouth are completely native to North America, and they're members of the sunfish family *Centarchidae* that began evolving about 400 million years ago when the first fishlike vertebrate creatures appeared on earth. Today's largemouth bass, however, almost certainly did not appear like anything modern fishermen would recognize until around 60 million years ago when the *Perciformes*, the largest order of fishes, began to evolve. This order is further divided into several families, one of which is *Micropterus*.

Although these fish were totally unknown to the first Europeans who reached American shores, the name *Micropterus* was actually assigned by a French naturalist named Bernard Germain de Lacepede (1756–1825), who received two slightly different fish samples in 1802. De Lacepede, appointed to study reptiles and fishes at the Museum National d'Histoire Naturelle in Paris, named one the largemouth, and the other a smallmouth bass.

Interestingly, only the smallmouth bass de Lacepede received was named *Micropterus*, meaning "little fin," while he named the largemouth *Labrus salmoides*, meaning "trout-like wrasse." Possibly this was because the smallmouth he received apparently had a broken dorsal fin, and he did not realize the accompanying largemouth belonged to the same genus. More than 90 years passed before taxonomists Barton Evermann and David S. Jordan straightened out the issue when they assigned the largemouth the name *Micropterus salmoides* in 1896 (de Lacepede's smallmouth name and classification remained, with only the spelling changed).

Fortunately, the naming problems were settled before fisheries experts realized there are really seven species of the black bass (largemouth, smallmouth, spotted, redeye, shoal, Suwannee, and Guadalupe) and to complicate the issue even more, scientists in 1949 determined there are two subspecies of the largemouth. Distinct differences in scale counts exist between these two subspecies, but anglers are far more interested in their size differences. Fishermen and biologists alike simply refer to them as the larger growing Florida largemouth (*Micropterus salmoides floridanus)* and the smaller northern largemouth (*Micropterus salmoides salmoides*).

Without question, one of the factors that elevated the largemouth to its lofty "gamest fish that swims" status is its nationwide accessibility. The fish thrives in common water. Whereas trout and salmon, long considered the royal gamefish of Europe, require cold, clear, and generally moving water, bass do best in shallow, warm, and often weedy conditions, including lakes, rivers, streams, creeks, and ponds. Never mind that bass are still sometimes referred to by some Southern anglers as "green trout," the fish steadily gained its own legions of devoted followers.

Indeed, bass were "stocked" in more than one waterway by engineers tossing them out from trains during their cross-country runs. In 1871, for example, officials in California requested bass from Hudson River authorities in the Northeast because they were concerned immigrant Chinese railroad workers—known to love to eat fish of any species—would deplete the Sacramento River of anything they could catch or seine.

Originally found only from the Great Lakes to Texas and across the South to Virginia and the Carolinas, by the 1890s the largemouth had spread one way or another throughout most of the nation. Today, the fish is located in every state except Alaska, in many South and Central American countries, several sub-Saharan African nations, Japan, and in parts of Europe.

Once the largemouth bass thus became widely established, fishermen themselves directed its future. Among the first things that happened was the development of the lure industry, initiated primarily by the largemouth's willingness to strike artificial lures. As early as the 1760s, naturalist William Bartram had observed the Seminole Indians in Florida catching fish with lures fashioned from deer hair, and in 1848 Whitehall, New York, inventor/fisherman J. T. Buel was awarded what is generally considered the first actual patent for a fishing lure.

In 1902 James Heddon built the first factory to mass-produce wooden fishing lures, and in doing so began to turn the sport into a true industry. As the story goes, one warm day in 1888, while waiting beside a pond for a friend, Heddon whittled a small piece of wood into the shape of a minnow, then casually tossed it into the water. To his surprise, a largemouth bass hit the wood figure almost instantly. A beekeeper by trade, Heddon borrowed $1,000 in start-up capital, and although his first lures were made and painted in an upstairs room of his Dowagiac, Michigan home, his company went on to become one of the most famous in the history of fishing.

Two other factors in the twentieth century helped move the largemouth bass into national prominence. The first, basically starting in the 1930s and continuing for more than fifty years, was the federally approved construction of large reservoirs to control river flooding and provide water resources to different regions of the nation. When this era of dam building began, there were probably less than a million acres of impounded water in the entire United States; half a century later, more than ten million acres had been backed up behind dams. More than 1,000 new lakes were created during this time, and the vast majority of them formed excellent bass habitat.

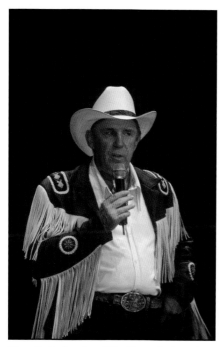

Ray Scott, founder of the Bass Anglers Sportsman Society, has done more than any single individual to unite America's bass fisherman and promote the sport of bass fishing worldwide. He established the ethic of catch-and-release fishing, and is given much credit for creating the entire $40 billion bass fishing industry.

As fishing interest continued to grow, especially in the immediate post–World War II years, demand for fishing knowledge followed, and that's when the second factor occurred. In 1967, a Montgomery, Alabama insurance salesman who loved bass fishing started an organization that has been providing that fishing knowledge ever since.

His name was Ray Scott, and his organization was named the Bass Anglers Sportsman Society, or B.A.S.S. Through newpaper and magazine coverage and eventually television, this organization became the unifying foundation for both the growing sport and the fledgling tackle industry.

Scott organized a series of bass fishing tournaments, then created his own magazine, *Bassmaster*, to publicize not only the results but also to describe the "how-to" techniques his tournament anglers used in catching their fish. There were actually national bass tournaments being conducted before Scott started his, most notably the World Series of Sport Fishing (in which contestants could catch several species), but only Scott's survived, not only because his rules were strictly enforced but also because he paid cash to the winning anglers. Over time, membership in his organization soared to well over 500,000, and remains nearly as high today. Those anglers needed boats to fish out of, and so the "bass boat" industry was created, to say nothing of the skyrocketing rise in fishing tackle manufacturers.

And the tournaments? They're alive and well, too, with winning payouts in today's biggest events reaching as much as $500,000, and in one case, a full million dollars. Professional bass fishing has become a full-time profession for some, who may drive as much as 50,000 miles a year to compete in different events staged from New York to Florida to California. Today there are numerous television programs devoted exclusively to largemouth bass fishing, and videos showing prospective anglers (and experienced ones, as well) the secrets of catching this singular species. Bass fishing is taught in some colleges, too, and even high schools are organizing bass clubs and competitions.

In many parts of America, particularly the South and Southwest, bass fishing is a year-round sport. Indeed, only a few states have closed seasons for this fish, and they are short. Surveys show the average bass fisherman in America today owns 14 rods and reels, four tackleboxes, a boat, motor, and trailer, and he enjoys fishing more than 50 days per year. The beauty of the sport is that the average bass angler can purchase the very same equipment used by his favorite tournament pros and fish the same lakes, and even in the very same locations. One individual store, the original Bass Pro Shops in Springfield, Missouri, that opened in 1971, still attracts some four million visitors annually, and today there are more than 60 Bass Pro Shops–affiliated stores around the nation.

What has basically been learned about the largemouth itself from both these professional fishermen, as well as the scientific community, is that the fish is a very intelligent creature, far smarter, in fact, than ever believed.

For instance, it is known that bass can see and discriminate between colors. The fish can smell fairly well (although not as well as some species) and constantly monitors its environment by pumping water in and out of its nostrils. It can hear sounds below and above water, and has a lateral line of nerve endings that allow it to sense water movement. And it has both learning and memory capabilities, to the extent the fish can probably detect even the most subtle differences in vibration patterns.

For fishermen, this means bass may recognize not only the type of vibration a certain species of prey makes, but also the vibrations produced by specific lures, and they learn to shy away from them. Scientists also believe bass may be capable of forming a mental image of its prey through this vibration recognition, a term known as hydrodynamic imaging.

Vision-wise, bass certainly do see, and appear to react to, the color red better than any other hue. Experiments conducted as early as 1935 established that bass could most readily distinguish red, yellow, white, green, and blue in that order, and more recent evaluations have essentially confirmed this same pattern.

One of the more interesting observations of the largemouth, and which certainly adds to the aura of mystery surrounding it, is what many experienced bass fishermen describe as a change of personality. This seems to occur at around four pounds for the northern subspecies, and at perhaps eight pounds for the Florida subspecies. In essence, the bass change from juveniles to adults, and their behavior becomes markedly different, quite possibly because as they increase in size they outgrow their predators. Instead of being dominated, they become the dominant ones.

These bass move to deeper water; they start feeding on larger prey (and lures) so they don't need to eat as often; and they seem to become much more cautious. If for no other reasons, this is why really large bass are not caught that often.

The thought of catching large bass, be it over 10 pounds, over 20 pounds, or even a new world record, has also added immeasurably to the largemouth's popularity. Until July 2, 2009, when Japanese angler Manabu Kurita caught a largemouth in Lake Biwa, Japan, weighing 22.311 pounds, the world record weight of 22 pounds, 4 ounces, had stood since 1932 and become the most hallowed of all freshwater fishing records. Because

Kurita's fish, verified by the International Game Fish Association (IGFA), did not break the 77-year-old record set by American angler George Perry by the required two full ounces, Kurita's fish is considered a tie for the world record.

Over the years, various firms have established huge financial incentives for anglers to go after a new world record largemouth. At one time the Daiichi/Tru-Turn/Xpoint Company, maker of fishing hooks, offered a $1 million bonus to the angler who caught the next world record largemouth on one of the company's XPoint hooks. In October 2011, a rival hook manufacturer, Mustad, announced a year-long contest in which the company would award $100,000 to the first angler catching a new IGFA-certified all tackle state record largemouth using a Mustad hook.

Other companies and organizations have offered as much as $8 million to anyone who caught a new world record, providing certain specific criteria were met. Numbers like these simply highlight the huge interest in the largemouth bass. Bass fishing is not just a sport, it has become a lifestyle.

Henshall himself was a dedicated student of the largemouth bass, and because he also had extensive experience fishing for them, a number of his own conclusions formed in the 1870s and 1880s accurately mirror the scientific data that followed decades later. What more than 12 million dedicated bass anglers most agree with is his assessment that the largemouth is, inch for inch and pound for pound, the gamest fish that swims.

Chapter Two

Ray Scott: "The One Thing I Am Most Proud Of"

Ray Scott, founder of the Bass Anglers Sportsman Society.

To anyone who has ever asked Ray Scott how he formed his idea of conducting professional bass fishing tournaments and unifying America's bass fishermen, his emphatic answer has always been that he had never, ever previously thought about it, but on March 11, 1967, when his epiphany took place, the sport changed forever. Scott did not know it then, but in just four decades his idea, his actions, and his charismatic leadership would transform bass fishing from a relaxing pastime into a global sportfishing industry valued today between $40 and $100 billion.

He is best known as the founder of B.A.S.S.—the Bass Anglers Sportsman Society—and the annual series of professional bass fishing competitions known as the Bassmaster Tournament Trail. Together, they unified hundreds of thousands of bass fishermen under a common cause that spurred new fishing tackle developments, the emergence of the bass boat industry, the growth of the outboard engine industry, a conservation awareness of

America's fish and water resources, and even the spread of bass fishing to other countries. Most agree he was the perfect man in the perfect place at the perfect time.

Born August 24, 1933, in Montgomery, Alabama, Scott remembers fishing as early as age six, using cane poles, worms, and crickets in the ponds and waterways with his family and friends. He wasn't a particularly good student in school, but he was definitely an early entrepreneur. In the third grade he started selling his homemade lunch sandwiches to his classmates for five cents each, and by the sixth grade he had graduated to mowing lawns and selling peanuts at the local Double A baseball games. It never stopped.

He played high school football at Starke University School, a military academy in Montgomery, and in his senior year he was good enough not only to be awarded All City honors, but also earned a football scholarship at Howard College (now Samford University) in Birmingham. He played for a year, but then dropped out after suffering a construction accident during a summer job. In May 1954, he was drafted into the United States Army, served with the 2nd Armored Division in Germany, then after his discharge in 1956, entered Auburn University on the G.I. Bill. He started selling insurance even before he graduated.

Scott was taking the day off from the insurance business to go fishing that fateful March day in 1967. By then, he was working four states—Alabama, Arkansas, Louisiana, and Mississippi—and he and his fishing partner Lloyd Lewis had been blown off Ross Barnett Reservoir by a hard rain. The epiphany came late that afternoon in the Ramada Inn in Jackson, as Scott was lying in bed watching a basketball game.

Only half-interested in seeing players running back and forth up and down the court, he suddenly had a vision. Why couldn't the court be a lake and the basketballers be bass fishermen having a tournament?

Ray Scott was not the first to dream of staging a competitive bass tournament. The credit for organizing the first tournament generally goes to Earl Golding of Waco, Texas, who in 1955 held an event he named the Texas State Tournament. Four years later, Hy Peskin, a *Sports Illustrated* photographer who happened to be listening to a group of professional baseball players discussing fishing, organized his own event, the World Series of Sport Fishing.

Peskin, who had never caught a fish himself, nevertheless tried walking on a big stage in that he dreamed in terms of state championships followed by regional eliminations that would eventually result in

12 champions who would then compete in a multi-day, multi-species event, the winner of which would be crowned world champion. His first event in 1959, won by Claude Rogers of Virginia, featured competition in both fresh- and saltwater. In 1960, the saltwater portion was dropped, and it became a freshwater-only event, although several species were still allowed to be weighed in each day.

Peskin held the World Series of Sport Fishing each year through 1968, with winners including such notable fishermen as Harold Ensley, Joe Krieger, Virgil Ward, and Glen Andrews, the only angler to win the event twice, in 1965 and 1966. Jimmy Houston won the final World Series in 1968. While the event drew a lot of attention in its time, it never succeeded financially for Peskin, and the winners themselves received only bragging rights, as no cash prizes were ever awarded.

Scott wanted to change that, and he remembers standing up on the bed, nearly bumping his head on the ceiling but nevertheless snapping his fingers and yelling, "I can do that! I can do that!" That night at dinner, he unloaded his idea on Lewis, who admitted later he thought Ray had totally lost it. Scott had just read a story in *Outdoor Life Magazine* about bass fishing on Beaver Lake in Arkansas, so that's where he decided he was going to have his first tournament, even though he didn't know exactly where Beaver Lake was located.

That was on a Saturday. The next day Scott took off for Little Rock, stopped at the tourism office to get directions to Beaver Lake, and after he did, brazenly telephoned the Chamber of Commerce in Rogers and asked if they'd be interested in sponsoring his tournament.

Not remotely, was the answer.

Undeterred, Scott then called the Springdale Chamber of Commerce on the opposite side of Beaver Lake. They were more receptive, saying they'd even heard of his organization, and invited him to make a presentation to their board of directors. Of course, he didn't have any organization at the time, but nonetheless, Scott made a beeline to Springdale and gave his presentation, but again was turned down. He'd asked for $10,000 in sponsorship fees, but they were afraid he would abscond with the funds.

It did not end there, however. Later that evening, Scott met the first of many benefactors who would prove to be instrumental in keeping his tournament fishing dreams alive over the next several months. His name was Dr. Stanley Applegate, owner of the Hickory Creek Boat Dock there on Beaver. When he learned Scott had been turned down by the

Springdale Chamber, Applegate wrote him a personal check for $2,500 to get him started. Scott then went to the Holiday Inn in Springdale, made a deal for the motel to be the tournament headquarters in exchange for two months of free rent plus a meal discount, and went to work trying to find 100 bass fishermen.

Scott also met with Glen Andrews in Rogers, the reigning champion who had won Peskin's World Series the previous two years and been runner-up two other years. He was rightfully considered one of the finest bass fishermen in the world at that time. Andrews not only provided Scott with a list of potential anglers for his first tournament (one of whom was a Memphis fisherman named Bill Dance who stayed at Andrews's home during the event), but was also instrumental in helping Scott establish the rules for the tournament, many of which are still in place today.

A highly successful and sought-after guide on both Bull Shoals and Table Rock Lakes, Andrews was a true student of the largemouth bass and was among the first to understand the relationship between bass, baitfish, and the structure, or depth changes, they preferred. He could literally catch bass when no one else could, and he passed this knowledge on to a number of others who eventually became outstanding professional anglers themselves, including Dance and Jimmy Houston. Because of his fishing knowledge, he had himself been victimized by Peskin's rule changes and he wanted to make certain Scott's rules applied evenly to all fishermen.

The desk clerk at the Holiday Inn introduced Ray to Darlene Phillips, who, for a salary of $250, became Scott's secretary for the event. He rented her an IBM Selectric typewriter, and with another part of Applegate's check he had a long distance WATS telephone line installed in his room. It was good for 13 states, but all Scott had when he sat down to start dialing were the names of four bass fishermen, three in Alabama and one in Georgia, so that's who he called first.

Each of those four, in turn, provided names of other anglers who then gave him even more names. Scott eventually ended up with the names and telephone numbers of more than 500 anglers. For whatever reason, and Scott has no idea why, he decided the tournament would last for three days. In that first event, like Peskin's World Series, he also allowed white bass to be weighed in, a rule he eliminated after the tournament.

Scott lost 20 pounds during the month he had to promote the tournament, but he pulled it off, paying the top ten places, including $2,000 in cash to an angler named Stan Sloan who won with a catch totaling 37 pounds, 8 ounces. Sloan's winning prize also included an all expenses paid trip to Acapulco or $500 cash; he took the cash. He was a sheriff's deputy at the time, but later went on to establish the Zorro Bait Company, which became one of the nation's most popular lure companies. Another angler, Ralph Polly of Lexington, Kentucky, won a waterfront lot on Beaver for bringing in the biggest bass of the event.

In the end, Scott lost $600 on this first tournament, but he knew his idea was right. He headed back to Montgomery where he planned to quit his insurance job. Along the way, in Cullman, Alabama, he stopped at the Chamber of Commerce to see if they'd be interested in sponsoring his second tournament, which they did just four months later.

In January 1968, Scott officially formed his organization, the Bass Anglers Sportsman Society, the name provided by Bob Steber of the Nashville *Tennessean* newspaper, with the initials B.A.S.S. Scott had provided him. The first member was Don T. Butler, a Tulsa businessman who had fished the Beaver Lake tournament. A few weeks later, Butler would almost single-handedly save the fledgling organization, and possibly the entire sport of competitive fishing, by sending the then-broke Scott a wire for $10,000 to pay expenses for a mass membership mailing. Scott made the mailing, and paid Butler back in six weeks. Butler would go on to become one of the key figures in bass fishing and putting his own name in the record book by winning Scott's 1972 Bassmaster Classic championship and the next year one of Scott's regular Tour events. Like the organization he had just started, Scott was off and running.

★ ★ ★

Of all that B.A.S.S. has accomplished over the years, the thing I am most proud of is starting the concept of catch-and-release, which I began promoting hard in 1972 at the start of our tournament season. By then, we had four years of tournaments under our belt, but essentially, none of the bass were being returned to the lake where we caught them. They were turned over to orphanages and other organizations to eat. The longer it continued, the worse the image looked for B.A.S.S., particularly since we were involved in numerous lawsuits we had brought against different firms for pollution and degradation of our water resources.

One day in my office in Montgomery, I received a phone call from Al Elis of Phoenix, a fly fisherman who had heard me speak about the lawsuits at a convention in Florida. He wanted me to come to the Federation of Fly Fishermen Convention in Aspen, Colorado, to talk to those anglers about the lawsuits.

I flew out and the last day of the convention they took me fly fishing on a small stream I could easily have cast one of my bass lures across. One of the anglers caught a 12-inch trout, and I couldn't believe how excited those fly fishermen got over such a small fish. In Florida, we used fish that size as bait for our big bass.

Then, with care and reverence, the angler released that trout back into the water. I was amazed, and a lightbulb suddenly went on in my head. On my flight back to Montgomery, I realized we could do that with our bass.

I had a big tank designed to keep our tournament bass alive, and then I decided to give a one-ounce bonus for each fish my pros brought in alive. That got everyone's attention, and led to the development of the first boat livewells; Don Butler, my first B.A.S.S. member, designed one and even received a patent for it. Today, livewells are standard on every bass boat, and companies spend a great deal of time designing them and making them even more efficient.

Everything continued just fine until our fifth event of the season, the Mississippi Invitational on Ross Barnett Reservoir in Jackson. The Game and Fish officials told us we could not release the

Don Butler, center, holds his trophy for winning the 1973 Beaver Lake Invitational, with Ray Scott, left, and Roland Martin, right. Butler was the first member of B.A.S.S., and helped Scott financially when the young organization was struggling to survive. Photo courtesy of B.A.S.S.

A successful and highly respected guide on both Bull Shoals and Table Rock Lakes, Glen Andrews is the only angler to have won the World Series of Fishing twice. He later helped Ray Scott formulate the original rules for B.A.S.S., and mentored future fishing stars Bill Dance and Jimmy Houston.

bass we caught. We had to keep them. They were afraid our stressed bass would contract some disease, then spread that disease to the healthy bass in the lake, even though there was absolutely no scientific research indicating that would happen.

Well, I was determined we were going to release our bass, and before our first weigh-in, the Game and Fish Department relented. The problem was, they collected our fish, then took them to a shallow bay they'd netted off from the rest of the lake. It was hot, and that water was probably close to 90 degrees. Only about 25% of our catch survived, but that only made all of us in B.A.S.S. work that much harder to keep our bass alive.

Over time, catch-and-release became standard among bass fishermen everywhere, and today, most anglers even release their trophy bass weighing more than 10 pounds. I have always allowed any B.A.S.S. tournament angler the choice of keeping a trophy fish he caught to have mounted, but so far, no one ever has, even though some weighed more than 13 pounds.

That's what I'm most proud of.

★ ★ ★

Ray Scott and his wife Susan live on their farm in Pintlala, Alabama, south of Montgomery, where he continues to be an active spokesman for the sport he created.

Chapter Three

Virgil Ward: "The Fishing Trip That Started My Lure Company"

Virgil Ward, left, son Bill, right, and grandson Gregory, center, all enjoyed successful bass fishing careers. Always known as a true gentleman, Virgil is credited with creating the first bucktail jigs, and his television show, Championship Fishing, *was one of the earliest and most successful programs on the air for more than 20 years.*

Somewhere out on one of the gently sloping timbered points of Bull Shoals Lake, there's a ⅝-ounce leadhead jig Virgil Ward snagged and lost during a fishing trip just after Christmas. It's about 15 feet underwater, and it's been there since 1955 so the chicken feathers he tied around it are long gone, but if ever a single lure can be credited with starting a legend, as well as foretelling the future popularity of bass fishing, it is that jig.

Ward, born May 25, 1911, in Easton, Missouri, had been moving toward that particular day on Bull Shoals since he was four years old, when he caught his first fish using a willow branch and a string. It was a chub, not a bass, but the species wasn't important. What was important is that Ward discovered fishing that day and spent much of the next 80+ years not only catching fish but also introducing millions of others to the sport. He accomplished much of that through his lure company, Bass Buster Lures. Located in Amsterdam, Missouri, at one time it employed more than half the city's population, and sold millions of lures during the 15 years he and his son Bill owned and operated it; many of Ward's lures, such as the Beetle Spin, are still popular today.

The lure company was only part of the Ward legend, however. In 1965, he began filming one of the earliest television fishing programs, *Championship Fishing*, which aired on one station in Springfield. For the next 22 years, when he finally turned the show over to his grandson Greg, *Championship Fishing* continually ranked at or near the top of the Nielsen television ratings, and at one time reached 2.5 million viewers per week. Ward fished from the Arctic to the Amazon for all species of fish, but largemouth bass were his favorite, and today thousands of middle-aged fishermen can say they became interested in fishing by watching his television program.

Throughout its long run—the show ended in 1991—the format remained the same: inform, educate, and entertain. To that end, Ward usually spent four days filming each show, and he did it with film, not video, which forced him to spend as long as 40 additional hours editing, a chore he did himself. Every scene was filmed as it happened, without staging or replays, and there were shows in which he caught no fish at all.

At the same time, Ward also hosted his own radio program that aired on more than 250 stations, and wrote a fishing column that appeared in 450 newspapers across the country. Thus, each week for years he talked, published, or televised fishing to tens of millions of fans, and no one ever did it more gracefully. Overall, he may have preferred largemouth bass fishing, but his favorite filming location was actually the Tree River in Canada, where, in August 1981, Ward and his two grandsons, Greg and Jeff, went to film a television show about Arctic char. On that trip, Jeff caught a world record 32-pound, 9-ounce char, but unfortunately it was too dark to film it.

Ward's dedication to fishing knew no bounds. One day right after World War II, after he and a friend had built an aluminum boat, they were in such a hurry to get it into the water they neglected to put in any type of floatation. They launched just below a power dam, hit a snag, capsized, and sank. Ward grabbed the motor, a brand new four-horsepower model, and went down with it. When he hit bottom, he looked up and could see the surface, so he let go of the outboard and swam to shore. He went to the powerhouse and asked the personnel there to turn off the power to lower the water, which they did. Then Ward waded back out and recovered the boat and motor.

Not long after, Ward actually started his original Bass Buster Lure Company, producing a series of cedar wood lures, including both topwater and diving models. His son Bill would come home from high school and paint them, but they simply could not make and sell enough of them to make a living, so in 1950 Virgil gave up lure making and started a plumbing and heating business, just to survive.

Of course, he never lost his interest in fishing, and because plumbers know how to work with lead, it wasn't long before Ward started molding those little leadhead jigs that eventually led him to that timbered point on Bull Shoals. In 1962, Ward won the World Series of Sport Fishing, which only increased Ward's, and his jig's popularity. He was inducted into the National Freshwater Fishing Hall of Fame, the International Fishing Hall of Fame, and the Bass Fishing Hall of Fame in honor of his storied career.

★ ★ ★

Back in 1955, just a few years after Bull Shoals filled, the bass fishing was really good, especially during the winter, so in late December between Christmas and the New Year, my son Bill and I took two days off from our plumbing and electrical business to see if we could catch some bass. Little did I know how those two days would change my life.

We rented an aluminum boat and because it was so cold, we took a little propane heater along to keep us warm. Bill was wearing an old flight suit his uncle had brought home from World War II, as well as his overalls and long underwear, and I wore the heaviest coat I owned. We warmed up pretty quick, though, because right after I pulled up on a timbered point and threw out a jig, I had a solid strike and brought in a three-pound bass.

We were both using ⅝-ounce leadhead jigs that we'd dressed with rough hackle feathers we'd purchased from the old Herter's Company in Waseca, Minnesota. We called them chicken feather jigs because that's what they looked like. We'd make a cast, let the jig sink about 15 feet, and just like that, a bass would hit it.

Well, the limit was 10 bass per person and 20 in possession, so each time Bill or I caught a good fish, we put it on a stringer and dropped the stringer back over the side. We didn't have a cooler in the boat. Soon, the stringers got so full some of the bass were still out of the water when we dropped the stringers back down. By about mid-afternoon we had 40 bass that weighed about 120 pounds.

The lake was quiet and we were sitting there catching fish when three fishermen in another boat nearby saw Bill catch a bass and noticed those stringers hanging over the side. We could hear them talking about our fish, and then they came over to see what we were using. I showed them our chicken jigs, and the next day he telephoned and asked us to tie 25 jigs for him, which we did. We charged him a dollar each, and that's exactly how Bass Buster Lures got started.

About a week later, Bill and I made another trip to Bull Shoals, and again we really caught the bass on those jigs. This time, we took them home in an ice chest and showed them Monday night on Harold Ensley's ten p.m. live television fishing show. Harold had both television and radio programs in the area, and he was a good fisherman himself, so he had a big following, and showing all our bass gave the jig a lot of publicity.

Afterward, Harold asked me if we'd make the jigs exclusively for Sears, Roebuck & Company in Kansas City if he could convince them to buy them. He did, and we did, so our little chicken jigs got even more popular.

A year or so later, Harold asked me to go with him to the White River below Bull Shoals Dam to do a trout fishing show with him. Well, I knew the chicken feather jigs were far too heavy for trout fishing, so I asked Bill to tie some ¹⁄₁₆-ounce jigs for me, but instead of using the rough chicken hackle, I suggested we use marabou. We'd tied a lot of marabou streamer flies for trout, and they were really effective because the marabou feathers just make the fly look alive. Marabou is much softer and fluffier than the feather material we were using, and I didn't see why they wouldn't work for a jig, too.

As far as I know, those were the first marabou jigs ever tied, and that day on the river with Harold I caught a limit of trout, including a six-pounder, on my little jigs, and that's how the marabou jig originated. A year later, Bill and I went up to Lake of the Woods to fish for trout and walleye. The guides wanted to use minnows because they didn't think the marabou jigs would catch anything, but before we finished, we'd caught more bass on our jigs than the guides had with their live bait. The lodge owner started buying and stocking the jigs and it spread from there.

Over time, we sold millions of marabou jigs. Bill had tied the first ones on the kitchen table, and then his wife Kay and my wife Cleda started tying them with him. Then we moved into a couple of buildings in town, and eventually we employed about 125 people, which I'm really proud of, because in those days Amsterdam only had a population of 200. We added other lures over the years, including the Beetle Spin, which was our jig with a spinner blade on it. I named it after the Beatles singing group who were popular at the time, but spelled it differently, and that sold well, too. In fact, one year we sold 10 million Beetle Spins, mainly because it caught all different kinds of fish for any angler using any type of tackle.

When I decided to sell the company in 1970 to Sam Johnson of Johnson Fishing, he wrote me a check for a million dollars. Who could have dreamed those little leadhead jigs we tied with chicken feathers would ever lead to something like that?

★ ★ ★

Virgil Ward died September 13, 2004, at the age of 93. Despite battling cancer, he still managed to make one final fishing trip just two weeks before his death.

Chapter Four

Tom Mann: "Leroy Brown Was Something Special"

Tom Mann gained lasting fame as an early lure manufacturer by creating, among others, the famous soft plastic Jelly Worms, which he sold in various "flavors." Mann was a highly successful tournament angler in the early days of organized competitive fishing as well as a tireless promoter of his own lures.

In the late 1960s, as bass fishing began its rapid change from a simple sport into a highly competitive business, one man was uniquely positioned to take advantage of this growth. He was Tom Mann of Eufaula, Alabama, who had already been manufacturing bass lures since 1958, several of which, including the Jelly Worm and the Little George, were nationally known.

Born in Penton, Alabama, in 1932, Mann could not remember fishing ever being a hobby. Rather, it was an obsession. As early as age six when he would fish for any species that might bite his bent safety pins, he was as interested in watching and studying the fish as he was in actually catching them. This intense desire to better understand his quarry became a trademark of his career and constantly manifested itself in his lures as he improved colors and designed more enticing actions.

Among the more than 3,000 lures Mann designed over the years, the Jelly Worm, which he created in 1967, is among his best known. Mann was making his molds out of aluminum, and one day after shining a worm mold with jewelry polish, he produced a transparent plastic worm. To create color, he simply added ink to the plastic. Mann's wife Ann remarked that the new worms looked and shined like the jellies she made, and just like that, a name was given to what would become one of the most famous bass lures in history.

In addition to using different colors of inks to make different "berries," Mann also contracted with a perfume company to create matching fragrances. Marketing them in packages of five for a dollar, he was soon selling as many as 50 million Jelly Worms a year.

In addition to designing bass fishing lures, Mann founded Allied Sports, maker of Humminbird electronic depth finders; and Southern Plastics, which became one of the nation's largest manufacturers and packagers of lures for other firms. He hosted bass fishing television programs on ESPN, TNN, and the Sportsman Channel; fished with two presidents, and was elected into the Fishing Hall of Fame.

★ ★ ★

I caught Leroy Brown one day in the 1970s while fishing on Lake Eufaula. He weighed about a pound and as I unhooked him, something about the little bass caught my attention. He looked kind of funny. His eyes were close together and positioned more on top of his head, and he had this little upturned nose, so I kept him instead of throwing him back in the lake.

This is Leroy Brown, the largemouth bass caught by Tom Mann in the 1970s in Lake Eufaula. When Leroy died on August 20, 1980, Tom held a formal funeral for the fish at Lake Point Resort State Park, which was attended by more than 500 people. Newspapers from as far away as the Soviet Union printed stories of the funeral.

I had a swimming pool without any chlorine in my backyard where I kept fish and tested lures, so I put him there. Almost immediately he started beating up the other fish, regardless of how much larger they were. My wife gave him the name Leroy Brown, after Jim Croce's popular song, "Bad, Bad Leroy Brown," and as it turned out, I learned more from that fish than any other bass I've ever caught. Leroy Brown was something special.

I moved Leroy to my 18,000-gallon aquarium at Mann's Bait Company where I could watch him more closely, and he immediately took control of the aquarium, just like he'd done in the pool.

Leroy grew fast, too, since we fed the aquarium fish well, and he always got his share. He would recognize my footsteps and be ready whenever I walked into the room, because he learned I was the one who always fed the fish. Before long, he would take food out of my hand. I even trained him to jump through a Hula-Hoop, too. After several years,

Leroy became a big tourist attraction, and started getting national media attention, which was great for my lure company.

Then I started trying to work with Leroy with lures. I caught him on a Strawberry Jelly Worm, but for the rest of his life, Leroy never actually struck another lure. I could toss a plastic worm into the aquarium and he'd pick it up by the tail and drag it around but he'd never actually strike it, and he wouldn't let other fish strike it, either.

When Leroy reached about three pounds, he began spawning with female bass in the aquarium, and he'd usually have more than one girl-friend. In fact, he would fight off all the other males and take care of all the female bass by himself, including Big Bertha, a 12-pound bass whose eggs Leroy fertilized for several successive years. In the aquarium the bass spawned between April and August, so Leroy stayed busy.

Leroy was more than seven years old and weighed six pounds, two ounces when he died unexpectedly one night. He had actually spawned eight females that year and looked healthy, but on August 20, 1980, I went in to the aquarium and found Leroy floating on the surface.

We wrapped him up and put him in the freezer. It happened that B.A.S.S. was coming to town soon for a big tournament on Lake Eufaula, and Susanne Newsome, my assistant at Mann's Bait Company, suggested we have a funeral for Leroy that week. She wrote an obituary that was printed in the local paper, then picked up by both the Associated Press and United Press International and distributed around the country. I received a telegram of condolences from country and western recording star Porter Wagner, and letters from fishing fans everywhere.

We held the funeral at Lake Point State Resort Park in one of the conference rooms that would hold 500 people; the room was packed and I think some 200 additional people were standing outside during the service. Susanne had stayed up until three a.m. the night before preparing Leroy's casket, a tacklebox she lined with satin.

Two pallbearers solemnly carried Leroy in, and at the service I read passages from Lamar Underwood's *Bass Fishing Almanac*. The Mann's Bait Company Choir hummed "Bad, Bad Leroy Brown," and then every-one walked by and dropped a Strawberry Jelly Worm into the casket.

I paid $4,000 for a hand-carved monument made in Germany. I'd sent them pictures of Leroy and they had carved his likeness in the marble, and we had it for the funeral. We buried Leroy next to the Fish World aquarium complex, but the next day we discovered the tomb had been robbed. The thieves took Leroy, 40 bags of Jelly Worms, and left a ransom note on a cardboard box demanding 1 ½ miles of Jelly Worms, and that they would be back in touch.

We didn't hear anything for two weeks. Then we had a telephone call from Braniff Airlines in Tulsa, Oklahoma. The voice said, "I've got Leroy Brown, now how do I get the money?" Well, right after Leroy was taken I had put up a reward of $10,000 for information leading to the arrest of the grave robber but not for the return of Leroy. When we told the caller that, he hung up.

Three or four days later we got another call from someone else at Braniff who said he had a box there at the baggage desk and it smelled really bad. Suzanne informed him the box was not sealed so he could open it to confirm if a fish was in it. He did, and Leroy was. They sent him back, and this time we gave him a private burial.

Today, more than 30 years later, people still come to see his grave and tombstone. We have a clipping from a newspaper in Russia that carried the story of Leroy's funeral, so I guess it was published all over the world.

★ ★ ★

Tom Mann died on February 11, 2005, from complications following heart surgery. He was 72.

Chapter Five

Glen Lau: "I Had No Idea a Bass Could Do That"

Glen Lau's film Bigmouth *was introduced in 1973 and completely changed how anglers viewed the largemouth bass. The first film to document a full year in the life of the largemouth, it was followed several years later by* Bigmouth Forever. *Both films are still being sold today.* Photo courtesy of Glen Lau.

In 1971, the total knowledge of what the world knew about the behavior of largemouth bass could be summed up in just a few paragraphs, and those paragraphs were largely being written by fishermen. Tournament competitors like Roland Martin and John Powell, as well as lure makers like Buck Perry and Fred Arbogast added immeasurably to the general pool of knowledge, but their knowledge came almost exclusively from their fishing experiences.

True, they were fishing different lakes and river systems around the country at various times of the year, and Martin and Powell rank among the finest bass fishermen of all time, but their experiences were also mixed with theories and guesses, and nearly always based on whether or not a bass hit their lures. At the same time, a handful of journalists, most notably Homer Circle, and Jason Lucas before him, were doing their best to answer the growing number of questions being asked by the public. What they all observed and experienced came from the seat of a boat; below the surface, the real world of the largemouth bass remained a mystery.

Enter then, a former Great Lakes fishing guide named Glen Lau, who in ten full years of guiding on Lake Erie had never come back to the dock without at least one fish. Lau had traded his guiding gear for underwater cameras and scuba diving equipment, and in 1971 began filming what turned out to be a movie that changed the entire world of bass fishing. The movie was named *Bigmouth*, and when it was released in 1973, some theaters showed it 40 and 50 times continuously. Lau had made 50 copies of the film, and within six months all but two had been stolen. The Shakespeare Company, which had helped finance the filming, went from an average rod and reel manufacturer to one of the top firms in the industry, where it remains today. Hundreds of thousands of copies of *Bigmouth* have since been sold, and are still being sold today. Lau himself went on to produce numerous series of outdoor programming for television, as well as another equally famous underwater film, *Bigmouth Forever*.

More importantly, Lau's work changed how everyone, especially fishermen, approached the largemouth after seeing the film. For the first time ever, anglers saw exactly how bass related to cover; the way the fish hit their lures or how quickly they could spit them back out; and how they actually spawned and then guarded their nest and newly hatched fry. Lau filmed for 18 straight months, during which time he was in the water every day except three, and shot more than 85,000 feet of film. Working in the clear water of Silver Springs, Florida, Lau sometimes spent as many as ten straight hours just sitting on the bottom observing and filming how bass acted. Although some sequences in the film last only a few seconds, they may have taken more than a month to capture on film.

Born September 15, 1935, in Ironville, Ohio, Lau did not discover bass fishing until he was 14, during a two-week summer stay at East Harbor on Lake Erie. In a johnboat with local fisherman Sam Oatley, it was Lau's first time to use baitcasting tackle, and when a four-pound largemouth hit the homemade topwater lure Oatley had given him, Lau was hooked as firmly as the fish. As he relates in his biography, *Bass Forever* (The Whitefish Press, 2010), after that two-week vacation, he began riding his bicycle the 47 miles from Ironville back to East Harbor just so he could experience the thrill of that strike again and again.

By age 17 he'd decided to become a fishing guide on Lake Erie, but it took him nearly six more years of grueling, sometimes menial jobs—he'd dropped out of school after the eighth grade—to save enough money to buy his first boat and actually start his business. It was 1958 and Erie was considered too polluted to have much of a fish population, but Lau quickly disproved that. Concentrating on smallmouth bass, walleye, and white bass, he started averaging as much as 200 pounds of fish a day on rod and reel, totals unheard of at the time.

That year he won the King of Ohio fishing tournament, despite not getting into the 12-week long contest until it was half over, but even with that disadvantage he still weighed in some 2,900 pounds of fish, and won by more than 1,000 pounds. The press attention he received for winning not only gained him more guide clients, but also allowed him to purchase a full set of scuba gear, which after just a few dives, made him decide to become an underwater filmmaker.

By 1971, after he'd made a number of films and television commercials, Lau had moved to Key West, Florida, thinking the filming opportunities there would be inexhaustible. Within just a few months, however, he found the spectacular saltwater fishing and the relaxed lifestyle there weren't exactly conducive to getting a lot of work done, so he decided to move. Along the way, he stopped in Ocala to visit his friend Homer Circle, whom he had met several years earlier. Circle was well-known and highly respected as the fishing editor of *Sports Afield Magazine,* and while he had traveled and fished over much of the world, Circle's special interest was the largemouth bass. Lau wanted to produce a film titled *The Bassin' Man*, about Circle's life.

That changed, however, after Circle took Lau to Silver Springs where he had permission to go diving; after two weeks of filming and studying bass behavior in the crystal clear water, Lau knew he wanted to see and film more of the life of the largemouth. Thus, the plan to film *The Bassin' Man* was dropped, and *Bigmouth* took its place. Just like that, the world of bass fishing took a quantum leap forward.

As a producer and director Lau created more than 200 television programs, including segments of *The American Sportsman*, the *Wild, Wild World of Animals*, *Quest for Adventure*, and *The Outdoorsman*. In 1996, after three years of work, he released *Bigmouth Forever*, another study of the largemouth bass, this time concentrating more on finding and catching the fish. That film won numerous awards, and like its predecessor *Bigmouth*, is still being sold today. Lau is also the founder of the highly successful Hooked on Fishing, Not on Drugs campaign, and he is one of the few anglers who have been inducted into both the Fishing Hall of Fame and the Bass Fishing Hall of Fame.

★ ★ ★

Even though the focus of *Bigmouth* changed from a story about Homer Circle to the life cycle of the bass, Homer played a major part in the filming and production of the movie. He was with me every day, casting lures to specific places I directed him to, and offering advice. Honestly, he was as excited as I was about what we were doing. We didn't have a written-out shooting script or definite plan we tried to follow. All I had was a basic idea in my mind of what I wanted, and I originally thought I could do it in two months. That turned into 18 months, and we could have gone longer.

Naturally, spending that much time with the fish, we learned a lot about bass behavior, and some of it was really surprising. One day, for example, I was down in an area with some bass off to one side, and I told Homer to put on a crankbait and make a cast in a specific direction so I could film a fish hitting the lure. Homer made the cast, and then I watched amazed as a bass swam up behind the crankbait, completely engulfed it, then spit it out, all in a fraction of a second. It actually happened twice. I had never seen anything like that before. I didn't know bass could do that.

I surfaced and asked Homer why he hadn't set the hook, and he replied that he'd never felt anything at all during his retrieve, except an almost imperceptible tick, as if the crankbait had touched a piece of grass. He was as surprised as I was that he'd never detected the fish, but from that moment on, he began setting the hook whenever he felt *anything* different during his retrieve.

Many fishermen, myself included, had always thought the female bass left the nest immediately after spawning, but through my filming I learned otherwise. In fact, the females remain around the nest for about 48 hours, although they're not always that visible. I even watched one female help guard her eggs for five days before swimming away.

It seemed like each week we were documenting some form of behavior no one had ever clearly observed before, and that we were breaking all the established "norms" that writers had been reporting for years.

I knew bass were voracious predators and often fed on baby ducklings, and I had seen it happen often during our filming but had never been able to capture it on film. Then, suddenly, there it was, and I captured the entire sequence, which in this case included showing the duckling actually pulling its head back out of the bass's mouth and escaping. I was so excited I took the film up to Jacksonville immediately to be processed so I could see what I had. Normally, I waited until I had taken about a thousand feet of film before I had it processed, but this time I just couldn't wait. To me, that duckling sequence remains one of my favorite parts of the film because I had wanted to nail it down the way it happened in its entirety. It had taken 34 days to get it.

While the bass are generally pretty efficient predators, it's amazing any of them really survive, because so many other creatures prey on them. It took about two weeks, but eventually I filmed an anhinga swimming underwater and actually spearing a bass, and I also filmed a great blue heron grabbing a bass and then swallowing it.

After 18 months of filming, we felt we had enough footage, and Parker Bauer, the son of outdoor writer Erwin "Joe" Bauer, wrote the script. I consider Joe Bauer my mentor in this business, and in my early years, he and I collaborated on a lot of stories that he wrote for both *Sports Afield* and *Outdoor Life* magazines. Then, with my final $9,000, I hired television actor Rod Serling to narrate Parker's script.

I had to borrow money to fly to Chicago in 1973 to the National Sporting Goods Association annual meeting. This was the fishing tackle show known today as ICAST, and when the movie was shown, people just seemed to go crazy because they'd never seen anything like it before. From that type of reaction I knew all those months and hours underwater had been worth it.

★ ★ ★

Glen Lau and his wife live on their ten-acre horse farm in Williston, Florida, not that far from Silver Springs where he made the film that defined his life.

Chapter Six

Stan Fagerstrom: "Giving Casting Lessons to a Princess"

Bass fishing was not on Stan Fagerstrom's mind very often while growing up on a small wheat farm in northwest North Dakota during the Depression until the day he found an old outdoor magazine and read a fishing story that sparked his imagination. He doesn't remember the author or even the magazine, but he knows it changed his life, so much so that when his family moved to Longview, Washington, in 1936 and Fagerstrom realized nearby Lake Sacajawea contained largemouth bass, he traded an old Montgomery Ward guitar his parents had given him one Christmas for his first rod and reel.

He couldn't afford any lures, but somewhere along the way he had acquired one spinner-type lure, and with bacon he'd convinced his mother to save, he fashioned a homemade pork chunk. Thus armed, he headed straight to the lake and promptly caught his very first bass. Although he was living on the Columbia River in the heart of some of America's finest steelhead and salmon fishing, Fagerstrom concentrated on Sacajawea's bass because he could walk or ride his bicycle to the lake. It took an automobile to reach the steelhead waters, and he didn't have one. He was 12 years old.

No writer has had as much influence in popularizing largemouth bass fishing in the Pacific Northwest as Stan Fagerstrom, who not only served as outdoor editor of The Daily News *in Longview, Washington, for four decades but also wrote fishing stories for the nation's top outdoor magazines. Fagerstrom is also an expert caster and has performed casting demonstrations around the world.* Photo courtesy of Stan Fagerstrom.

Today, millions of fishermen throughout the United States and numerous foreign countries are thankful the young angler concentrated on bass, because for more than 60 years Fagerstrom has been teaching them how to fish through his writings, his casting demonstrations, and his seminars. He pioneered bass fishing at a time and in a region when the species was barely known and often considered a trash fish; today, he is one of the most highly respected outdoor writers in the world. He has been elected into both the Fresh Water Fishing Hall of Fame and the Bass Fishing Hall of Fame, and won too many awards to list.

It started in 1946, after Fagerstrom returned home to Longview at the conclusion of World War II. He'd enlisted in 1942 at age 19 and served with Company G, 167th Infantry Regiment in the 31st Infantry Division, the famous Dixie Division that saw heavy fighting in New Guinea and the Philippines. He went to work full-time for *The Daily News,* where one of the first things he did was start an outdoor column titled "Nibbles & Bites," which would continue for the next 40 years.

Although he was careful to write about the area's steelhead fishing, he also included bass fishing in his column, and every week brought letters of protest and questions from the salmon fishing readers who asked why he devoted even a single line of editorial copy about a fish many described as second cousin to a carp. At the same time, however, Fagerstrom helped nurture a growing interest in bass, especially among a group of Seattle fishermen who had formed the Western Bass Club, one of the oldest such fishing clubs in the nation. Then, the Oregon Bass & Pan Fish Club was formed not far away in Portland in 1958. He took area steelhead guides bass fishing to teach them about the sport, eventually leading one of the area's best-known anglers to change his allegiance entirely to bass.

Not only was Fagerstrom writing about bass for *The Daily News* in Longview, but also in the *Vancouver Columbian,* a rival newspaper where he had to use a pen name for 11 years. He began writing fishing articles for leading national outdoor magazines, hosted a radio program about fishing, and in 1973 wrote a book, *Catch More Bass,* that is still being quoted today. No writer has had as much influence in popularizing bass fishing in the Pacific Northwest; his work was exactly what the sport needed at that time to be able to grow in a region where few had ever considered bass a true gamefish.

Along the way, Fagerstrom developed a strong friendship with Jason Lucas, the popular and widely read fishing editor of *Sports Afield*

Magazine and one of the earliest proponents of bass fishing in the national media. The two found common bonds in bass fishing and in their efforts to publicize the fish at a time when trout fishing was far more popular. Fagerstrom considers Lucas a guiding force in his career, and the two remained close friends long after Lucas left *Sports Afield* in 1968; Fagerstrom still has a box of letters the two writers exchanged through the years.

Realizing there were always many elements involved in a day of fishing he could never control, Fagerstrom began concentrating on those he could control, one of which was accuracy in his casting, putting his lure right on target time after time. Using two reels, a Langley Streamlite and a Lurecast, he began practicing every chance he had, and soon word began to spread about his prowess. One day in 1952, a man named Nate Buell walked into Fagerstrom's newspaper office and put two reels on his desk; Buell represented the Abu Garcia Company and the reels were brand new Swedish-made red Ambassadeur 5000s, the first ever seen on the West Coast. Once again, Fagerstrom's life changed in a way that would impact millions of fishermen over the next half century.

Buell invited him to demonstrate the reels at the huge outdoor recreation show in the Pan Pacific Auditorium in Los Angeles, where Fagerstrom spent 11 days casting eight to ten hours each day. Other appearances followed as both his reputation and his repertoire of casting tricks grew. Not only could he consistently drop a small casting weight into a coffee cup at 30 feet, or pop helium-filled balloons floating away, he could seemingly make a lure change directions—90 degrees.

The rods and reels Fagerstrom used were not special-made; they were exactly the same ones any angler could purchase for himself, and while he made his casts, he not only explained how he was accomplishing them, he also provided a running commentary of why casting accuracy was important, especially in bass fishing.

He made two trips to New Zealand to demonstrate his casting skills, the first performance of this type ever made in the country; and he did the same in São Paulo, Brazil. In both countries he was also featured in the local newspapers as well as on nationwide television, and thousands watched him in person. In São Paulo, he signed autographs for three hours the day after he appeared on television, and even the attendants on his return flight to the United States asked for his autograph. He was in such demand at sports shows throughout the United States he was hardly home for more than a few hours at a time during the annual January to mid-April show season. When he was home, he was either writing or fishing.

Early on, he became known as the Master Caster, and requests to give casting demonstrations continue to come in today. More than once he's been approached by strangers who thank him for teaching them to cast a fishing lure 30 or 40 years ago.

★ ★ ★

One year, while performing one of my casting demonstrations at the International Sportsman's Exposition in San Mateo, California, I noticed a group of Japanese gathered at the far end of my casting area taking photos of me. It wasn't distracting, but I wondered what it was all about. Soon enough, I learned.

One of the gentlemen came up to me after I'd finished and told me they planned to show their photos to the directors of a big sports show in Tokyo to try to convince them to hire me to do my casting demonstrations there. I immediately said I'd be interested, and not long after, one of the directors flew over and made a formal invitation.

Stan Fagerstrom giving a casting demonstration in Tokyo, Japan. Photo courtesy of Stan Fagerstrom.

Stan Fagerstrom gives a demonstration to Princess Nobuku. Photo courtesy of Stan Fagerstrom.

Not totally sure of what I was getting into, I flew to Tokyo and was soon ushered to my accommodations in one of the city's newest and grandest hotels, which, fortunately, was within walking distance of the auditorium where I would be performing.

The opening ceremony was very formal and filled with dignitaries, all of whom were dressed in black suits. Princess Nobuku, one of the nation's more revered citizens, cut the ribbon to open the show; you can imagine how I felt, dressed in casual slacks and wearing a vest with my fishing sponsors' patches all over it!

Shortly after Princess Nobuku cut the ribbon, one of her representatives came to me and mentioned that the Princess liked to fish occasionally, and wondered if I would consider giving her a private casting demonstration, since the public had not yet entered the building. "Of course," I answered, but then I started wondering how in the world I would communicate with her to describe what I was doing. I did not speak one word of Japanese, and working through a translator would be difficult if he did not understand fishing.

I should have known she could speak excellent English, for she was highly educated, and for 15 minutes we talked back and forth as I made my various casts and my nervousness disappeared. I don't believe I converted the Princess into a bass fisherman, but it was one of the most enjoyable casting demonstrations I've ever been privileged to perform.

★ ★ ★

Stan Fagerstrom is still writing regularly, and practicing his trick casting, from his home in Sun Lakes, Arizona.

THE TACKLE

———

Chapter Seven

How One Fish Changed the Tackle Industry

An angler is silhouetted in the late afternoon sun with a nice largemouth bass. Although the fish tend to be most active at daylight and again at dusk, fishermen go after them at all hours of the day and night.

The bass that changed the entire fishing tackle industry was not the world record 22-pound, 4-ounce giant George Perry caught in 1932. Instead, it was a little 2 ½-pounder an angler named Bill Dance caught just after daybreak on June 6, 1967, throwing a 7 ¼-inch blue Fliptail plastic worm to a sunken roadbed on Beaver Lake in Arkansas.

It was Dance's first cast of the morning, and is widely acknowledged as the very first cast by anyone in the All American Bass Tournament being conducted on the lake that week. The All American, in turn, was the first event conducted by what would soon become the Bass Anglers Sportsman Society, a fledgling fishing tournament organization that quickly became the unifying voice for millions of American bass fishermen.

Just as importantly, that unification led to the most rapid expansion the fishing tackle industry had ever experienced. Fishing lures, as well as rods, reels, and other equipment, were already being manufactured, of course, in some cases for more than 60 years; the first patent for a fishing lure was actually issued in 1848. But Dance's fish, along with those caught and weighed in by his fellow competitors—another fisherman named Stan Sloan won the three-day event with 37 pounds, 8 ounces—created a wave of excitement that continued to build and grow for decades to come.

More changes took place in the tackle industry during the next 25 years than in all previous years combined because anglers like Dance, Sloan, and the others were not only learning new techniques, they were teaching those techniques to others. That led to the formation of new manufacturing companies, as well as competition between them, which spurred growth and development even faster. The new industry followed the new tournaments, and more than one competitive fisherman started his own tackle company, either because he needed an item not then available, or if it was, he thought he could make it better.

This is not to detract in any way from James Heddon, who is rightly credited with creating the first American fishing lure manufacturing company in 1902, James Heddon & Son. The business was located in southwestern Michigan in the town of Dowagiac, which, incidentally, translates into "many fishes" in the language of the nearby Potawatomi Indian tribe. Heddon had already been extremely successful in the beekeeping business, but he suffered from asthma; his father and grandfather had both enjoyed fishing occasionally so he was no stranger to the sport himself. Besides, he felt being on the water helped him feel better.

On one such excursion in 1898, Heddon is said to have whittled a stick down to a small size as he waited for his fishing companions to arrive there at the mill pond in Dowagiac, and then absently tossed the carving into the water where it was immediately hit by a bass. Heddon, who had long been intrigued by topwater fishing, then began carving additional lures, attached hooks, and selling them to his friends. These "frogs" resembled little more than a section of broomstick and included a bottle cap at the head of the stick to create action as the lure was retrieved, but they caught fish.

This crude, stick-like lure evolved into the Dowagiac Perfect Casting Bait, and became Heddon's first commercial lure. Although he initially made them in his home, with the paint baked in his wife's oven, in 1902 the first permanent lure factory was set up on the second floor of a clothing store in downtown Dowagiac.

Other fishing companies began about this same time, and some actually preceded Heddon. What is known for certain is that the beginning of the fishing tackle industry gradually emerged during the next two decades. Firms like Creek Chub, Hildebrandt, Shakespeare, Pflueger, and South Bend opened their doors, but none could have possibly imagined the future of what to that point was still only a casual pastime.

Surprisingly, perhaps, some lures from this long-ago era are still being manufactured and used regularly by today's bass fishermen. Without question, one of the most famous is the Zara Spook, a topwater lure Heddon introduced in 1922 as the Zaragossa Minnow. The lure had been designed by Heddon's son Will at their family home in Florida, and named for a well-known street in the red-light district of Pensacola where ladies of the night regularly walked the sidewalks.

The lure became an instant success because of its side-to-side action, which soon became known as "walking the dog." This term also refers to those imaginative ladies on Zaragossa Street, who, after being forbidden to approach potential customers on the sidewalk, simply began walking their pets on leashes along the same route.

Some lures were named for famous personalities, such as the Little George, produced by Eufaula, Alabama, angler Tom Mann, who fished against Dance in that first Beaver Lake tournament. Mann had been a game warden and one day while on a stakeout along a stream he whittled a lure that immediately caught bass. Mann named the lure after Alabama's governor at the time, George Wallace.

One lure, the Gilmore Jumper, was even sold with a snakeskin covering. As the story goes, a bass fisherman was having a fabulous day on the Buffalo River in Arkansas catching bass with a brown painted Jumper, but lost the lure when his line broke. On his way back to town to purchase a new brown lure, he ran over a snake on the road, and seeing the snake's brown coloration, the angler immediately skinned it, glued the skin on another lure, and started fishing again.

In many instances, other lure changes came in bits and pieces over the years, especially in the decades of the 1970s and 1980s. Spinnerbaits, for example, were popular before Dance caught his Beaver Lake bass; the basic safety-pin design still in use today was patented on June 28, 1966, by Chicago inventor Jesse M. Shannon, but it was improved on in March 1970 by John R. Hudson who patented his design of placing the spinner blade on the wire so it would help make the lure snag-proof. Alabama angler Bill Huntley added ball bearing swivels to the lures, as well as made the change from steel piano wire to satin stainless wire. Skirts eventually evolved from plastic to rubber, and blades began to change shape from round to long, narrow, and pointed.

Stan Sloan, in fact, winner of that first Beaver Lake tournament, used his expertise and name recognition to launch his Zorro Spinnerbaits; Don Butler, another competitor in that same tournament, started his Okiebug Spinnerbait company; and Charles Spence and Ray Murski, who also competed at Beaver Lake (Murski finished fourth) were poised to take Spence's fledgling spinnerbait company to heights undreamed of by either of them.

The previous year, Spence had purchased a small garage-based lure company in west Tennessee and immediately renamed it Strike King. Spinnerbait blades were punched out by a single machine that simply dropped the blades into a cardboard box on the floor, and the wire frames were created by bending a piece of wire around pegs on a small board. In 1968, Murski started selling them across the southern United States—he was one of Sam Walton's original salesmen—and the rest really is history.

Murski was a huge supporter of bass fishing in general and of Ray Scott's professional tournament idea specifically. He fished 11 of Scott's events, and earned a check in all of them, so he not only knew how to fish, he knew what fishermen wanted, and they wanted spinnerbaits, as well as anything else that would fool a bass. In 1995, Murski bought Strike King from Spence, and added additional tournament anglers to his pro staff. He didn't just pay them to wear his logo at tournaments, however; the anglers played a very active role in designing Strike King's lures, and then winning with them. Today, Strike King is regarded as one of the world's foremost lure manufacturers, with a lineup that includes dozens of baits in both hard and soft plastic designs.

Although a spinnerbait blade design known as the willowleaf had been around for several years, it hit national prominence in 1984 when several anglers won national tournaments using it, including a Florida-based pro named Roland Martin, who had done his best to keep the long, narrow, pointed-end blade a secret. Once Martin's secret lure was discovered, no one helped fishermen learn how to use it more than Martin himself, and today the willowleaf spinnerbait blade is the standard blade of choice among bass fishermen everywhere.

While many lure changes were small and incremental, others were sometimes monumental, such as what happened to crankbaits in 1972. Prior to that year, these types of lures, which had been around for half a century, looked remarkably similar. Most featured generally elongated bodies and a front diving lip, most often made of metal. There were other styles, but in 1972 a lure named the Big O changed everything.

The Big O was a hand-carved balsa diving plug, created by Fred Young of Maynardville, Tennessee, and named after his 6-foot, 6-inch football playing brother Odis. The lure incorporated several features never before combined so successfully in a single plug: it dived quickly on retrieve and swam with a strong side-to-side wobble, then floated right to the surface if the retrieve was stopped. Until then, most crankbaits had a very slow, lazy action. The Big O also featured a short, squared-off bill so it deflected off cover well, and instead of being long and skinny, it was short and squatty, almost fat. One writer of the time described it as a pregnant guppy.

At the June 1972 Tennessee Invitational tournament conducted on Watts Bar Lake by the Bass Anglers Sportsman Society, a professional fisherman named Billy Westmorland (who had been using the Big O secretly for months) accidentally let the lure be seen by his competition, and a virtual stampede to find Big Os started. At that tournament, the lure rented for $5 a day but cost $25 if you lost it. A new one, if you could locate one, sold for as much as $50.

In Hot Springs, Arkansas, a leading lure manufacturer of the time, Cotton Cordell, secured the manufacturing rights to the Big O from

Young, and began producing them in plastic; during the next 12 months he sold more than a million of them. Helping the Big O's reputation during this time was the fact that a tournament fisherman, Larry Hill, caught more than 60 pounds of bass in an hour with the lure en route to winning a national bass tournament competition in Florida.

That type of success led other manufacturers to bring out their own similar-looking lures, and practically overnight the age of the "alphabet plugs" was born. Companies like Bagley, Norman, and others called their creations the Balsa B, Big N, and similar names. The most important legacy the Big O created was that practically every crankbait made today includes some of that lure's same original design and offers the same basic action Fred Young carved into his original lure. Many are thinner and others will dive much deeper, but all have a distinct wobble.

Plastic worms, widely used today, had been around since the early 1950s. Imitation worms made of rubber and designed for fishing had been tried nearly a century earlier, and later models impregnated with special scents appeared in the 1930s. In the years immediately following World War II, however, as bass fishing continued to grow as a sport, a number of individuals developed worms from plastic. Among them were Dave DeLong, Nick Creme, and Charles Burke.

During this time, as competition between manufacturers began to increase, worm designs started to change. Although the worm itself remained straight, body styles varied considerably. Bing McClellan of Burke introduced the Buckshot Worm that looked like just that, a string of beads or "buckshot" with a floppy tail. Others concentrated on color and length, with DeLong producing worms more than 12 inches in length.

In 1973, however, the plastic worm grew a new tail that changed the lure forever. This change started during the summer of 1973 when R. J. Benson, president of a Rockaway, New Jersey, firm named Generic Systems, showed a French lure named the Sosy Eel at the American Fishing Tackle Manufacturers Show in Chicago. The lure featured a thin, flat curving tail that produced a dramatic swimming action when retrieved, and cried Benson, it was being illegally copied by several American firms.

Indeed, the swimming tail concept was so revolutionary it was quickly adopted by other manufacturers. The first to bring their own such worm to market was Carver Plastisols Co. (later to become Mister Twister, Inc.) of Minden, Louisiana, and after its introduction in early 1974, more than three million had been shipped by April. They retooled their manufacturing facility to be able to produce half a million worms a day.

The impact on the industry was so stunning that nearly all the major manufacturers had curly-tail or swimming-tail worms on the market within weeks. Included were Cordell's Pigtail, Mann's Jelly Twister, Burke's Wig-Wag, Bagley's Screw Tail, Lindy's Swirltail, and Pico's Streaker. A Cordell rep reportedly sold $9,000 worth of their worms by demonstrating one in a toilet bowl.

Although several of these firms are no longer in business, this particular design continues to be one of the most popular and is offered by all of today's manufacturers. The overall concept remains unchanged, although the design has been altered slightly over the years, and is now incorporated in plastic lizards, grubs, minnows, and other creatures.

If the curled, swimming tails created a more realistic look for soft plastic lures, then colors and new paints did the same for hard plastic and wood lures. Realism was the catchword of the day, as manufacturers tried different techniques to make their lures appear as natural as possible. Photo-imprintation became popular for a short while, while others kept adding more and more coats of paint. In Bagley's case, each lure received a total of 17 coats as it moved down the assembly line.

Not all developments in the fledgling fishing industry were lures, of course. Realizing the growing legion of anglers also required rods, reels, and fishing lines in order to use their new lures, various firms entered this new arena specializing with those products. The first "multiplying" reel, a forerunner of today's popular baitcasting reels, had been introduced as far back as 1770 by Onesimus Ustonson of Britain, but it was not until 1896 when William Shakespeare, Jr., of Kalamazoo, Michigan, created the first true level-wind reel that these types of reels started to grow in popularity. Level-wind allows line to be wound back evenly on a reel after a cast, and is standard on all baitcasting reels today.

Shakespeare started his own reel making company the following year, and by 1902, as James Heddon moved his young lure business from his home to a dedicated factory, Shakespeare's company already had a dozen employees. For more than a century the firm, now headquartered in Columbia, South Carolina, has continued to introduce new and innovative reels as well as rods and fishing line. In 1947, Shakespeare introduced the first fiberglass rod, the Wonderod, revolutionizing the market and all but making bamboo and steel rods obsolete.

Shakespeare entered the fishing industry by design; others, like the little company that would eventually become a giant in the sport and one of Shakespeare's strongest competitors, Zebco, moved into the fishing world completely by coincidence.

In 1948, still nearly 20 years before Dance caught that Beaver Lake bass, the Tulsa-based firm was known as the Zero Hour Bomb Co., making time-detonated bombs for use in oil exploration and drilling. By 1948, however, with their patent on bombs about to expire and new technology threatening to make their explosives obsolete, the company began looking for new products to manufacture.

They found it in fishing, when a West Texas angler/watch repairman/inventor named R. D. Hull walked in with something none of them had seen before, a reel that would not backlash. Actually, Hull didn't show them a fishing reel because he hadn't made one; what he did show his future bosses, Harold Binford and Marion Parry, was a Folger's coffee can lid fastened to a piece of plywood. However crude it was, the concept—a fixed spool from which line came off on demand (casting) but was controlled, and could then be "reeled" back onto that spool—impressed Binford and Parry enough to invite Hull back with an actual prototype model.

Hull built his prototype in less than a month and returned to Zebco to show his new creation. Hull's reel was not the first fixed-spool "spinning" reel—British angler Alfred Holden received a patent for one in 1905 and others had been imported and even built in the United States since the 1930s. While certainly easier for the casual fisherman to use than the revolving-spool baitcasting reels of the day, these early spinning reels still had problems, namely line spilling freely off the spool. That's what Hull's coffee lid stopped; he put a cap over the spool and controlled line flow by use of a pin located inside that cap.

Hull was hired on the spot, and on May 7, 1949, the Zero Hour Bomb Company's first closed-face reel, the Standard, came off the production line. The firm soon shortened its name to Zebco as improvements in their new product, which became known as a spincast reel, continued. In 1954, Zebco introduced the model 33, featuring a push button spool control, and during the next 32 years more than 185 million had been sold, and the reels continue to be sold today. The decision by Harold Binford and Marion Parry, neither of whom knew anything about fishing, has to be considered one of the most fortuitous in the entire history of sport fishing, because Hull's plywood board and coffee can lid literally opened up the world of fishing to the masses.

His invention offered an alternative to the revolving spool reel, which had been around in various forms for well over a century. A Kentucky fisherman named George Snyder invented what is considered the first reel that actually paid out line during a cast; the term "baitcaster," still in use today, came from the fact that virtually all fishing at that time was done with live bait, since there were no artificial lures.

At Beaver Lake in 1967, Dance fished with a baitcaster made by the Swedish firm of Abu, which by that time pretty much controlled the revolving spool reel market. Their signature reel was painted red and designated the 5000. By today's standards, the 5000 would be considered primitive, since it was fairly big and heavy, featured a 5:1 gear ratio, and had no adjustable spool braking system. Once tournament fishing truly became the moving force spurring tackle development, changes in reels came quickly.

Today, baitcasters continue to evolve as bass fishing continues to grow and thrive. Braking systems, usually with a set of tiny internal magnets, have all but made these reels backlash-proof. Gearing varies from 4.7:1 to higher than 7:1, a range that allows a great deal of variation in lure retrieve speed that was never available in Dance's red 5000. The gears are stronger, too; the overall size is smaller and more streamlined; and numerous companies like Shimano, Shakespeare, Pure Fishing, and Ardent compete for angler dollars. Abu reels themselves have changed dramatically, as well, and are part of the Pure Fishing Company lineup.

Another reel, the open-face fixed spool spinning reel, had been introduced from Europe into the United States in 1935 but had not gained a following until the years following World War II. This particular design permitted the weight of the lure to pull line off the stationary spool, a feature that allowed the use of extremely light lures. Changes in these reels were also gradual, until 1963 when the Japanese company, Matsui Manufacturing, under its American umbrella, Daiwa Corporation, began importing its first fishing reels.

In 1970, just three years after Dance's tournament on Beaver Lake, Daiwa imported an open-face spinning reel with a skirted spool, a feature that provided far greater line control than previous models, and by 1971 virtually every company making these types of reels offered this feature, which continues to be the standard design of today.

Most of the anglers in that first Beaver Lake event also used 5 ½-foot, hollow fiberglass rods with short pistol-grip handles, but practically no one offers models like this today. The first pistol grip had been whittled out of wood by Cotton Cordell and taken to Japan by Cordell and another rod maker friend from Alabama, Lew Childre. The Japanese produced a handle for them overnight, which Childre then began using on his own rods, known as Speed Sticks and which quickly became the most popular handle style in America.

One of Childre's employees at the time was a former football player named Shag Shahid, who had traded in his pads for fishing gear. He designed Childre's Speed Stick rods, and as early as 1960 had made a V-shaped spool for baitcasting reels, a design to help reduce backlashes because the line speed slowed automatically during each cast. Childre introduced the reel in the mid-1970s, and while it did not become an overnight success, it led to the emergence of one of today's industry giants, Shimano, the world's largest bicycle component manufacturer. They were the company who did the original manufacturing of Shahid's reel, the Speed Spool.

In 1976, Shimano introduced its own reel, the Bantam 100, which was the first true, small, lightweight baitcaster. Additional baitcasters, spinning reels, and rods followed—all of it starting just nine years after Dance and Sloan had fished that first major tournament and basically shown the world new ways to catch largemouth bass. Today Shimano is one of the foremost rod and reel manufacturing companies in the world.

Cordell had also been experimenting with a lighter, stronger, more sensitive material with which to build his rods, and by 1971 he'd found it: graphite. He wanted to enter that Beaver Lake tournament, but wasn't allowed to, since he'd been making fishing tackle for more than twenty years at that time and was considered a "pro."

During the mid-1970s, Cordell decided to get out of the rod business so he could concentrate on lures, and called another rod-making friend in Washington State to come get all his equipment if he wanted it. That friend was a man named Gary Loomis, who accepted Cordell's offer and hauled everything back to Woodland. There he established the G. Loomis rod company, which today is one of the most highly respected rod companies in the world and is now owned by the aforementioned Shimano Corporation.

Another West Coast company, Fenwick, introduced their own graphite rods in 1972, and through their highly successful marketing program, quickly established themselves as a leader in the field. Graphite is available in many different grades, often measured in a modulus, or strength, and during the next two decades Fenwick, G. Loomis, and other rod companies raced each other to see who could create rods with the highest modulus rating. This type of research and development cost hundreds of thousands of dollars, but by then demand by the nation's bass fishermen for lighter, stronger, more sensitive rods could support it.

Another segment of the rapidly growing bass fishing industry, electronics, was, at the same time, growing nearly as fast as the rod, reel, and lure business. Fishermen had been using sonar-type equipment prior to 1967, much of it produced by Carl Lowrance, who was using his Navy electronics experience now in freshwater. In 1957, Lowrance introduced what is generally called his "blue box" unit, since most of his equipment was fairly boxy looking and all were painted blue. A year later he produced the "gray box." Basically, these units told fishermen how deep the water was, but not much more.

In 1959, Lowrance introduced his "green box," and suddenly anglers could begin to see not only the bottom, but also had a clearer view of the bottom contour as well as objects on the bottom. Thus, the concepts of fishing "cover"—those objects—and "structure"—the contour—became realities. The tournament anglers had already figured out the rudiments of both concepts, but now they began to refine them in an ever-growing circle of knowledge. In 1972, tournament pro and lure maker Tom Mann, who had also started his own depth finder company, Allied Sports (later to become Techsonic Industries), did a quick survey of 25 top tournament anglers to determine what they regarded as their most important tool for catching bass; 19 said it was a depth finder.

By 1973, Lowrance had introduced paper chart recorders that literally graphed the bottom, and a decade later they introduced the first computerized model, the X-15. Two years later, paper units were already on the way out, replaced by liquid crystal recorders. Today, bass fishermen can look at objects in the water and on the bottom far to either side of their boats, not just in a small area underneath them, and they can tell exactly how far away it is so they can fish it that much more efficiently.

The overall concept—showing water depth, bottom contour and cover and fish above it—is still the same. The visual information is simply being presented in new and more exciting ways, and Dance, still an active fisherman and teacher, admits amazement at all that has happened not only in electronics but also rods, reels, and lures since that remarkable morning on Beaver Lake.

He did not originate the sport of bass fishing when he caught that little 2 ½-pounder. What he, Sloan, and the others did was far more important. Symbolically speaking, they opened the curtain on a brand new world. They were like explorers seeing another continent for the very first time; everything they did was new and fresh and exciting, and the fishing public embraced them because they could feel and experience that very same excitement.

Chapter Eight

Trig Lund: "We Wanted Anything New or Good We Didn't Have"

Trig Lund, shown with some of the fiberglass rods he helped design during his years working with Heddon. Lund was hired by John Heddon in 1945 and remained with the firm for the next 23 years, eventually serving as vice president. Photo courtesy of the Heddon Museum.

No one in James Heddon's family ever took credit for creating the first artificial lures for bass fishing, not even after idly tossing his little carved stick into the mill pond of Dowagiac Creek and seeing a bass hit it. Indeed, two firms that would become serious rivals, Pflueger and Shakespeare, had already been producing fishing lures since 1886 and 1897 respectively.

There is some evidence that also suggests Heddon himself may have been influenced by an earlier topwater lure he probably fished, a cork frog made by Charlie Harris of Mackinaw City, Michigan. The frog, which Harris was selling as early as 1896 and which he patented a year later, featured a hook in each leg, as well as a third hook in the body.

Heddon did not establish his own company, James Heddon and Son, until 1902, but what he did better than anyone else was recognize the business potential of producing fishing tackle. Heddon had long been a bass fisherman himself, so he understood both the fish as well as the anglers who pursued it. He and his cousin, W. H. Tuttle, had discovered fishing at an early age while exploring the Tuttle farm in southwestern Michigan. When the Heddon family moved to Dowagiac when he was 15, James began fishing the mill pond created by a dam across Dowagiac Creek.

Just as importantly as his interest in fishing, Heddon also became an expert in marketing, as evidenced by his worldwide success and recognition in the beekeeping industry. By the 1880s when he was still just approaching his 40th birthday, he had already invented and patented several products that dramatically improved the beekeeping industry.

Thus, it really comes as no surprise that the fishing lure company succeeded as quickly as it did. The original Dowagiac Perfect Casting Bait, his first commercial lure, was soon followed by other wood lures, both floating and sinking, including the Dowagiac Underwater; the company was selling as many as 6,000 lures a year within a short time.

When James Heddon died in 1911, his son Charles, who had really been the driving force behind the company for several years, became president. His brother Will, who had moved to Florida in 1903, continued to be associated with the company, but only in a modest role, and not one of leadership. Charles' son John, who had spent most of his early years in southern California where he had a Lincoln automobile dealership, returned to Dowagiac in the early 1930s, but he was not a major force in the company until 1941, when he became president after his father died of a stroke.

John was the last member of the Heddon family to lead the company, and he guided the company through World War II, but before the war ended in 1945 he hired a young engineer named Trygve Lund, better known as "Trig," who, for the next 23 years, would continue to push the Heddon name to the forefront of the lure-making industry. Born August 15, 1913, in Stillwater, Minnesota, Lund had been using Heddon lures for years while fishing for bass and walleye in the St. Croix River.

Interestingly, he never asked Heddon for a job. He had graduated from the University of Minnesota in 1941 and was working for Kimberly-Clark, buying tools for the war effort. He knew several Heddon salesmen, and during a business trip to Dowagiac he stopped at the plant to meet John Heddon. Heddon took him through the factory and along the way Lund suggested some minor changes in the hook arrangements in several of the lures he'd been using in the St. Croix River. Seeing Lund's experience not only as a fisherman but also as a quality control engineer, Heddon offered him a job.

During his career, Lund not only worked in developing and promoting new lures but also helped design the company's fiberglass rods. They made both solid and tubular models, and suitable for a variety of fresh and saltwater species. In time, Lund became supervisor of the manufacturing plant and later was named vice president of the company.

Initially, Lund's work at Heddon centered around improving existing lures and organizing the production and assembly of those lures. He spent thousands of hours testing and evaluating products, and even found time to develop new lures himself. One, a plastic worm with a light-reflecting, fish-attracting band around it that also served as the hook holder, received a patent in 1961.

Lund also helped smooth the transition between different owners. In 1959, John Heddon sold the company to the Murchison brothers of Dallas, who later also purchased Daisy Manufacturing, the famous BB gun company, and combined the two firms to create Daisy-Heddon. The Murchisons sold Daisy-Heddon in 1967, a sale that marked the beginning of more than a decade of ownership changes along with the separation of the two companies again.

Eventually, in 1977, Heddon was purchased by the Walter Kidde Company, and six years later they sold to EBSCO, a Birmingham, Alabama–based publishing/subscription service firm. Today, EBSCO's reach extends deep into the bass fishing industry as the owner of PRADCO (Plastics Research & Development Corporation), a group of well-known bass fishing brands that includes not only Heddon but also Bomber, Rebel, Arbogast, Cotton Cordell, and others, and is based in Ft. Smith, Arkansas.

For today's bass fisherman, one of Lund's greatest traits was the fact he seldom, if ever, discarded anything, even lure prototypes and designs that were never developed. Today, these items form the basis for the National Heddon Museum, located in the business office of the original Heddon factory building, which had been closed since 1984. Two long-time Dowagiac residents, Don and Joan Lyons, bought the factory in 1991, and after acquiring Lund's amazing collection, opened the museum in 1995.

Although the mill itself is gone, the pond where James Heddon tossed his little piece of carved wood still exists. Officially, it is now named James Heddon Park, but bass fishermen the world over know it as the place where the fishing tackle industry really got its start.

★ ★ ★

The plant had been well established before I came, and my first job was working with new baits. In those days, we did design and produce some of our own original lures but most of the time we went to fishermen themselves. We had salesmen and field testers all over the United States, and if they heard of a local guy catching a lot of bass, they would get to that fisherman and find out what kind of bait he was using. If it was one he had made himself, they would get samples of his lure and send them to us. We wanted anything new or good we didn't already have.

Once we got a bait like that, we'd fish it and see if we could improve it. Lots of times, we'd go fishing with that fisherman and get him to tell us all the fishing tricks he knew, and we'd use that to advertise and promote that lure. If we needed to, we would patent the lure and pay the fisherman for the rights to produce it.

The first thing we'd look at was to determine how hard it would be to make that lure. We had two big test tanks inside the factory where we did a lot of testing, and if we really liked a lure, we'd take the bait to other good fishermen we knew around the country and see how they liked it, and get their suggestions for improving it. I did a lot of that kind of fishing, traveling all over the United States to fish with these different anglers. My biggest bass ever weighed between 11 and 12 pounds, and I caught it in Florida when we were testing a lure like this.

We had to do all of this in secret, because there were other companies out there that did the same thing. That's how so many lures were developed in those days. There were also spies trying to see what we were doing, so we wouldn't show any lure we were testing to anybody. That's one reason we got patents. After we had a lure or a design patented, we'd start making them and selling them, and that's the first time any of our competition knew about it.

Sometimes the competition would find out about one of our lures and beat us into production, so we had some lawsuits to stop them, but sometimes we didn't stop them completely. We'd let them make the lure but we would limit them on how many sizes or colors, and we would let them advertise, too. Then we'd go ahead and manufacture and advertise our lure, so their advertising would help us sell our baits, especially because we'd have colors they couldn't have.

A lot of the lures we made took between three and six months from the time we received a patent to the time we were actually selling that lure. Some were faster than others, and some lures we just couldn't make because it just took too long or was too expensive. Almost all of the baits our salesmen sent us were hand carved from wood, and that fisherman never paid any attention to how long it might have taken him to carve it, but that was really important to us because we had to simplify it without changing it.

I always thought it was important to try to find out why a fish went after a lure, whatever it was, so I always told fishermen to look at what was in the stomach of the fish they caught. That's how we learned what kinds of colors attracted the fish, and that's what we tried to copy. We spray painted our lures, and a good sprayer could hold five different colors in her hand and spray them.

We sold most of our lures for about $1.50, and we did a lot of promoting and selling through sporting goods stores. We would make up a display to put in a store, then we would run down to the boat dock and give any fishermen we saw samples that they could give to other fishermen. We gave them the best colors, too, so after they used them and caught fish, they could go straight to the sporting goods store and buy that same color. It really worked, and we did that for years.

★ ★ ★

Trig Lund bought his home from John Heddon in 1954 and lived there until his death on December 17, 2004, at the age of 91.

Chapter Nine

Cotton Cordell: "I Never Had a Pocket without a Lure in It"

Red Fin. Hot Spot. Gay Blade. Boy Howdy. Crazy Shad. Sonic. Big O. Twin Spin. Near Nuthin. Vibra King and Vibra Queen. In the pantheon of famous bass fishing lures, these are always near the top of the list, and while some of today's younger bass fishermen may not have used them, an older generation knows them well.

What even some of the older anglers may not realize is that all of the above lures were created by the same person, Carl "Cotton" Cordell, Jr., of Hot Springs, Arkansas. He may have designed and created more fishing lures than any single individual in history—he has no idea how many, but it easily numbers in the hundreds and perhaps thousands. Cordell did not limit himself to lures, either; he produced a successful line of fiberglass fishing boats named the "Going Jessie," built an extensive line of rods, and produced high-speed gears for Abu Garcia reels.

Born in 1928 in Benton, Arkansas, where his father had a furniture store, he was always known as "Carl Jr.," but that ended before he turned 15, because by then his hair had turned snow-white. His nickname quickly became "Cotton" and has stayed with him his entire life. Even though his father took off every Thursday to drive the 25 miles to Hot

No single individual has designed and produced as many bass fishing lures as Cotton Cordell. Among his best-known creations are the Spot, a rattling, vibrating minnow imitation, which he carved from a piece of pine bark while sitting on a deer stand.

Springs and fish Lake Catherine, Cotton became more interested in high school sports, where he played center and defensive end on the school football team. It was not until he was in the 11th grade, after his father bought the boat landing on Catherine and they moved to Hot Springs, that he truly became interested in fishing.

The facility didn't include an actual dock, just a collection of 14-foot wooden boats customers would pull up on the bank. It was 1946, and with the end of World War II, people were fishing for food. The lake and river that fed it, the Ouachita, were filled with largemouth bass, white bass, crappie, and catfish, and Cotton, helping his father manage the landing, quickly learned the best methods and places for catching them all.

One day he stopped to watch another man fishing, and he simply could not believe how many fish he was catching. What Cotton learned changed his life, for the man was using a leadhead jig he'd taken out of a surplus B-52 bomber survival kit. The kits, available for $2 from Jack's Trading Post in Hot Springs, measured about six inches by eight inches, and included a small knife, some twine and bandages, and the 3/8-ounce jig. Cotton asked his wife (he'd gotten married at age 20) for $4 to buy two survival kits so he and his fishing buddy, a house painter named Zoom, would each have a jig.

The two of them caught 35 to 40 fish that day on their new jigs, before losing them in the rocks on the bottom of the river, so they decided to try to make some themselves. With the help of Cotton's father, they made a mold from plaster of paris in a cardboard box, melted lead in a pot on the kitchen stove, took the hooks off an old trotline, and produced about two dozen jigs before the mold wore out. Then a friend who worked in the nearby Alcoa Aluminum plant fabricated a mold for them and gave it to Cotton. He painted his jigs with fingernail polish, but when he started looking for hair to finish them, his heart sank when his father told him the survival jigs had been dressed with bucktail from a whitetail deer. Cotton had hunted as much as anyone but he'd never seen a deer in the wild near Hot Springs, so he did the next best thing: he cut hair from the family's English setter to finish his new lures.

The problem was, the dog couldn't grow hair back as fast as Cotton could sell his jigs; one morning his wife sold 60 of them for a dollar each to two visiting fishermen who'd never seen anything like them before, and another salesman simply took everything Cotton could make because the world was ready for them. Not long afterward, the plastic worm hit the market, and Cotton added a weedguard to his leadhead jigs, put two in a package and labeled them as "worm hooks"; he couldn't build them fast enough, either.

While it must be noted that this white-haired man from Hot Springs entered the world of bass fishing at precisely the right time in history to sell his new creations, it must also be recognized that Cordell was an exceptionally knowledgeable fishermen himself, and he never stopped fishing, or learning what types of lures fish seemed to hit best. That's why he was able to create such a long list of very successful baits, many of which are still being sold today, even though they were developed more than half a century ago.

For roughly 30 years, between about 1950 and 1980, Cordell produced some of the best-known lures in bass fishing history. He made them not only for his own company, Cordell Bait Company, but also for other major firms, including Heddon, Pflueger, Creek Chub, Crème, and Burke. In 1980, when he sold his company to EBSCO, which still produces lures under his name, Cordell employed more than 500 people and was producing more than 20,000 lures a day.

Those lures weren't all made in Hot Springs, either. Cordell was the first fishing lure manufacturer to move offshore; in his case, the location was El Salvador, the smallest country in Central America. He had a salesman in Baton Rouge who called one day in the early 1970s to tell him the State of Louisiana had an agreement with that country—if anyone would start a factory there, El Salvador would provide the workforce. With a sample package of baits in hand, Cordell flew to the capital, San Salvador, where he met Alfredo Herrodor, then the Minister of Industry, but he was still skeptical because, after all, no one in the tackle business had done this before.

He'd hardly returned to Hot Springs before the phone rang again. This time it was Alfredo, who announced he had resigned from the government, rented a building, and was ready to start making fishing lures. All he needed to do was fly to America and learn how to set up a lure-making plant. Alfredo arrived on a Wednesday afternoon and Cordell put him in a motel room to rest, stating he couldn't visit that evening because he and his wife always attended midweek church services. Alfredo asked to go along, and Cordell picked him up at six p.m.

Alfredo was so moved by the service he received his baptism that evening, and by the time he left for El Salvador a few days later, he and

Cordell had made a deal to let him start making fishing lures. Cordell sent him molds and bodies to assemble, then flew back to San Salvador just to see how Alfredo was doing. What he found was an operation set up exactly like Cordell's Hot Springs plant, turning out lures by the thousands.

Cordell was forced to buy a truck to take components down to New Orleans for shipment, and he'd return with a load of finished products perfectly ready for America's anglers, an arrangement that continued until he sold the company in 1980. Just as significantly, Cordell's success opened the door for other tackle manufacturers to also move offshore, a common and widespread practice that continues today.

In 1988 Cordell was inducted into the National Freshwater Fishing Hall of Fame in recognition of his lifetime in the fishing industry and the many contributions he made.

★ ★ ★

I never had a pocket that didn't have a lure in it, or at least a piece of wood that I was whittling into a lure. I always say I started making lures because I couldn't afford to buy them, and that's the truth. When we had the boat landing on Lake Catherine, each summer when the water was low I'd go out and pull up all the fishing line I could find because that's how I collected my own fishing lures. I couldn't afford to go buy new ones.

Some of my lure ideas came about in strange ways. For instance, one fall day in about 1962 I was deer hunting near Pryor, Arkansas, sitting on the ground against a big pine tree with a .30-30 across my lap. Nothing was happening, so I picked up a piece of bark and started whittling out a swimming minnow type of lure. I had used some lures like this before and liked how they performed. I just made the top flat and rounded off the bottom real pretty, but I didn't finish snubbing off the head the way I planned, because about then I heard the hounds getting closer.

I laid the piece of bark and my pocket knife on the ground, picked up my rifle, and shot a little three-point buck. I forgot about my whittling, but when I came back that night to retrieve my pocket knife, I saw the piece of bark I'd been working on, and it looked so good I picked it up and put it in my pocket.

When I went up to a tackle show in Chicago not long afterward to sell my jigs, I still had that piece of bark in my pocket, and when I showed it to someone who made lure molds, he agreed to make me one for $300. When I started painting them, I put a black spot on them, just like a shad has, and that's how that lure was named. At first, I called them Hot Spots, but then I learned someone else already had a lure named the Hot Shot, and after we visited, I dropped the name Hot, and just called it the Spot. It was really popular, too, and the only reason I didn't sell three million of them the next year was because I couldn't build that many.

One of the most successful lures I ever made was one I didn't design myself, the Big O crankbait. Fred Young of Maynardville, Tennessee, designed and carved that lure, and he was happy to sell them for $5 each. I got some of them, and really liked how they vibrated in the water, and they caught bass like crazy, too. So I had a mold made and made a Big

Cotton Cordell with some of his many creations.

O out of plastic. Then, I called a friend of Fred's, Bill Nichols, and asked them to come to Hot Springs so we could talk about the lure. They arrived the next day.

I offered Fred a five-cent commission on every dollar's worth of Big Os I sold if he'd let me make them. Nichols, whom I'd been supplying lures to for his own fishing, backed me up, since Fred and I hadn't met before they came to Hot Springs, but Fred just wasn't sure I could create the same wobbling action in plastic.

That's when I handed him a Big O I'd already made, and invited him to walk down to the lake to try it. He caught a bass on his very first cast, and that's how I got to make the Big O. I sold 1.3 million of them in the first 13 months I had it, which even surprised me. I knew the lure would sell, but I had no idea it would be that popular. I had borrowed $3 million from the bank to do the production, and I paid it back in less than 18 months.

I think my own favorite lure is the Gay Blade. If I was starving to death and had to go catch a fish to keep from starving, I'd pick a ¼-ounce Gay Blade. It started one day when I was in a retail tackle store in Tyler, Texas, in the early 1960s, when the owners showed me how they were taking a piece of tin, bending it back on itself, and soldering it together. All that took a lot of time and work, and they asked me if I could build it. Of course I could, and for only $3 a dozen. They gave me an order that I filled in two weeks, and I didn't have to solder it.

I've been really fortunate my entire life. I've met and worked with some truly wonderful people who really helped me, and I've gotten to fish all over the country. There was a time I fished five straight years without missing a single day. I remember one day fishing down on Lake Amistad with a writer named Stan Slaton out of Houston. We were out in the middle of the lake when we saw a boat barely moving across the water. It was sitting really low, and as it slowly passed by us I was sure we'd have to go rescue them because the boat looked like it was going to sink.

They were heading toward a point on the Mexican side of the lake, and as they got closer, we saw a truck start backing down out of the woods. It didn't have a trailer, so we weren't sure what was going on. When it reached the edge of the water, two men jumped out, and when the boat reached the point, those guys jumped out, too, and all four started pulling the boat up on land. It had the trailer attached, which was why it had been sitting so low in the water. They hooked it to the truck and drove away. Stan and I just looked at each other dumbfounded. That's how they steal boats down there.

★ ★ ★

Cotton Cordell lives in Hot Springs, and on most days he's still in his shop designing new lures.

Chapter Ten

Bill Lewis: "It Was Just a Plain Accident"

Bill Lewis created one of the most iconic lures in bass fishing history, the vibrating, rattling swimming lure known as the Rat-L-Trap, which continues to be a top seller today, four decades after its introduction. Lewis began selling them out of the trunk of his car, and today Rat-L-Trap sales have topped 200 million lures.

Bill Lewis began making fishing lures because he did not like selling insurance, and fishermen the world over have been thankful ever since, because all Lewis did was create the icon lure of the entire industry, the Rat-L-Trap. In the three-plus decades since the first 'Trap was assembled, well over 100 million (actually closer to 200 million) have been sold. The lure, known as a "lipless crankbait" in bass fishing terms, is today manufactured in six different sizes and painted in more than 300 colors; it is the best-known lure name in fishing, even though nearly a dozen copies are now on the market.

It wasn't an easy road. One day in the late 1950s, Lewis, who studied advertising and commercial art in Chicago but who had always had a passion for fishing, met a tackle representative who sold him $500 worth of old lure molds and convinced him to become a lure maker. Using those molds to make spinnerbaits, leadhead jigs, and other items, Lewis and his wife worked night and day to eventually create an inventory worth about $2,200, which they then gave to the tackle rep to begin selling.

As an advance against future commission fees, Lewis also gave the rep his 16-foot johnboat and 7 ½-horsepower outboard. They never saw the man again; Lewis went out of business and he and his wife even lost their home in the aftermath.

As devastating as that experience was, Lewis remained in the tackle business, eventually opening the Witch Doctor Lure Company in Jackson, Mississippi. The company was named after his spinnerbait, which had gained an immediate following throughout Louisiana. Soon after, Lewis and his wife moved to Alexandria where Rat-L-Traps are still made.

★ ★ ★

My own favorite lure had always been the Bayou Boogie, a shad-type vibrating, swimming lure that was being made in Monroe, Louisiana, so I designed one and named it the Rattletrap. I had formed the Red River Lure Company in Alexandria with some partners and this was one of our offerings. As far as I know, the Bayou Boogie was one of the original, if not the original, lures of this design.

Initially, I designed my lure with screw-in eyes, and you had to get them put in just right or it would completely change the lure's action. I also made the very first Rattletrap with a single balancing weight in the body cavity, but it wouldn't run right at all, so one day I just started filling it with BBs to balance it, and suddenly bass started biting it like crazy. I never even counted the number of BBs we put in it. It was just a plain accident.

When the Red River Lure Company split up in 1972 or 1973, I walked out the door with my Rattletrap and nothing else, and started my own lure company, Bill Lewis Lures. I added two crankbaits with lips, the Little L and the Big L, but nobody ever remembers them anymore. I had a lure maker in Chicago make the lures and paint them for 16 cents each, and I started selling them out of the trunk of my car.

I bought the rights to the Rattletrap name and changed it to Rat-L-Trap, and I did get it trademarked, but I never got a patent because I couldn't afford it. I couldn't get money for loans for manufacturing or anything else unless a banker happened to like fishing, and in those days not many did.

So I went from fish camp to fish camp from Texas to Florida trying to sell my Rat-L-Traps. One day in 1979 I stopped at Raymond Gauthier's Mid-Lake Marine business on Toledo Bend. Over the years he had become one of the biggest boosters of Rat-L-Traps and one of my regular customers. This time, knowing how much I enjoyed fishing myself, he suggested I buy a new boat, from him, of course.

I didn't even have enough money to buy gas to get home to Alexandria, much less buy a boat, but Raymond said I could pay for it with Rat-L-Traps, so I gave him everything left in the trunk of my car and drove home that afternoon with a 16-foot Skeeter SS Fisherman with a 115-horsepower Evinrude. I had it paid for in one season, too.

Little by little the lure's fish-catching action began to spread. I once received a letter from a fisherman in Florida who wrote about a great blue heron that had accidentally wrapped a leg in his line as the man was fishing his 'Trap, and as the bird struggled across the water a bass hit the lure. He landed them both, and released the heron.

Another time I got a letter from a fisherman who'd lost his Rat-L-Trap to an alligator. Somehow he and his partner managed to land the 'gator and then pulled the 'Trap out of its jaw with pliers, even as the 'gator's tail was thrashing everything in their boat. Letters like this, and I received many, many similar letters over the years, were really inspirational to me in the early days because I knew I had a successful lure and fishermen were willing to do all kinds of things to keep them.

Over the years as the Rat-L-Trap's reputation continued to grow, a number of firms tried to buy my company. In fact, I used to get three or four inquiries every week from interested parties. Heddon wanted to buy me out, and later even Humminbird, the depth finder electronics company, made an offer, although I have no idea why they wanted into the lure market. The Daiwa rod and reel company tried, and so did the Southland Corporation, which at that timed owned the 7-Eleven convenience stores.

Sometime back in the mid-1970s, one man even offered me $50,000 for exclusive rights to the Rat-L-Trap. It was at a time when I didn't have any money at all to spare, but I refused him and just kept on driving from lake to lake and camp to camp.

What's most amazing to me is that the original design I started with, once I stumbled onto the right weight and balance, has barely changed at all, and as I said, that was just a plain accident.

★ ★ ★

Bill Lewis died June 17, 2005, after a long illness.

Chapter Eleven

Glynn Carver: "How the Plastic Worm Grew a New Tail"

Glynn Carver, shown here on the shore of Toledo Bend Reservoir with a nine-pound bass, revolutionized the lure industry in 1974 when he introduced the first plastic worm featuring a swimming-style tail. Carver sold tens of millions of the new worms, which are standard in the industry today.

To the tens of millions of bass fishermen he influenced during his career, there is little doubt among them Glynn Carver was born to make plastic worms. Certainly, catching his first bass at age five on a worm—even though it was a real worm, not an artificial one—had something to do with it. So probably did his professorship at McNeese State University teaching biology. But mainly, it was his deep-down determination to create something new in fishing lures, which he did not once, but many times.

As the founder of Mister Twister Lures in Minden, Louisiana, Carver created the original curl-tail plastic worm in 1973–74, a totally new lure design whose impact is still being felt now, more than four decades later. The curl-tail design not only changed how anglers fished the lure, but also how manufacturers created them. Today, the curl-tail design dominates the soft plastics industry; millions upon millions have been sold, and continue to be sold today.

The Mister Twister Worm wasn't all Carver created. He is also the father of an incredibly popular soft plastic grub named the Sassy Shad, which he created in 1975. Originally designed for bass fishing, fishermen quickly exploited the lure's potential for other species, and bought more than 25 million Sassy Shad lures the very first year. Today's small plastic "swim baits" that have become extremely popular are only slightly modified versions of Carver's creation.

At its height in the mid and late 1970s, Carver's Mister Twister plant operated 23 lure-making machines 24 hours a day, seven days a week, and frequently produced more than a million individual items a day. These included not only the curl-tail worms and Sassy Shads, but also other soft plastic lures as well as the lead jigheads to use with them.

Born July 20, 1936, in Georgetown, Louisiana, Carver was wading the bank of Fish Creek, about 40 miles north of Alexandria, the day he caught his first bass. He'd never seen one before, and to his five-year-old eyes the 3 ½-pound fish looked like it weighed 15 pounds. He was using a cane pole that he tried to give to his father because the fish was pulling so hard and scared him so much. Still, to use a well-worn cliché, that bass hooked him, and Carver has never stopped fishing.

He graduated from Louisiana Tech in 1958 with a degree in biology, and earned his doctorate from LSU four years later. He taught there for a short time, then accepted a faculty position at McNeese State University in Lake Charles, eventually becoming chairman of the biology department. The problem with being a college professor, especially the head of a major department, was that it did not allow Carver enough time for fishing, so in 1971 he resigned to go into the fishing business full-time.

He quickly joined forces with another fishing enthusiast in Dallas, with the goal of developing an improved plastic formulation for fishing lures. Both Nick Crème and Dave DeLong were already producing plastic worms, but Carver was convinced he could produce a better one, particularly with his strong educational background in chemistry. Their first product was a kit including both plastic and molds so a customer could make his own worms.

Then his partner ran out of money. Carver, determined to remain in the tackle business, took his entire $7,000 university retirement fund and moved to Shreveport and started his own company, Carver Manufacturing, and began creating custom plastic formulations for other already established lure companies, including Mann's Bait Co., Crème Lures, and Cordell.

In 1971, Cotton Cordell bought Carver's little company, which consisted of little more than 14 Sears, Roebuck & Co. pressure pots used to make his worms. Carver moved to Minden, a few miles east of Shreveport, convinced ten investors who also loved bass fishing to put up $10,000 each to finance a new manufacturing plant, and started producing his own soft plastic lures. One of his first products was the curl-tail worm.

A year later, Cordell called Carver back up to his shop in Hot Springs, Arkansas; Carver had the very first six-inch prototype of his curl-tail worm in his pocket and ready to offer to his friend, but when Cordell asked if Carver wanted to buy his company back, Carver did, and Cordell never saw the radical new design until Carver introduced it to the market a short time later.

Carver called his new company Mister Twister, and it was a perfect match for the new curl-tail worm. He introduced it in February 1974, and by August he had sold more than $1 million worth of them; the next year he sold more than $3 million.

Despite the amazing success of his Mister Twister Worm (Carver introduced a different size or style each year for a decade) he still found time to create new plastic lures. In 1975 he had the first prototype of the Sassy Shad in his pocket at the national AFTMA tackle show when one of America's most respected fishing writers, Homer Circle, approached him on the show floor. When Circle asked if he had anything new, Carver gave him the prototype.

Several weeks after the show, Circle called him. Carver was having problems with the Sassy Shad mold and had forgotten about the prototype. Circle, long time fishing editor of *Sports Afield Magazine*, informed Carver he'd never seen a lure that caught so many fish, and that he was planning to write a full feature on the lure in his magazine.

"But I don't even have a mold for it," Carver cried.

"Well, you'd better get one!" replied Circle.

Carver solved his mold problems in record time, and that first year he sold 25 million Sassy Shad lures. Even that, however, was less than the number of Mister Twister Worms he sold. In 1981 when he sold Mister Twister to Sheldon's, producer of the famous Mepps spinners, the company was selling more than $9 million worth of lures annually. Carver did not sell the manufacturing rights, however; he moved his plant to the shores of Toledo Bend Reservoir, and kept right on producing Mister Twister products, as well as lures for other soft plastics manufacturers.

In 2000, after 35 years of producing bass fishing lures, Carver closed the Toledo Bend plant. Outside the city of Many, he opened a retail tackle store specializing in top-of-the-line fishing tackle and featuring an indoor grill where fishermen could swap lies and tips over hamburgers and coffee. It was so popular Carver soon had to expand, and he has since added more space a third time. The store is named Toledo Town and Tackle, and it remains one of the most popular shopping spots on the lake.

★ ★ ★

At the 1973 American Fishing Tackle Manufacturers Association (AFTMA) show in Chicago, I saw a lure named the Sosy Eel introduced by a company named Generic Systems. The lure was French-made and while it was not a plastic worm—it looked more like a mouse to me—it did feature a fairly large curved tail shaped somewhat like a sickle. We'd all been thinking of developing a curved tail for plastic worms for some time, but no one had. When I saw the tail on that Sosy Eel, I saw the full potential of such a design.

That AFTMA show was in late summer, and I came back to the shop and started designing and trying to make some prototypes. I had some ready by February, and took them to Toledo Bend where I just walked out on a pier and starting making a few casts to study the worm's action. Initially, I had five people watching me. The next time I looked up, 75 people were crowded around watching. They'd never seen anything like it in plastic worms.

I had an employee at the plant, Sid Gibson, who was a genius at keeping the lure-making machines working, but he had never fished a day in his life. I gave him some prototypes, a rod and reel, and asked another fisherman I knew to take Sid fishing on Lake Claiborne not far from Minden. I told him to just rig the six-inch worms with an open jighead.

Sid couldn't cast, but whenever he'd get his lure in the water, he'd just let it sink and then start reeling back, and he'd catch a fish on every try.

The worm was that easy to use; not only had no one ever seen anything like it, neither had the bass!

Then I went down to Mexico and shot some film at one of the bass lakes, and started showing them, along with the worms, in various store promotions. The word got out so quickly it still amazes me. Word of mouth is the greatest tool in the world for selling fishing tackle. I officially introduced the worm in February, and by August we'd sold more than $1 million, and the next year, more than $3 million.

The curl-tail worm pretty much sold itself because it was such a new design. All of a sudden, fishermen had a lure with built-in action, and we demonstrated it at sport shows around the country. We even developed a special little tank with moving water that showed the worm's swimming tail action, and we ended up making and selling those machines, too. I heard stories of Mister Twister Worms being demonstrated in bathroom sinks and practically anywhere else a little water was available.

A sports writer friend living in Houston at the time had some of my earliest Mister Twister Worms and took them to Lake Livingston where he fished at least once every week. It had rained buckets that morning, he told me, but his guide friend at Livingston told him to come up anyway. When he arrived, he demonstrated my worm by swimming it through one of the mud puddles in the road. None of them had seen it before, and my friend told me afterward every guide up there who watched made him give them some, or they wouldn't take him out anymore!

One day a buyer came into my office and told me he wanted to buy some Twister worms. I told him I was so far behind filling orders it would be a long time before I could deliver anything to him. He just asked for a piece of paper, and I pushed a yellow notepad across my desk to him. He wrote, "I want $50,000 of Mister Twister Worms, any size, any color," and signed it and left it on my desk. In 1974, that was a huge order.

Of course, the lure industry being what it is, the Mister Twister Worm started being copied immediately by other companies. It was not a particularly hard lure to design, especially after I had perfected the original six-inch model, but I did make a mistake when I made the four-inch version. I made the tail too thick for the length and diameter of the worm, but I didn't catch the mistake and we released the lure anyway.

Well, all those other companies immediately copied it, too, even with the wrong tail. When we corrected the tail, our sales went even higher. Eventually, I had 17 design patents on the different Twister tail lures, but they weren't worth much, since anyone could change the design just a tiny bit and not be guilty of infringement.

I remember getting a phone call one day before the Mister Twister Worm was introduced, from the CEO of another lure company who wanted to buy Mister Twister. When I refused, he told me I was such a small operation I'd never make it. That just made me work even harder to succeed. I remember several years later, when my marketing manager, Rick Welle, and I were so exhausted after working weeks of 16-hour days without a break that we took an afternoon off just to go fishing.

The first thing we saw when we arrived at the landing was three young boys walking and casting along the shoreline, and all three were using Mister Twister Worms. That's when I told Rick I thought we'd made it.

★ ★ ★

Glynn Carver lives on Toledo Bend Reservoir where he can walk out on his dock anytime and still catch bass on his favorite plastic worms. He's a regular at Toledo Town and Tackle most mornings, too, where he's happy to talk to visiting bass fishermen.

Chapter Twelve

Lee Sisson: "I Made a Lot More Lures That Didn't Work Than Did"

Local fans gather to cheer their favorites as professional bass anglers tow their bass boats down a city street in Syracuse, New York, prior to their tournament on nearby Lake Oneida.

Even though his parents jokingly called him Peter Pan, a reference to whether he was really ever going to grow up and have a real job, Lee Sisson likes to thank a football player for making sure he stayed in fishing rather than continue in football, and for nearly four decades the bass fishing world has been thankful Sisson took the player's advice. Sisson can be considered the father of deep diving crankbaits and the highly productive fishing technique of deep cranking; his DB-3 lure was the first such fishing plug that could reliably be reeled down to depths of 15 feet and deeper, thereby opening a brand new world of fishing to American anglers.

Nearly 40 years after its introduction, the DB-3 remains one of America's most popular fishing lures, and untold thousands of them line the bottoms of the country's bass lakes, snagged on roots and stumps where fishermen had to leave them as they explored water farther and farther offshore. Today there are other crankbaits that actually dive deeper under certain conditions, but all are based on the original DB-3 design Sisson created.

Born March 29, 1948, in Baton Rouge, Louisiana, Sisson grew up fishing the bayous and canals of southern Louisiana at the very time American bass fishing was becoming popular as a recreational sport. Even though as a youngster he became known as someone who would fish a six-inch deep mud hole with a string just to see if he could catch a crawfish, Sisson always wondered what he would catch if he could just get his lures a little deeper. The best crankbaits of the day only dived to about six feet.

At Louisiana Tech University in Ruston, Sisson continued to fish periodically, although not seriously. He played offensive tackle on the Tech football team, and his main job was to protect their quarterback, a fellow Louisianan named Terry Bradshaw. The two became close friends, for as Sisson likes to say, he taught Bradshaw how to be a scrambling quarterback. Bradshaw also happened to love to fish, and one day he took Sisson fishing with him to Lake D'Arbonne north of Farmerville.

There, the two of them found a school of active bass, and by the time darkness fell, Sisson had not only caught more bass than ever before in his life, he had also caught his life's career path. Whereas before that trip he had just played at fishing, that single day's experience with the future Hall of Fame pro quarterback made him realize that what he really wanted to do in his life was fish.

He'd always been a tinkerer. Even during his college days, if he was going to fish a bass tournament, Sisson would collect all the used and split plastic worms he could find, melt them back into liquid and add a touch of black dye, then re-pour them into handmade plaster molds. He used the dye to turn every worm black, since he melted worms of every color together. He also learned how to make jigging spoons, too, by whittling holes into a thin block of wood and then filling the holes with lead. He wouldn't even paint the lures, because he didn't need to; they caught bass 15 feet deep because the fish had never before seen lures at those depths.

After college, Sisson started fishing even harder. He often fished False River, a lake near Baton Rouge, where he caught bass off the ends of some of the deep piers. Owners had put piles of brush out where the water was 15 to 18 feet deep, and if he dropped a plastic worm down into that brush, he could catch bass. The problem was, Sisson liked to fish lures fast, believing that if he could expose his lure to more fish, he'd catch more of them.

Fishing fast meant using a crankbait, but there were no crankbaits made that could reach those brushpiles. To be sure, there were deep-running lures, but they were designed to be trolled behind a moving boat; Sisson wanted a lure he could cast and reel down 15 to 18 feet. So, he started trying to design one.

He began with balsa wood, primarily because it was easy to work. He never carved or whittled the wood, but rather, shaped it with a sander. He knew a long lip or bill would make the lure dive, but he didn't know any of the real nuances of crankbait design, such as lip angle, line-tie location, or even body size. No one did, because it had never been done before.

A Tennessee lure maker named Fred Young had recently created a new standard with his Big O crankbait, and lure makers everywhere began copying his basic design, including Sisson. But the Big O didn't dive deep enough, so essentially Sisson would create a lure body, stick a diving bill in it, and go fish it.

★ ★ ★

Believe me, I made a lot more lures that didn't work than did. Some of my lures were right on the edge of being what I wanted, and finally I came up with a long-lipped balsa lure that did get deeper than all the others. It was a pretty ugly creation because the wood body extended out to support the lip but it ran straight, vibrated, and dived. I patterned it after what had by that time become known as the "alphabet lures," which, of course, had been started by Fred Young. Originally, my deep diving lure did not have a name, but I did manage to sell a few to a local tackle store.

To make my baits more attractive, I started playing with different paint colors. Most lure paint patterns were pretty plain, such as chartreuse/black back or pearl/black back. I obtained some very fine powdered pigments from a local ceramics class, and mixed the pigments with my regular paints. The result was an iridescent color that had never been done on lures before.

I had a small spray painter, but no compressor to run it, so I used big tire inner tubes for air pressure. I'd go to a service station each morning and fill up all the inner tubes I could find, and back at home I'd hook my sprayer to the tube valve. When the tires were full, the sprayer worked pretty good, but as the tube's air pressure went down, I'd have to sit on the tube to force more air out. Then, when it was finally flat, I'd have to hook my sprayer to another tube.

Lee Sisson can rightfully be described as the father of deep water crankbaiting, because his lure for the Jim Bagley Bait Co., the DB-3, was the first crankbait that would reliably reach depths of at least 15 feet. Photo courtesy of B.A.S.S.

One day Jim Bagley, who had his own established lure company and was coming to town to do a seminar, happened to see some of my painted diving crankbaits in a tackle store. He'd seen some of my lures earlier and wanted to meet me, because he was having problems with the paint on his lures.

We talked for 10 or 15 minutes, and then he asked if I would go to work for him. I agreed, and two weeks later I had moved to Winter Haven, Florida, where Bagley Baits was located. Jim didn't hire me to design and build lures for him, but rather, to paint his lures. He already had several very successful balsa lures in his lineup, including the Bangalure.

I had given some of my deep diving lures to a fisherman in Texas named John Fox, who had a television show and was promoting some of Jim's lures, and one day not long after I started working for Bagley, Fox called and asked to speak to me, not Jim. He wanted some more of my deep divers because he had really been catching a lot of bass with them.

We were talking and finally Jim picked up the phone and asked which lure we'd been talking about for so long. I told him, and two weeks later we were building and selling that deep diving crankbait, which we named the DB-3. Jim was already making a crankbait he had named the Balsa B 3, so we just added a D to the name, which stands for Diving.

It became really popular because it was the first truly deep diving crankbait of its type, but one year after DB-3 sales slipped a little, Jim took it out of the Bagley catalog, and that year we sold more DB-3s than ever before.

★ ★ ★

Lee Sisson left Bagley Bait Company after 12 years to start Lee Sisson Lures, building his own brand of lures, as well as producing them for other firms. He sold his company to Yakima Bait Co. in 2006, and today produces lures through his newest company, Old School Tackle, located in Winter Haven, Florida.

THE LAKES

Chapter Thirteen

The Largemouth's New Home

Although the largemouth bass lives comfortably in creeks, quiet river backwaters, ponds, and swamps, the fish thrives in large lakes. *Micropterus salmoides* had survived in many of the natural lakes created by the gouging flow of the ice age 10,000 to 15,000 years ago, but not until midway through the 20th century when the US Army Corps of Engineers, the Tennessee Valley Authority, and other smaller agencies began constructing dams across many of the nation's rivers did the largemouth find its real home in the newly created reservoirs behind those dams.

Here the fish had not only the basically shallow, current-free habitat it prefers but also abundant food resources. Many of the new reservoirs—a French word meaning "storehouse"—were located in the South, too, where waters remained warm throughout most of the year so that in some areas both the bass and its forage spawned several times annually, not just once in the spring.

The results were not immediate but they were far-reaching. Largemouth populations increased a hundred-fold with the increase in available habitat, while at the same time the fish thus became more accessible to the masses. The new reservoirs were a critical, but totally unplanned, step in turning bass fishing from a quiet pastime into a sport and eventually a multibillion-dollar industry.

The United States, of course, did not have a monopoly on dams and water storage. The earliest recorded dams were built on the Nile around 2700 BC to provide water for the city of Memphis, the ancient capitol of Egypt. The oldest dam still in use, a rock wall standing about 20 feet high, was constructed in 1300 BC at Orontes in Syria, and the Kallanai Dam

A bass fisherman is silhouetted at dawn. The largemouth bass is found in every state except Alaska, as well as in several foreign countries. Tournament competitions are conducted practically every weekend on lakes throughout the United States.

on the Kaveri River in southern India, built sometime prior to 200 AD, also remains in use, as well.

In America, dams of varying sizes had been constructed practically since Colonial days, but even as late as 1900 the number of reservoirs larger than 500 acres barely topped a hundred. As the population increased and the demand for both flood control and water resources continued to grow, more and more dams were built so that today there are more than 1,500 reservoirs larger than 500 acres. Included among these is massive 231-mile-long Lake Oahe near Pierre, South Dakota, the fourth largest reservoir (by water volume) in the United States.

Unfortunately, not all the dams that have been built have held. Historically, probably the most famous dam failure occurred in 1889 when the South Fork Dam above Johnstown, Pennsylvania, gave way and the resulting flood caused the loss of more than 2,200 lives. The Teton Dam in Idaho failed in June 1976, as did Barnes Lake Dam near Toccoa Falls, Georgia, in November 1977, among others.

Although the Corps of Engineers had been in existence since 1776, it was not until June 22, 1936, when President Franklin D. Roosevelt signed the Flood Control Act, that the Corps became recognized as the nation's primary federal flood control agency. Although the engineers had often studied flood control, they had not been in the dam building business prior to this authorization.

They had spent much of their time, instead, improving America's transportation system by surveying and mapping roadways or eliminating navigational hazards in rivers. They had actually recommended construction of several dams on the flood-prone Savannah River as early as 1890, and had been struggling with the Mississippi River since 1917 when Congress had passed the very first Federal Flood Control bill. The Corps had also been busy constructing military fortifications in different areas, and even been tasked with managing the Army's West Point Military Academy.

With Roosevelt's go-ahead, the Corps quickly initiated a number of building projects, one of the earliest being the Surry Mountain Dam across the Ashuelot River in New Hampshire. The Ashuelot is a tributary of the Connecticut River, and the dam, completed in 1941, created the 265-acre Surry Mountain Lake, which today remains a popular fishing and outdoor recreation lake in the region. Since 1936, Congress has authorized the Corps of Engineers to construct 375 major reservoirs.

Roosevelt had already made an earlier move toward flood control three years prior to the passage of the Flood Control Act, when he created the Tennessee Valley Authority (TVA) as part of his New Deal program for economic development. In an effort to keep the Tennessee River Valley from flooding, provide electrical power, and maintain the river for year-round navigation that was critical to both the region and the nation, TVA was authorized to immediately begin constructing dams on the river.

Ironically, because this new agency had no experience building dams, they relied heavily on survey work previously conducted by the Corps of Engineers. The site of their first dam had been identified more than a decade earlier, and in fact, several private companies had applied for permits to build it. The location was a spot on the Clinch River where it empties into the Tennessee River near the city of Kingston, and within months, TVA began working on it. The dam, completed three years later, created 33,840-acre Norris Lake, the first of nearly four dozen dams TVA has since built across rivers in Tennessee and Alabama.

Actually, the Norris Dam was not the first dam on the Tennessee River. More than 100 miles downstream near the city of Muscle Shoals, Alabama, where the water cascaded over a long sweep of sharp, steep rocks, the US War Department had completed construction of the Wilson Dam in 1924. The dam itself is 137 feet high and has a lock lift of 94 feet, the highest single navigational lift on any river east of the Rockies.

Later taken over by TVA and designated as a National Historic Landmark in 1966, Wilson Dam not only solved that particular navigation problem, it also created 15,500-acre Wilson Lake, which over the ensuing years has been recognized as one of the premier bass fisheries in the nation. Indeed, the lake produced a world record smallmouth bass weighing ten pounds, eight ounces (the record has since been broken) in 1950 by Birmingham angler Owen Smith. It was the first smallmouth bass weighing more than ten pounds ever officially recorded.

Overall, however, the construction by any agency of a dam and the creation of a reservoir behind it does not guarantee a successful bass fishery. Rather, success is determined by the presence of various forms of microscopic organisms collectively known as algae. These are among the oldest known organisms on earth, with fossil remains dating them back more than three billion years.

There are more than 25,000 species of algae, but in the case of a newly impounded reservoir, the most important are those that float freely through the water at the mercy of the waves and wind. They're known as phytoplankton and zooplankton, and because they can reproduce through photosynthesis several times a day, they form the beginning of the food chain in a new lake. They also do best in standing water, rather than current, which the new lakes created in abundance.

The amount of algae and phytoplankton present in the beginning depends to a great extent on what the impounded water covers. Overall, lowland reservoirs, such as those in the South, have richer watersheds that include not only better soil but also abundant vegetation, which in a very short time become available as nutrients in the water through leaching and decay.

A pair of bass fishermen head out at sunrise to begin a day of pleasure fishing. Today, the largemouth bass is well established in every state except Alaska, and is actively pursued by millions of anglers.

These nutrients, including the major building blocks of potassium, nitrogen, and phosphorus, allow the plankton to thrive. That growth creates a "bloom," in which the plankton reproduces so rapidly it may literally change the water color from blue to green. The bloom attracts tiny insects that begin feeding on the bloom, which in turn attract small minnows that feed on the insects.

This food chain, as it is commonly called, is not really a chain, but rather, a web of life, because different food "chains" exist in any aquatic environment and many are interwoven. In the case of impounded reservoirs, two other extremely old and naturally occurring species form critical links in this web. These are the gizzard shad, *Dorosoma cepedianum,* and its cousin, the smaller threadfin shad, *Dorosoma petenense,* both of which are favorite foods of bass. The threadfin is particularly important not only because its basic range is limited to warm waters where the largemouth does best but also because it is smaller and thus remains as bass forage longer than the gizzard shad, which can outgrow a bass.

These two fish don't eat the plankton floating on the surface, but instead, root along the bottom and feed on decayed matter—those plants and other materials that were covered by the flooding water as well as other organisms that died and sank. More importantly, these shad are among the first to expand into the new lake habitat because they're stimulated to spawn by rising water. They are broadcast spawners, meaning they do not create a special nest or bed in which to lay their eggs, but instead release them in open water, usually adjacent to rocks, logs, or pilings in the shallows.

Obviously, shad spawned in river systems long before the first TVA dams began backing up new lakes, but never to the extent they did once the newly flooded habitat became available to them. The same is true for the largemouth. Although they were present, bass populations were never large in those rivers, nor were there large populations of big bass. One of the primary reasons is because most rivers, especially those in the South, are turbid so photosynthesis by plankton is greatly diminished. Riverine habitat is also much more limited since plants grow in only the shallowest water depths light can penetrate.

Algae cycles, bass, and bass fishing were far from anyone's consideration when FDR created the TVA and Corps of Engineers. His initial mandates to them were primarily to impound water to help control flooding, produce electrical power, provide an irrigation source, and to supply urban areas with drinking water. Thus, the creation of such ideal habitat and of the food chain to support the fish in it came about essentially by accident. And because the new habitat was vacant, the bass enjoyed huge and successful spawns just like the shad since there was no competition for that habitat.

This initial explosion of new life in any reservoir lasts about a decade, and typically, unless something changes, this decade will be the best the lake will have. The complete web of life then becomes dependent on the continued inflow of nutrients from the watershed it drains. This is why some reservoirs do not offer the continued quality of fishing that others do. High desert lakes like Mead and Powell in Arizona, for example, even though huge in size and fed by the Colorado River, are not as fertile as Georgia's Lake Seminole or Lake Fork in Texas, primarily because of the lesser amount of nutrients being washed into them.

Another element that affects the quality of bass fishing in a lake as it ages is the amount of habitat available to the fish away from the shoreline. This can include rocks, stumps, standing timber, and vegetation. All create additional surface area for different organisms like algae to grow. Insects come to eat the algae, and some even lay their own eggs on it so the web of life is repeated again in a slightly different manner. Even non-native plants like hydrilla are beneficial to some extent because of the cover they provide to various fish species, including bass and forage.

In many of the new lakes created by the Corps of Engineers and other agencies timber was left standing, either by accident or design, but which provided this extra habitat for bass. Some of the early lakes in which the timber was not removed, such as 186,000-acre Toledo Bend along the Texas/Louisiana border, continue to be excellent bass fisheries today, nearly half a century after impoundment.

In the case of Toledo Bend, created by a dam that flooded the rich, timber-filled Sabine River valley and adjacent woodlands, the bass actually received an unexpected gift. The trees were so thick and the lake so large that special harvesting equipment was needed to clear the lake, but unusually heavy rains began filling the lake before it could be cleared and at least one of the bulldozers is reported to still be sitting on the bottom where it was stuck. Local anglers know where it is, and report it to be an excellent place to catch bass, too.

Chapter Fourteen

Jack Wingate: "The Fishing Stories Were True"

Jack Wingate's name will forever be linked to Lake Seminole, where he owned and operated the famous Lunker Lodge for 41 years. The lake quickly became famous for producing trophy bass in the early 1960s, and no one promoted Seminole or bass fishing more than Wingate.

When the US Army Corps of Engineers impounded Lake Seminole in 1957, no one could foresee the impact the new reservoir would have on American bass fishing. From the very beginning, the fishing was excellent, due in part because the lake was filled two feet at a time as construction continued. That gave bass plenty of time to grow and multiply, because the all-important new shoreline habitat kept arriving in stages.

That wasn't all. Located near the city of Bainbridge in southwestern Georgia's Seminole County along the Florida border, more than 5,000 acres of weeds and mossbeds eventually flourished in the warm conditions and added even more habitat for both bass as well as various forage species. The Corps left 12,000 acres of timber standing, and approximately 250 separate islands were formed by the rising water. The two major rivers forming the lake, the Chattahoochee and the Flint, brought in a continuous supply of nutrients; and dozens of natural-flowing springs provided small, hidden pockets of clear water year-round. By the time Seminole filled to its 37,500-acre capacity, it was already producing ten-pounders; the lake was so stunningly beautiful anglers fully expected every cast to be hit by a big bass.

Many of their casts were. The lake record stands at 17 pounds, a fish caught on live bait. Jack Wingate, who purchased the first fishing camp on Seminole, Lunker Lodge, in 1959 and managed it until 2000, personally saw and weighed several bass topping 15 pounds, including the present lake record caught on an artificial lure, 16 pounds, 4 ounces.

Wingate, born September 1, 1929, in Faceville, just six miles from where Lunker Lodge would be located, had grown up fishing the Flint and Chattahoochee, and had always wanted to own a fishing camp. As a youngster, he'd helped his parents in their bait shop and barbecue stand; he'd get up before dawn, pound a piece of stump wood into the moist ground, and then scrape it with a broken car spring, a Deep South technique known as "worm grunting."

Others sometimes used a saw instead of the car spring. Whatever the instrument, the vibrations brought earthworms to the surface so quickly it was impossible to grab them all. Wingate would usually fill a gallon jug with the worms, then return home by eight a.m., in time to sell them to the fishermen driving by their bait shop.

After serving in the US Navy during the Korean War, Wingate hitchhiked back home in 1951 to help his parents at the bait shop, which had grown into a small grocery store. To augment the bait business, he started making and selling barbecue the following year. Wingate became so well-known for this that he was soon catering to special parties in the

Bainbridge area, once serving 5,500 people in just 45 minutes. In fact, in 1957, Wingate catered the party dedicating the new Jim Woodruff Dam that impounded Lake Seminole.

Initially, none of the old-timers, Wingate included, thought the Corps could build a dam across the river, and if they could, the old-timers weren't sure they really wanted a lake, anyway. To those who lived on the Flint and Chattahoochee Rivers, the fishing was already the best there was and they didn't want anyone to change it. Personally, however, Wingate was excited because it meant he could sell more bait and barbecue.

One day, however, en route to Oklahoma to visit his wife Joyce's parents, they drove by Lake Texoma, the massive 89,000-acre reservoir along the Texas/Oklahoma border that had been impounded more than a decade earlier in 1944. Wingate had never seen so many people in one place, all of them fishing. That, he thought, was exactly what they needed to do at Seminole, so when he and Joyce returned to Bainbridge, he purchased Lunker Lodge, which consisted of a boat dock and four little brick cabins at the water's edge.

Seminole was still off the radar then, and Wingate struggled with his new acquisition. The first month he and Joyce were in business, their total income was $43.00. He and Joyce cooked, cleaned cabins, and guided fishermen for $15 a day. The bass fishing was unbelievable in the new lake, but no one knew about it.

Then one day, a bass fisherman named Dick Bostick and three of his friends drove in from Hopkinsville, Kentucky, and during their stay they caught dozens of quality largemouths. More importantly, they returned to Hopkinsville and told their friends about the lake, and later that year, 25 of those friends came to Seminole and Lunker Lodge, and became regular customers for years. That is what turned Wingate's business around and put the lake on fishing maps everywhere. Bostick, in fact, continued to return to Lunker Lodge every year for more than two decades.

Because of the water conditions and warm climate, Seminole became known for its topwater fishing, which also happened to be Wingate's favorite technique. He teased his two favorite lures, either a Heddon Baby Zara Spook or a Tiny Torpedo, across the surface to the tune of "Shave and a Haircut, Two Bits." Anyone fortunate to be in the boat with him also realized that Wingate talked to the bass he was trying to catch, chastising them for passing up a perfectly good lure, then telling his observer he was scared of big bass and if he saw one coming he always tried to get his lure back before one ate it.

It was this type of humor, total informality, and of course, Wingate's wonderful hospitality and barbecue that kept fishermen returning year after year, regardless of how successful they had been catching bass. Once, two visiting anglers pulled into Lunker Lodge after an all-day drive, and Wingate had them on the lake fishing before they had a chance to properly park their truck. They threw their tackle into Wingate's boat, signed licenses, and went fishing.

Wingate's boat, an ancient 17-foot burgundy red Ranger, was possibly the hardest-used bass boat in the South. Lures were usually scattered from bow to stern; Wingate didn't use a tacklebox. At one time he kept them under control in a small tin bucket, but after Joyce confiscated it to use as a flower pot, Wingate simply left his lures on the boat deck.

In those days, topwater fishing ended at dark, not just because that's when the mosquitoes came out but also because Wingate's restaurant stopped serving dinner at 9:00 p.m. Fish and barbecue were the main dishes, but if a customer didn't see what he wanted, Wingate occasionally let him into the kitchen to fix whatever he preferred, especially at breakfast, when fishing days began at around 4:30 a.m. The restaurant was open every day of the year except Christmas; at Thanksgiving the cooks started preparing the holiday meal a week in advance and usually served about 100 people that day.

The front office of Lunker Lodge was as informal as Wingate himself, and only added to the aura of a Deep South fishing camp. Visitors sometimes commented that, after registering for their stay at Lunker Lodge, that they'd literally stepped back in time. Wall shelves in the tiny front office were stuffed with everything from lures, maps, and minnow nets, to turtle shells, cans of pork and beans, and baseball caps. Plastic worms were sold out of cut-down mustard and mayonnaise jugs. The dining room was lined with deer antlers, Indian arrowheads, plaques and pictures, and all of Wingate's guides sat at one table closest to the coffee pot.

But, of course, it was the fishing that initially drew anglers to Seminole. The lake filled and began producing its biggest bass in the early 1960s, coinciding perfectly with the growing excitement of bass fishing across the South.

★ ★ ★

Even as the lake was filling and I was trying to get fishermen to come to the lodge. I could go out in an hour and catch all the bass anybody would want in a whole day. By 1963–64, after word began to spread and more and more fishermen started coming, I had as many as nine guides working every day.

I did not see the 17-pound bass that was established as the lake record for Seminole, but I did see Charles Tyson's 16-pound, 4-ounce fish, the largest bass caught here on a lure. He fished out of a canoe with a little seven-horsepower outboard; in fact, he and I were flyfishing together the day President Kennedy was shot.

Anyway, Tyson had caught a 16-pounder three weeks earlier but hadn't weighed it on the proper scales, so the Georgia Department of Natural Resources officers wouldn't give him the lake record. Well, he was mad about that, so Charles went out and caught the 16-4 in the same place. This time he weighed the bass on certified scales and I drove with him to Atlanta with all the paperwork where this time the game and fish people gave him the award.

Another time, I was guiding Mary Keen and her husband from Knoxville. It was close to midnight, and her husband was stretched out sleeping on the boat deck because we'd been fishing steadily since nine a.m. I was sculling the boat from the back. We already had a nine-pounder in the boat, and she picked up a Bomber Spinstick lure and threw it up beside the stump and moved it once. There was an awesome strike, but the fish dove into the weeds, and by the time I could get the boat up to the stump, I was sure she'd lost the fish.

I had to climb over her husband with the net, and when I shined a flashlight in the water I could see she still had the fish. I got the net under it but I scooped up so much grass she couldn't see it, but she almost fainted when I lifted it up. That bass weighed 15 pounds, 8 ounces, one of the largest ever caught in Seminole.

Back in the early days most clients would keep the bass they caught and I'd sometimes be up until midnight or later cleaning and filleting and then icing their catch for them. Once I had a client I was guiding who had to leave at noon, and I was cleaning his morning catch. He had caught a 10-pounder that somebody else wanted to keep and mount, so I asked my client if he'd accept two 5-pounders for the 10, and he agreed. I went out and caught the two fives for him in less than half an hour. The fishing was that good.

When I was struggling to make a living right after I bought Lunker Lodge, I never dreamed the sport would grow so big. I fished Ray Scott's very first tournament on Beaver Lake in 1967 and had so much fun I told the Bainbridge Chamber of Commerce we had to have a tournament like that on Seminole, and the next year Scott came, the third tournament in B.A.S.S. history. It snowed most of the first day and a northwest wind howled so hard the US Coast Guard made the contestants follow behind them as they crossed the lake and flattened the waves.

Even in that terrible weather, I couldn't believe how many spectators came to see the fishermen weigh in their bass, and I couldn't believe how many bass they caught. I probably shouldn't have been surprised, since I already knew Seminole really was a place where the fishing stories were true.

★ ★ ★

After selling Lunker Lodge in 2000, Jack Wingate continued to live by the lake and fished nearly every day until his death on December 8, 2011, at the age of 82. He was posthumously inducted into the Bass Fishing Hall of Fame in 2013.

Chapter Fifteen

Tommy Martin: "We Caught 'Em and Caught 'Em and Caught 'Em"

By 1968, Lake Seminole, the crown jewel of Southern bass fishing, had already given up the biggest bass it would ever produce, even though the lake was only 11 years old. Sam Rayburn Reservoir, impounded in 1965, had been producing a lot of quality bass, but its best years were still to come. Amistad, far out of the mainstream in Del Rio on the Texas/ Mexico border, was still a year away from completion. In a simple act of timing and geography, then, the door swung open for another impoundment to capture the hearts and minds and imaginations of America's growing legions of anglers. That lake was Toledo Bend.

Located less than 30 miles from Rayburn in southeast Texas, Toledo Bend had been under study since 1949, and actually under construction since 1961. Formed by a dam across the winding Sabine River between the towns of Hemphill, Texas, and Many, Louisiana, Toledo Bend was never designed for flood control, as were most of the lakes of the era. Rather, the new lake was created for water storage, and, in a remarkable act of forethought, for recreation. Even today, Toledo Bend remains the only major reservoir of its type constructed without any federal funding.

Building the lake wasn't easy, given the miles of dense forest covering the ridges and channels throughout the flood zone. Indeed, a special

*In 1972 Tommy Martin resigned his job at an investment company to become a
full-time guide on Toledo Bend. He is credited with solving the mystery of fishing the
lake's thick hydrilla by adding extra weight to his jigs so they would penetrate the
vegetation, since heavy jigs were not available at the time. Martin also won the 1974
Bassmaster Classic as a rookie.*

55-ton tree crusher with a 26-foot wide rolling blade was built just to
remove the timber, and frequently more than 20 bulldozers worked simul-
taneously moving dirt and debris. Because of the thick forest growth,
more than 175 miles of north–south and east–west navigational boat lanes
were cut to aid the lake's future bass fishermen.

Impoundment began in 1966, but unusually heavy rains that year
caused the lake to fill faster than expected. So fast, in fact, that the tree
crusher couldn't complete its task and so instead of wide open water,
Toledo Bend initially looked like an ocean of flooded trees. It stretched
for some 65 miles north of the dam, and in places the lake was more than
five miles across, a total of 186,000 acres. The total shoreline measured
some 1,200 miles, about as far as from Dallas to Denver.

The lake was dedicated in special ceremonies on October 11, 1969, with dignitaries from both Texas and Louisiana taking part. More than a thousand people came to watch, forced to stand more than a mile south of the dam itself since there still weren't any roads available to take them closer. Holy water, collected from the Tajo River in Toledo, Spain, and blessed and sent for the occasion by the archbishop of Toledo, was poured into the gently lapping waves of the Sabine River.

Area merchants did not wait for the new lake to fill before trying to take advantage of what was to come. One of those entrepreneurs was a man named George Pickett, who purchased land near the small community of Six Mile, Texas, determined to build a first-class fishing lodge. He named it the Fin and Feather Resort, and had a boat ramp and covered boat stalls in place before he could even see any of the rising water. Unfortunately, the water rose higher than calculated and the roofs had to be raised so people could actually stand on the dock, but that was quickly remedied.

Pickett's dream reached fruition by the early 1970s, as word of Toledo Bend's spectacular bass fishing spread like wildfire across the nation and the Fin and Feather was ready to serve the thousands of anglers who flocked to the lake. More than 60 fishing guides worked out of the resort, many of them booked as often as 300 days a year. Oil field companies rewarded their employees with trips to the lake, sometimes flying in as many as 100 people at a time. More than a few of them had never been bass fishing before, but the action was so hot that even these newcomers could catch 50 bass a day.

Other facilities sprang up around the lake, and the fishing attracted not only fishermen but also other guides, one of whom was a thin, 30-year-old angler already gaining a reputation for his bass fishing skills at nearby Sam Rayburn. His name was Tommy Martin, and like every bass fisherman at that time, he was going through various learning stages, honing his skills in locating fish through the seasons and using different lures in different situations. Over the coming years, his name would become as intertwined with Toledo Bend as Jack Wingate's had at Lake Seminole.

Martin was different from most in that he had already made up his mind to make a career in bass fishing, working not only as a guide but also as a tournament angler and a spokesman with the growing bass fishing industry. As early as 1968 he'd already entered his first bass tournament, held on Lake Livingston not far from Rayburn, and finished 30th, high enough to get his $100 entry fee back. He wanted to fish the national events he was reading about, but he knew he needed to prepare himself, so he concentrated on smaller tournaments, several of which he won, and on his guiding, in which he built an ever-increasing clientele.

Finally, in 1974, Martin entered his first B.A.S.S. event on the St. Johns River in Florida. People had told him not to throw a spinnerbait at Florida bass because they wouldn't hit it, but after two days of fruitless casting with a plastic worm, Martin realized the Florida water he was fishing looked exactly like what he fished on Toledo Bend with a spinnerbait, so he changed lures and promptly caught his first two Florida bass, both over five pounds. Later in the competition, he caught fish over seven and nine pounds, and finished third in the event.

Confident then that he could compete successfully on a national stage, Martin finished well at the next B.A.S.S. tournament on Sam Rayburn, and won in his third outing at Beaver Lake in Arkansas. Later that year, he won the Bassmaster Classic world championship at Wheeler Lake in Alabama. Much of his success he attributed to his time on the water at Toledo Bend.

Toledo's huge size—it is still the fifth largest manmade lake in the United States—created so many different conditions and fishing situations that Martin was literally able to choose how he wanted to fish practically every day. If he wanted to fish deep diving lures, for instance, he could go to an area where he could use them, and there was such a high bass population then that he would catch some of them. It was the perfect learning lake, since catching bass, in turn, immediately allowed him to perfect his presentations even more; he could, and did do this day after day, even when he wasn't guiding. Other guides also fine-tuned their skills this way; in the 1980 Bassmaster Classic championship, no less than seven qualifiers, including Martin, could trace their fishing backgrounds directly to their time on Toledo Bend.

As good as the lake was, in 1975 Toledo Bend received a present that made it even better, and which has continued to sustain the fishery ever since. That present was hydrilla, a non-native, fast-growing weed that thrives in quiet, shallow water. It appeared in Sam Rayburn at the same time, and likely was transferred from one lake to the other on a bass boat trailer or boat hull.

Hydrilla grows up from a stem and eventually mats on the surface. Baitfish spawn on top of it, feed on the algae that collects around it, and hide in it when predators approach. Bass likewise use the hydrilla for their own protection, and also as ambush spots for those baitfish that don't hide fast enough. The problem was figuring out how to catch those bass hiding in the thick vegetation, and not surprisingly, Tommy Martin was the one who figured it out.

He'd successfully used heavily weighted plastic worms to catch bass in the flooded timber at Sam Rayburn, but for the hydrilla he needed a denser, more compact lure like a jig, but no manufacturer did or would make one heavy enough to penetrate the mat, despite Martin's urging. Curious to know what the water looked like underneath the surface mat, Martin donned a diving mask and swim fins and swam down to take a look. Discovering fairly open water below the mat, he solved his fishing problem by adding a slip sinker, just like the ones he used for plastic worms, to his jigs, and over the next several years he won five or six tournaments on Toledo with the technique. That included a B.A.S.S. event in which he weighed in more than 80 pounds of bass in three days.

Eventually, of course, Martin's successes led lure manufacturers to begin making heavier jigs, and his technique became the accepted strategy on virtually all lakes where hydrilla is found. Today, Toledo Bend's bass still hide in the hydrilla as well as around the thousands of acres of stumps hiding just underneath the surface, the remains of all the trees left standing during impoundment. In recent years, some of those bass have weighed more than 15 pounds, leading many to believe that this huge reservoir on the Sabine River is still one of the best ever constructed.

★ ★ ★

In the fall of 1967 I was living in Lufkin, Texas, working for Southwestern Investment Company and spending every weekend fishing on Sam Rayburn Reservoir, but I kept hearing stories of how many bass were being caught over on Toledo Bend. Toledo had flooded a few months earlier, so a friend and I decided to make a trip over to the new lake.

We had an aluminum boat with a trolling motor and an 18-horsepower outboard, and we launched near Pendleton Bridge at what was known then as White's Landing. It was a Sunday morning in early November and so foggy we probably couldn't see 30 yards in front of us; we didn't have any idea where we were going, so we slowly motored out to a dim line of flooded timber we could just make out in the fog.

Each of us had the same lure, a Cordell Redfin that basically wobbled across the surface. One of us had a solid chrome model and the other a chrome/black back color, but color didn't matter that morning. We started catching bass on every cast. I mean every cast. The fish ranged from ten inches to three pounds, and we probably caught 125 or more. We caught 'em and caught 'em and caught 'em.

We didn't have a depth finder on the boat so we didn't know the water depth, but we were catching so many bass we didn't care. We just kept trolling around out there because wherever we went we caught fish. Bass were schooling everywhere. You couldn't throw out a lure without catching a fish. We could hear cars going across the Pendleton Bridge and sometimes we'd see their headlights, but it stayed foggy until about noon.

When the fog finally broke and we could see where we were, we realized we hadn't gone anywhere. Our car and trailer were in plain view at White's, not 500 yards away. I've never had a day of fishing like that again.

The next time we came back to Toledo, the water was colder and we didn't catch nearly as many. Back then, we didn't understand cold water fishing, and when the bass stopped biting our surface lures and plastic

Tommy Martin solved the mystery of how to fish through thick hydrilla on Lake Toledo.

worms, we didn't know what to do. A lot of the techniques we use today for deepwater fishing had not been developed then.

A few months later I bought a fiberglass bass boat with a 55-horsepower outboard, and in June 1968 I started guiding on Sam Rayburn every weekend. I never forgot that day on Toledo Bend, however, and returned often. Finally, in January 1972 I bought an interest in Housen Bay Marina on Toledo Bend, quit my job at the investment company in Lufkin, and moved to Toledo Bend and started guiding full-time. Forty years later, I still consider it one of the best decisions I ever made.

★ ★ ★

Tommy Martin still guides and fishes regularly on Toledo Bend when he isn't competing in tournaments or presenting seminars around the country. He lives in Hemphill in the home he built at the water's edge in 1982, less than a mile from the spot where he launched on his very first visit to the lake in 1967.

Chapter Sixteen

Jackie Thompson: "This Place Is a Fish Factory"

In February 1967, the first day Jackie Thompson fished Alabama's Lake Eufaula, he caught 15 bass weighing 98 pounds. Thompson later began guiding on the famous impoundment, and through the years has taken clients from all over the world fishing there. Photo courtesy of Strike King Lure Company.

The timing could not have been better. In 1966 when the Corps of Engineers began filling Lake Walter F. George on the Chattahoochee River in southeast Alabama, bass fishing was quickly gaining both publicity and popularity. Lake Seminole, located further down the Chattahoochee along the Florida line, had already been producing more and larger bass than anyone ever imagined, and in Texas a 114,000-acre reservoir named Sam Rayburn, impounded just a year earlier, was attracting anglers from all over the country.

Almost immediately, the new lake—named for US Senator Walter Franklin George of Georgia—became known as

Lake Eufaula, after the historic antebellum city through which the river flowed, and one February day in 1967, a fisherman named Jackie Thompson launched his boat on the lake for the first time. Thompson had moved to Eufaula the previous October from Augusta, Georgia, because he'd been hearing stories of the new lake; an employee at the new Mead Paper Company mill just north of town, he'd been too busy at work to have a chance to fish until that February morning.

He'd been working swing shifts, and finally, when he did get some time off, Thompson had a full five days free. The first thing he did was purchase a 15-foot boat with a 35-horsepower Johnson outboard from the local dealer, throw in his open face spinning tackle, and launch at Cheneyhatchee Creek. He had a solid strike on his first cast to the shoreline brush, but the bass broke his 12-pound line. The next five fish he hooked also broke his line.

With that, Thompson returned to the ramp and put his boat back on his trailer, then drove into Eufaula to the first fishing tackle store he could find. He purchased an Ambassadeur casting reel spooled with 20-pound line, and went right back to Cheneyhatchee Creek. Two hours later he was back at the same tackle store, this time, however, with an Igloo cooler filled with 15 bass that weighed 98 pounds.

Thompson was no stranger to bass fishing, but that first outing on the new lake left him stunned. Born December 27, 1930, in Tallassee, Alabama, he had learned about bass fishing by walking with his father along the shoreline of Lake Martin when he was just eight years old. The thrill and the challenge of catching largemouths had never left him. Even while living in Augusta he'd been guiding part-time on Clarks Hill Reservoir, and when he hauled that cooler full of bass into the Eufaula tackle shop, he knew he would never doubt the wisdom of his move to the new lake.

Later that same year, Thompson brought another 15-bass catch weighing about 85 pounds into the marina where a spectator named Tom Mann happened to be present. Mann was already making a name for himself as a lure manufacturer there in Eufaula, and although he'd been hearing stories about Thompson's big catches, the two had never met. Mann introduced himself, and asked Thompson if he'd start guiding some of his business clients. Thompson agreed, and so with a handshake began a career showing others how to catch bass on what was destined to become one of the most famous bass fishing lakes in the world, a career that has continued for more than 45 years.

Thompson was present to watch the first national tournament on Eufaula, the 1968 Eufaula National conducted by the then fledgling Bass Anglers Sportsman Society, which was won by an Alabama angler named John Powell with a three-day catch weighing 132 pounds. And he was also there the warm June day in 1972 when his friend Tom Mann and another local angler, David Lockhart, brought in 25 bass weighing 155 pounds, topped by Lockhart's 13-pound, 2-ounce monster.

Embracing more than 45,000 acres, the lake produced catches like this for years because of its remarkable configuration. Essentially, Lake Eufaula consists of a river, the Chattahoochee, running through the middle of huge flats extending out from the edges of the river channel. Those shallow flats, themselves laced with smaller ditches and filled with rock piles, brush, trees, stumps, and vegetation, formed an ideal bass habitat that stretched for miles up and down the river. Additionally, Eufaula has more than half a dozen large tributary creeks that flow into the main Chattahoochee, rich in structure, cover, and nutrients.

It's the structure—those places where the water depth changes—that have made Eufaula so famous, because no matter where bass live in the world, structure seems to be one of their first requirements. On Eufaula, there are literally thousands of places where the depth changes gradually from about 2 feet to 10 to 15 and so on down to about 30 feet. Bass come up to feed on the shallow flats, then drop back down these stair-stepping ledges to whatever depth is most comfortable to them.

In the early days when Thompson first began fishing the lake, the bass on the flats weren't disturbed, simply because no one really realized they were there. As for fishing the structure, Thompson used a weighted rope he dropped to the bottom to determine the water depth; when he found water between 6 and about 12 feet deep, he dropped anchor and started fishing. The rest of the time, Eufaula fishermen just cast to the brush-filled shoreline.

Gradually, anglers and guides like Thompson and Mann began to put the pieces of the fish-finding puzzle together and learned how the bass lived and moved on Eufaula, and their catches reflect that growing knowledge. Thompson, who was usually guiding 130 to 150 days a year, had one client who, on two separate occasions, caught 10-pound bass on back-to-back casts. He himself once caught nine bass weighing 55 pounds in 45 minutes from a spot less than 30 yards long, and that included losing two bass each over 12 pounds right at the boat.

Catches like that, of course, could not continue indefinitely, and on Eufaula they didn't. All lakes go through various stages of decline as they age, as cover deteriorates, and the forage base changes. On Eufaula, the forage base that supported those huge bass catches was threadfin shad, a species notorious for its own boom-and-bust spawning cycles. As long as there are plenty of small threadfin available after a good spawn, bass up to about 16 inches in length will continue to feed and grow. Larger bass, however, suffer because they have to expend a large amount of energy chasing a very small meal. If there is a poor shad spawn, or a die-off in unusually cold weather, both of which Eufaula experienced a number of times, all the bass suffer. The surviving adult shad are too large for the smallest bass but too small for the largest bass.

Between 2000 and 2001, aquatic vegetation, primarily hydrilla, began growing in the lake and, as expected, fishing was excellent, because heavy vegetation changes the bass diet. In weed-filled lakes, bass feed more on sunfish like bluegills, a diet far more stable than shad because the sunfish live in and around that vegetation their entire lives and the bass quickly adapt. Anglers have learned bass stay around this type of shallow vegetation, so they concentrate their fishing efforts around it.

In 2007, however, the Corps of Engineers released more than 13,000 grass carp into Eufaula, and two years later added 5,000 more, in an effort to reduce the aquatic greenery. The Corps also sprayed herbicides as they tried, and succeeded, in greatly reducing the amount of hydrilla. That forced the bass back to a diet of shad, which had been suffering from several successive poor-spawn years Once again, there wasn't enough food for the larger bass; within a year, from 2009 to 2010, the weight needed to win a one-day, five bass tournament on Lake Eufaula dropped from 25 pounds to about 13 pounds.

Back in the 1970s and 1980s, there likely were fluctuations in the shad populations as well, but no one noticed. There weren't as many bass fishermen on the water then, and guides like Thompson kept the bass they and their clients caught. Today, fishermen tend to release all the bass they catch, a practice that, ironically, has likely also contributed to a slowdown in the overall quality of fishing on the lake. There are literally too many small bass in the overall population, so there isn't enough food for the larger bass, the very fish that made Lake Eufaula so famous.

★ ★ ★

The lake has had its ups and downs but it always seems to bounce back. I've certainly seen that during my time here. We don't catch as many big bass as we once did, but none of the famous bass lakes of the 1970s produce fish like they did back then. Still, this is a lake where you might catch a big bass on any given cast.

The biggest bass I personally ever landed on Eufaula weighed 12 pounds, 2 ounces, but I've hooked heavier bass but didn't get them to the boat. I remember it was early February, which is normally rainy, dreary, and too cold for fishing, but one day the weather turned sunny and I just couldn't help myself. I had to go fishing.

I launched about mid-lake and started heading south. At that time, Tom Mann's lure company was making a balsa crankbait named the Wooden Deep Pig, which was their only venture into wood lures, and I had one tied on. I started casting on the points looking for staging bass, and I caught two 5-pounders with the lure. I left that particular point and went on down south a mile or so and caught several more, but something kept calling me back to that first point.

I finally turned around and went back, and on my first cast as the crankbait came off the edge of the point, it just stopped. I had a 12-pound line and when I set the hook, the fish just took off. All I could do was follow it with my trolling motor and let it do whatever it wanted to do.

When I got it to the boat, that fish actually scared me. It was huge, the biggest bass I'd ever seen at that time. I didn't have a livewell so I put some water in a cooler and put the fish in it. When I got back to the boat landing I took the bass to a little grocery store where they had a pair of hanging scales where people weighed their vegetables. The bass weighed 12-2, and to this day is still the heaviest fish I've ever put in the boat, although I've seen larger bass caught here by other fishermen.

Eufaula is probably the most amazing lake I've ever seen. This place is a fish factory.

★ ★ ★

Jackie Thompson and his wife Mary live in Eufaula where, at age 82, he still fishes and occasionally guides for bass.

Chapter Seventeen

David Wharton: "One Year I Caught 1,700 Bass from the Same Spot"

Only one thing could have kept David Wharton from becoming a school teacher. After all, both his father and mother had been teachers; his father taught school for 43 years, his mother for more than 30. And, on December 20, 1972, he'd just graduated from Stephen F. Austin University in Nacogdoches, Texas, with a degree in education and vocational agriculture, a course he planned to teach in high school in Center, Texas.

The one thing that could have stopped his teaching career was bass fishing, and it did. Literally, as he sat by a window filling out his teaching application at the high school, Wharton thought about how the bass were probably biting at Sam Rayburn Reservoir just down the highway. He stood up, turned in his unfinished application, and walked into bass fishing history as one of the most popular and successful anglers to ever step into a bass boat.

Born February 10, 1950, in Timpson, Texas, Wharton and Sam Rayburn Reservoir were made for each other, and, like Jack Wingate and Lake Seminole in Georgia, it is practically impossible to think of

David Wharton made his first guide trip on Sam Rayburn Reservoir in 1969 while still in college, and continued to guide there for more than three decades; no angler knew the 114,000-acre reservoir better than he did. Wharton also enjoyed an outstanding professional tournament career, winning four national Bassmaster events.

one without the other. The two grew up together. Rayburn, all 114,000 acres, had filled by March 1965, and Wharton conducted his first guided trip there in February 1969, while still a sophomore in college. He was 19 years old, had to fish out of a borrowed boat, and received $40 for the day. He continued to guide on weekends throughout his college years.

It's easy to understand why Wharton, who became known through-out his career as gracious and reserved but with a quick and agreeable smile, decided on bass fishing instead of teaching. Growing up just four miles from Lake Murvaul, the original Texas trophy bass lake, Wharton started fishing there with his father when he was only five years old. When he was 12, he caught a bass there weighing 10 pounds, 6 ounces.

As Rayburn was filling, his father actually started guiding there on his weekends and in all likelihood set his son's career path in motion at that time. The two could catch 100 to 200 or even more bass during a day on Rayburn in those early years, and that kind of action drew excited bass fishermen from all over the United States. Several factors separated Rayburn from other new impoundments of that era and contributed to the quality of fishing there. A primary factor was that Rayburn was one of the very first reservoirs in which the US Army Corps of Engineers left trees standing, instead of removing them as they had done in most of their previous lakes.

That provided a lot of additional habitat for fish; in some coves the trees, logs, and brush were so thick fishermen could not get to the bass, even though they could hear them splashing in the shallows. Indeed, it took three or four years before enough timber rotted to allow anglers access into some of these places. Because of his earlier years of experience, however, Wharton found plenty of other bass for his clients, so much so that by the time he became a full-time guide in 1974 he already had a large and regular clientele that continued to support him for many years.

He guided out of the M Motel in the town of Broaddus, which, through the aggressive advertising of the motel's owner, Marge Miller, had become the center of the Texas bass fishing universe. Wharton was one of more than 40 guides she used, and in 1978, Wharton guided an astounding 311 days. He was fishing out of a 16-foot Super Skeeter with a 33-horsepower outboard so he could not make the long runs today's anglers do to reach their favorite fishing spots, but he didn't need to. Even though the larger-growing Florida strain of largemouths would not be stocked until the early 1980s, Rayburn was still filled with solid four- to six-pound northern strain largemouths; on one trip, he and two clients from Port Arthur caught 9 fish over seven pounds in one day.

As great as the fishing was during that first decade, Rayburn then began to decline, following a normal progression common in many man-made reservoirs. Much of the timber had rotted so the habitat disappeared, and so did most of the big bass. For a period of about two years, Wharton and the other guides could only find small fish for their clients. Then, four events occurred that put Rayburn back on the path to becoming one of the best bass lakes in America, and keeping it on that path for decades to come.

First, it stopped raining in East Texas, and for at least a year, Rayburn remained about 15 feet below full pool level. During that time, weeds, small brush, and willows grew along the newly exposed shoreline. When the drought finally broke in 1982, this new shoreline habitat was flooded, providing instant cover for small bass. At about this same time, hydrilla also appeared for the first time, and to their credit, the Corps of Engineers did not immediately try to eliminate it. It provided even more habitat for the fish.

The third thing that happened was that the Texas Parks & Wildlife Department began stocking the Florida-strain of largemouth into the lake. Agencies across the South were doing this in other reservoirs, and at Rayburn, biologists netted the entrances to coves in Indian and Pigeon Roost Creek, as well as several others, treated them with rotenone to kill everything in the coves, then filled them with Florida bass fingerlings. Rotenone is a natural toxin produced by several tropical plants and has been used in fisheries management for more than 80 years. It is one of the most environmentally benign toxins in that humans and wildlife are comparatively insensitive to it, whereas fish usually die within hours of exposure.

When the fingerlings grew large enough, the nets were removed and the bass swam into their new home. Along with the new fish came new rules, too; the ten-bass, 10-inch minimum size limit was changed to five bass with a 14-inch size limit, which remains in effect today. Adding those four inches allowed the bass another year or more to mature, during which they spawned at least once and usually twice before they could be harvested.

Although the lake has had other ups and downs during the decades, the introduction of Florida bass, the very limited control of hydrilla, and the more stringent size restrictions have all combined to not only produce larger bass more consistently—the lake record stands at 16.8 pounds—but also to produce staggering numbers of quality catchable bass for more than three decades.

Professional bass tournaments came to Sam Rayburn for the first time in 1968, when Bill Dance won the B.A.S.S. All-American with a three-day catch of 72 pounds, 13 ounces, another testament to the quality of fishing there, since Dance's fish were all northern strain largemouths. Wharton stood on the sidelines as a spectator; he did not enter his own first professional tournament until 1974. He was too busy as a guide, and he did not think he could afford the tournament entry fees and travel, but once he did become a tournament pro, few could match his sheer competitiveness on the water. What he had learned on Rayburn often applied to the lakes where he competed. He won four of the 264 tournaments in which he fished, winning more than $800,000 during an era in which anglers seldom took home more than $15,000 for a victory.

And yes, he did win on Rayburn, taking first place in the 1987 Texas Invitational, where he brought in 37 pounds, 2 ounces during three cold, blustery days in March. It certainly wasn't vintage Sam Rayburn, but it was vintage David Wharton.

★ ★ ★

The thing that always amazed me about Sam Rayburn was that the great fishing was purely an accident. Back in the 1950s and 1960s when the Corps was constructing all the new lakes, fishing and recreation were not at the top of their priority list. None of us really knew much about how bass need and use structure and cover, but purely by accident the Corps created a lake full of absolutely ideal bass structure.

For example, during my guiding years I kept a lot of notes about where I caught bass, and one year I noted that of the more than 5,000 bass I had caught with my clients, 1,700 of them came from one spot. It was a long ridge where a creek channel cut in from one side, then turned and formed a loop and came right back in around the end of the ridge. You could sit on the point and cast left or right and hit that channel, which was also full of brush. You couldn't draw a better spot, and the Corps, fortunately, left it there.

*David Wharton guided and fished on the Sam Rayburn
Reservoir for over three decades.*

There's another place I know that's been just as good, located a short
distance north of Caney Creek. It's right around a place we know as
Peckerwood Point, where two shallow creek channels intersect. Between
them is a little flat that's about five feet deep, and the creeks are 14 feet
deep. Some years there's an inside hydrilla line that falls right into those
channels; it's a natural place for bass moving shallow to spawn.

One February morning in 1990 during a tournament, my partner
and I pulled up on the spot, and I caught a 12-pound, 10-ounce bass on
my first cast. My partner had made a cast, but left his lure in the water as
he netted my fish. He was just staring at the size of the fish when he felt
a strike and set the hook on what proved to be a 10-pound, 8-ounce fish

that I then netted for him. We'd been fishing 30 seconds and already had more than 23 pounds of fish in the livewell. On my next cast I caught a 7-pounder, and for the day I had five fish weighing more than 33 pounds.

The next morning I went back to that spot and caught another bass over 10 pounds. That's how good Rayburn is. I still catch bass on that point where the channel loops in, and I've been fishing it for than 30 years. There are hundreds of places just like that all over the lake. In all my years of guiding, during thousands of days on the water, I only had one trip during which I never caught a bass. It was with two clients from Dallas with whom I had fished often, but just before their trip it started sleeting and the water temperature hovered in the low 40s. I telephoned and asked them not to come, but they just wanted to be on the water, and none of us caught a bass in three days.

Wharton won four national Bassmaster events.

That 12-10 was the biggest bass I ever weighed in, but I have caught larger fish, including one I believe weighed nearly 14 pounds. The bass would have easily qualified for the Parks & Wildlife Department's Share-Lunker program, but going through all that would have taken most of the rest of the day. I was practicing for a tournament and really needed the time on the water, so I just turned the fish loose. I have often thought Rayburn had bass weighing between 15 and 20 pounds in it; one year the lake produced at least seven bass weighing more than 13 pounds for the ShareLunker program.

In the 1990s when the largemouth virus hit Rayburn, I went out on the lake and saw dozens of bass in the 10- to 15-pound class floating dead, but within a year the lake was producing big fish again. It's just a very special lake, and the fishing quality was really just an accident.

★ ★ ★

David Wharton died suddenly of a heart attack on February 16, 2009, just a week after turning 59. At his request, his ashes were spread on the lake he loved and fished for more than 40 years.

Chapter Eighteen

Guy Eaker: "We'll Never See Fishing Like That Again"

Guy Eaker was already 20 years old when he fished the Santee Cooper Lakes, Marion and Moultrie, for the first time in 1959, and never in his dreams could he have imagined how the 17-year-old twin South Carolina impoundments would change his life. Already employed as a dispatcher at Carolina Freight Company in Charlotte, the Cherryville, North Carolina, native started fishing the lakes regularly, became a highly successful guide there, and eventually resigned at Carolina Freight to become a full-time bass tournament pro who would fish around the world, design fishing lures, and share a bass boat with two US presidents.

He and his father weren't even after largemouth bass that fateful day. Instead, they were looking for crappie, which thrived in the lake's heavy cover and shallow water. That changed, however, when Eaker saw a school of huge fish break the surface feeding a short distance away from where they were jigging their minnows. Those fish weren't largemouths, either, but rather, striped bass, and in short order the big fish totally wrecked all the tackle father and son had with them that day.

They drove the 185 miles home, refitted themselves with stronger rods and line, and were back on the water the next day where they redeemed themselves, catching fish up to about 16 pounds.

The big silvery fish with the dark lateral stripes had been in the lakes from the beginning. Migrating up the Santee River from the Atlantic to spawn, they'd inadvertently been trapped when the Wilson Dam on the

Guy Eaker honed his tournament skills by fishing and then guiding on the Santee Cooper Lakes, Marion and Moultrie. A successful tournament angler known for his expertise with a spinnerbait, Eaker first used the blade lures with another well-known tournament pro, Roland Martin, at Santee Cooper more than 45 years ago.

Santee River closed and began impounding what would become the 100,500-acre Lake Marion and the Pinopolis Dam closed on the Cooper River to begin forming 60,000-acre Lake Moultrie. The year was 1942, but damming the two rivers—the Santee was the fourth largest river on the East Coast—had been dreamed about for more than a quarter of a century.

The two lakes are connected via the seven-mile-long Diversion Canal; rarely, however, does any fisherman refer to either lake by its real name. They are known simply as Santee Cooper, from the rivers that create them, and they are actually quite different in character. Whereas Moultrie offers more open water and hydrilla, Marion is shallow, stumpy, and in its early years contained vast areas of flooded swampland so dense anglers frequently got lost in the timber.

The stripers survived because of the forage that came with them out of the Atlantic: mullet, herring, needlefish, and several species of shad. All found the generally warm, nutrient-rich water and abundant cover to their liking. And because the entire ecosystem remained virtually undisturbed during the years of World War II, the striped bass not only spawned but also thrived. When anglers began returning to the lakes in the late 1940s they found a monster they'd never before seen in freshwater.

No one had; at the time, it was unheard of that striped bass could survive in freshwater. Over the years, the Santee stripers, which grew to weights of 40 and 50 pounds, were propagated in hatcheries and stocked in lakes across the nation, creating an entirely new fishery for America's anglers. Later, these same Santee Cooper striped bass would be bred with the common white bass to create a new fish, the hybrid striper, which have also been stocked throughout the United States.

The heyday of the Santee stripers lasted from the late 1950s throughout the 1970s. Not only were the fish big and plentiful, they were relatively easy to catch because of their ravenous appetites, and they were themselves good to eat. The limit was 15 fish per person per day, and often an angler and his guide could catch their limits fairly quickly, put the fish in a cooler, and head back out to catch another 30 before sunset.

That's the world Guy Eaker discovered the day he and his father Earl first visited Santee Cooper. Born November 23, 1939, in Cherryville, Eaker discovered largemouth bass fishing on Easter Sunday when he was five years old. After church, his father had taken him to a favorite fishing spot on the nearby Catawba River known as the Round Hole where they caught five bass weighing between three and eight pounds. The younger Eaker caught the three-pounder, and although he and his father fished frequently for other species as well, his primary interest quickly became largemouth bass. There were plenty of opportunities for bass, too, since father and son fished nearly every weekend on Lakes Hickory, Wylie, or Wateree, or the Catawba and Johns Rivers.

That first experience with striped bass on Santee Cooper, however, drew him back again and again, usually to a fishing camp named Jones Landing. Eaker was working a three days on, three days off schedule at Carolina Freight and usually spent at least some of his free days at the two lakes. On one of those trips he met another enthusiastic angler who, although in the Army and stationed at nearby Fort Jackson, also spent his off days fishing Santee Cooper. That angler was named Roland Martin, and he, too, loved bass fishing.

The two became fast friends and frequent fishing companions, and eventually Martin talked Eaker into becoming a fishing guide there on the lakes, but it was for striped bass, not largemouths. In 1960 when he started, few clients wanted to fish for bass when they could quickly load the boat with the much larger stripers. It was easy fishing for Eaker, and he earned $100 a day for it. That certainly beat fishing by himself, when he would sell his striped bass catch for 20 cents a pound to local fish markets just to help pay for his gas, meals, and lodging.

Hardly anyone, except Eaker and Martin, realized what was happening then to the lakes' largemouth population in those days. All the attention being given to the stripers allowed the largemouth to grow and thrive, just like the stripers had during the war years. In fact, he and Martin prayed for rain during Eaker's guiding days so his clients would cancel and he and Roland could go bass fishing instead. Neither man realized it at the time because the first true professional bass tournaments were still several years in the future, but every trip they made together for largemouths was in reality preparing them for those tournaments.

One of their favorite largemouth spots was a large, stumpy area on the southern shore of Moultrie known as the Hatchery, since bass favored it as a spring spawning area. They had to slide a boat over a sandbar to get into the place, but once in the Hatchery, Eaker and Martin could easily catch 100 bass a day, at least one of which would nearly always weigh between 8 and 11 pounds. Eaker began guaranteeing his clients 50 bass a day if his clients would agree to go after largemouths instead of stripers.

Today, the Hatchery is still an attractive area for bass fishermen. Eaker remembers catching two bass over 11 pounds there, and probably 15 over 10 pounds during his guiding years, and in a one-day club bass tournament there he once brought a 10-fish, 65-pound catch to the scales. He can also remember losing larger fish. The Hatchery is a huge stump field with scattered lily pads and vegetation, and all Eaker did that day was cast a spinnerbait, start winding, and hold on. That's how good Santee Cooper was in the beginning.

With catches like that, combined with Eaker's pure love of fishing, it's easy to understand his transition into full-time professional bass fishing. Lakes that offer lots of bass, as well as lots of ways to catch them, are always the best teachers, and Santee Cooper was one of the best. Eaker, like his friend Roland Martin, went on to enjoy a stellar career in the sport, winning events at all levels, and competing in ten Bassmaster Classic world championships. Always in demand as a public speaker, he often made as many as 40 seminar appearances annually. He was inducted into the Bass Fishing Hall of Fame in 2011.

★ ★ ★

The thing about Santee Cooper in those early days that sometimes gets overlooked is that the lakes filled and the bass fishing peaked at just the right time to become part of the growth of the sport. The fishing was so good it attracted more and more fishermen, and when they caught a lot of fish, they told their friends and they came down. It just grew and grew, and the lakes were located in the perfect place, too, to draw anglers from up and down the East Coast.

One problem every angler faced, however, was that it was a dangerous lake to fish, in that there was so much brush, logs, and timber just below the surface, and every time a big storm blew through the area, a lot of that cover changed locations. We didn't have the big boats and faster engines then that we do today, and when Marion or Moultrie got rough, it really was hard to navigate. For instance, when we fished the Hatchery, we had to cross 14 miles of lake to get there, and we thought that was really dangerous. Years later, during a Bassmaster Classic where I finished second, I drove more than a hundred river miles *one way* to my fishing spot, and I did it for six consecutive days of practice and competition. Santee Cooper is where I really learned to drive a bass boat.

There was so much water to fish on the two lakes, too. When it was really hot during the summer, another tournament pro who really got his start at Santee Cooper like Roland and me, Hank Parker, and I would fish the swamps in Lake Marion. We'd throw buzz baits and ten-inch plastic worms in the open pockets in the trees, and one day it was so hot the reel seats on Hank's rods were practically melting so each time he'd set the hook on a big bass, his reel would fly off.

We used those big lures because we were after big bass, and we caught them. If we used a small crankbait, we never got it back because you just couldn't control a fish with the lighter line we had to use with those lures. Even 20-pound test line wasn't always strong enough in the logs and stumps. During my career I've caught 58 bass over 10 pounds, and more than half of them have come from Santee Cooper.

I never fished very much above the I-95 bridge that crosses the upper end of Lake Marion, but early one March I did fish up there during a club tournament. The area I chose had been off-limits all winter as a waterfowl sanctuary, so when I went in, I knew it hadn't been fished for months. I caught 48 pounds the first day and 52 pounds the next, just by throwing a spinnerbait around the cypress trees.

When you talk about Santee Cooper as a training ground for myself, Roland, and Hank, I always remember one day in 1964 or 1965, when some visiting fisherman showed Roland and me a spinnerbait. I had never seen one before; Roland and I fished the big plastic worms, topwater plugs, and Johnson spoons. We didn't have much of anything else, but at Santee we didn't need anything else.

Anyway, Roland looked at that spinnerbait—it didn't even have a skirt, just a blade, a hook, and a plastic worm on the hook so it would have some wiggling action—and decided he could make some. A few days later he was back at the lake with a handful of the new spinnerbaits, and we caught bass with them until the lures were so torn up they wouldn't work anymore. Roland caught a ten-pounder, and I caught two weighing nine and eight pounds. I don't know how long we fished them before we ever tried putting skirts on them, which are standard today.

That experience is what set me on fire as a spinnerbait fisherman, which continued throughout my professional tournament career. It's been the lure I've depended on more times than I can ever remember, and Santee Cooper was the perfect place to learn to use them because of all the flooded stumps and trees, as well as the big fish population. Both Roland and Hank also became excellent spinnerbait fishermen because of their time on Santee Cooper. Hank actually won two Bassmaster Classics with spinnerbaits, and several of Roland's tournament wins came with spinnerbaits, too.

Looking back, I realize now what an unbelievable experience it was, and I know we'll never see fishing like that again.

★ ★ ★

Guy Eaker and his wife Pat live in Cherryville, North Carolina, and although he has retired from full-time competition, he still competes several times a year in Professional Angler Association events and makes seminar appearances.

THE BOATS

Chapter Nineteen

Boats Built for Bass

When the winner's name was announced at the Dixie Invitational B.A.S.S. tournament on Lewis Smith Lake on October 22, 1967, it was not Forrest L. Wood, but it should have been. In the standings, the tall, slim Arkansas angler was somewhere in the 30s, but all Wood did that week was jump-start the bass boat industry.

A guide on the White River and nearby Bull Shoals Lake where he also built the wooden boats he and other fishermen used there, Wood showed up at Smith Lake with a 16-foot wooden flat bottom with 18-inch sides and powered by a 55-horsepower outboard engine. He was willing to build them for other fishermen for $650, and he started receiving orders for them the day the tournament started. Just that quickly, Wood totally changed the way America fishes.

Although it made an impact, Wood's 16-footer was not the original bass boat. Boats for specific purposes, such as navigating rivers or stump-filled lakes, had been being built and sold for years. The first boat many consider designed specifically for pursuing one species of fish, the large-mouth bass, had actually been built almost two decades earlier in 1948 by Holmes Thurman, a Louisiana fisherman who'd grown tired of being blown across the water by the wind and getting wet when waves lapped over the gunwales. To solve these problems, he'd made a 13 ½-footer in his garage in Shreveport, a flat-bottom craft designed with high, inward-sloping sides and a sharply pointed bow.

It reminded him of a mosquito so Thurman called his boat a Skeeter, and, because of its stability and improved performance over other boats of

Professional anglers like Billy Westmorland, shown here fishing a tournament in Florida, helped spread the popularity of bass boats by their visibility in national tournaments. The boats were truly designed specifically for fishing for the largemouth bass, and designs improved each year. They were not only fast, but also able to maneuver quietly in shallow water where the largemouth is commonly found.

the era, fishermen quickly started buying them. Thurman's business soon outgrew his garage and he moved across the state line to Marshall, Texas, where, within a decade, the business had grown large enough that he began making the boats out of fiberglass, one of the earliest manufacturers to do so. In those days, fiberglassing was a messy, miserable, and potentially dangerous process, but it allowed Thurman to not only create different sizes and styles of boats, but also to produce them much faster. Even with these improvements, however, he still could not build them fast enough.

In 1961, Thurman sold his little company to the Stemco Corporation, which relocated to a still larger facility in Longview, Texas, and named their new operation Skeeter Marine. They added forward-mounted stick steering and eventually a tri-hull design. In 1983, the Coleman Company, long known for its camping equipment, purchased Skeeter, and in 1996 they sold the company to Yamaha Marine, the present owners.

By this time, had Holmes Thurman lived to see them, he would not have recognized the craft that still carried his name. The boats were now more than 20 feet in length, designed not with a pencil but with a computer, and capable of handling outboard engines producing more than 200 horsepower.

No one, including Forrest Wood, could foresee any of this during the Dixie Invitational. What Wood did recognize, however, was that he liked to build boats practically as much as he liked bass fishing, and that tournaments like the Dixie Invitational offered a natural avenue of national publicity he could use to sell them. In 1968, just a few months after he drove back home to the little town of Flippin on the White River, he opened his own company, Ranger Boats.

Wood continued to divide his time between boat building and bass tournament fishing, often writing boat orders during meals on restaurant paper napkins. Initially, he custom-built every boat, incorporating the various features each angler wanted. After a while, he realized most fishermen wanted pretty much the same things, so he standardized his designs, and like Thurman, could barely keep up with demand.

Although Ranger and Skeeter, both alive and well today, were among the first to tap into the spreading and soon-to-be lucrative bass fishing market of the 1960s and 1970s, they were not the only companies doing so. Improvements in fiberglass technology gave new companies like Terry in Louisiana and Kingfisher and Sidewinder in Texas quick opportunities, and each added their own specializations. Kingfisher, for example, reinforced its hulls with balsa, claiming the lightweight wood added extra floatation as well as strength. Sidewinder used foam instead of balsa, but added a special battery storage compartment underneath a seat.

During this same time, near Knoxville, Tennessee, another boat builder was heading in a different direction. His name was Paul Allison, and although he initially repaired beat-up cars for a living, what he really wanted to do was go faster on the water than anyone else. Within a few short years, the technology gained by "Saturday afternoon racing," as Paul describes their runs across Ft. Loudon Reservoir, would be transferred directly to bass boats. Paul was the second generation of the Allison family to enter the boating business; his father James had built his first boat in 1917, a flat-bottom 12-foot barge powered by a Harley-Davidson motorcycle engine that reached the then unheard of speed of 12 miles an hour.

The construction of that 1917 barge, as inauspicious as it may have been at the time, marked the beginning of the most remarkable family legacy in American boat building history, which continues today with Paul's son Darris at Allison Boats in Louisville, Tennessee. Forrest Wood receives much of the credit for starting the bass boat industry, but what Wood really accomplished with Ranger was to *popularize* bass boats, spreading the belief that owning a bass boat would make anyone a better fisherman. Ranger advertised heavily, donated boats as prizes in tournaments everywhere, and sponsored bass fishing pros, bass fishing events, and bass fishing causes. This is exactly what the fledgling sport needed, and no one could have handled the task better than the lanky, quiet-spoken Wood.

Wood was so busy promoting the sport that his own Ranger research and development programs began to lag, and in 1973–74, he approached Darris Allison about doing design work for Ranger. He also bought Allison's year-old hull molds for both 15- and 17-foot models, and began building some of his Rangers around them. They were originally named and sold as Ranger-Allison boats. What made them special was the fact the hulls were the first bass boat Deep V models with a running pad, a design Allison had created, perfected, and incorporated in Allison Boats several years earlier. The Deep V bottom was not only faster but also handled rough water much better.

Surprisingly, the Deep V hull was slow to gain acceptance in the bass market, so Allison created the Tri-hull V bottom, which revolutionized boat design and was eventually copied by nearly 100 other boat companies. Allison's attorney was 30 days late filing the patent application so it was refused and as a result, Darris missed out on a small fortune in royalty fees for the design.

The Deep V and Tri-hull V are but two of more than a hundred innovations Paul and Darris introduced and which are now standard across the business. Among the others are foot throttles, hydraulic engine trim units, pedestal seats, molded-in depth finder transducer boxes, raised flipping decks, self-latching compartment lids, and set-back jack plates, to name a few. Darris was just eight years old in 1955 when he helped his father rebuild an old 13-foot plywood boat, and two years later, at only 15, he built his own first boat, and he's never stopped. Indeed, the entire bass boat industry owes much of its existence today to the Allison family.

The outboard engine industry is much older; in fact, the first true gasoline-powered outboard, known as the American, appeared in America in 1896. It was a four-cycle air-cooled model producing about two horsepower, and it would move a 15-foot rowboat along at more than six miles an hour. Records indicate, however, only about two dozen of them were ever manufactured.

The American was followed by another outboard known as the Waterman, which first appeared in 1905. It was water-cooled, which is how today's outboards are cooled, and by 1907 as many as 3,000 engines were being built, and within a decade more than 30,000 had been sold. Despite these successes, however, the company was out of business by 1924. That opened the door for a young man named Ole Evinrude to leave his mark in bass boating history.

It started on a hot August afternoon in 1908 as Evinrude struggled to row against a strong wind blowing across the Wisconsin lake where a young lady named Bess Cary waited for him at an island picnic. She had decided ice cream would be a nice treat, and Evinrude, seriously wanting to please her, had rowed two miles back to the mainland and purchased a box for her. Now, the ice cream was melting fast in the summer heat as he worked the oars to get back. The very next morning he began drawing the plans for an outboard.

The son of Norwegian immigrants, Evinrude was perfectly suited for just such a task. He had worked in various machine shops and even built his own gasoline-engine-powered automobile, and by April 1909, less than a year after the picnic, he had his first outboard ready to try. He carried it down to the Kinnickinnic River outside Milwaukee, rented a little wooden boat for 50 cents, and immediately started chugging across the water, to the cheers and waves of everyone who saw him.

Evinrude (who had married Bess despite the melted ice cream) quickly made improvements to the engine, and after a friend borrowed it for a fishing trip and came back with orders for ten engines, he was in business. It was a single cylinder, two-cycle motor that developed about 1 ½ horsepower, and Evinrude sold them for $62. Although he did not actually develop the first outboard engine, he did produce the first outboard that was commercially successful.

He and Bess sold their company, The Evinrude Detachable Rowboat Motor Co. in 1914, but by 1919 he was back in the business, this time with an aluminum twin cylinder three-horsepower outboard. In 1929 he merged with his former company and six years later bought the Johnson Motor Company to create what eventually became one of the true giants in the bass boat outboard engine world, Outboard Marine Corporation. In time, they became the largest manufacturer and supplier of outboard motors in the world.

They would be challenged repeatedly, however, by another outboard engine manufacturer, who, like so many others in the bass fishing industry, started his company by accident. His name was Carl Kiekhaefer, and the mechanical cheese separators he had planned to build for the local dairy industry in 1939 turned into the Mercury Marine Corporation.

When he bought the old, defunct Thor outboard engine factory in Cedarburg, Wisconsin, Kiekhaefer really only wanted the technology to make the separators the company also owned. In the factory, however, he found several dozen broken Sea King outboard engines, the little motor Thor made exclusively for mail-order catalog giant Montgomery Ward. Kiekhaefer, needing funds for his new separation machine business, decided to rebuild the outboards and send them back to Montgomery Ward. He not only repaired them, but also improved them so dramatically Montgomery Ward placed another order.

Just that quickly, Kiekhaefer forgot about cheese separators and turned his attention to the marine industry. The Thor nameplate was replaced by Mercury, for two reasons; Mercury was the messenger of the gods in Roman mythology, revered for his running speed; and it was also the name of the new automobile just introduced by the Ford Motor Company, so name recognition was automatic.

Internal improvements to the engine resulted in a faster, more dependable outboard, and the public responded, for at the 1940 New

York Boat Show, then one of the largest in the country, Kiekhaefer took orders for more than 16,000 outboards.

Kiekhaefer's mechanical genius continued to shine during the years of World War II, during which his little company produced chainsaws for the military, as well as small, lightweight two-cycle engines to power drone aircraft. By 1947, however, as recreational boating began to explode in popularity after the war, Mercury quickly returned to outboard production, and to help promote those engines, Kiekhaefer turned to stock car auto racing. Among the drivers he hired between 1954 and 1956 were Tim Flock, who won the 1955 NASCAR championship with 18 victories in 38 races; and Buck Baker, who won 14 races during the 1956 season.

Turning his full attention back to outboards after withdrawing from racing following the 1956 season, Kiekhaefer and his chief engineer, former MIT instructor Charlie Strang, continued to push engine development to new limits, and in 1961 the company merged with the Brunswick Corporation, long a world leader in recreational products. That same year, the sterndrive MerCruiser engine, developed years before by Strang, was introduced, followed by 100- and 125-horsepower outboards.

Originally, all Mercury engines were white, but Kiekhaefer, not only a mechanical genius but a marketing genius as well, thought the white engines looked too big. Strang mentioned this to his mother, who mentioned that women often wore black dresses because it made them look slimmer, so Strang painted one of the engines black, just to see. Kiekhaefer loved it because it did indeed make the outboard appear smaller, and Mercury outboards have been painted black ever since.

As tournament bass fishing came of age in the 1970s, both Mercury Marine and Outboard Marine Corporation became sponsors of many different fishing events as well as professional tournament anglers themselves. Strang left Mercury and later served as the president, CEO, and finally chairman of the board of the Outboard Marine Corporation until his retirement in 1990. Outboard Marine was acquired in 2001 by the Recreation Products division of Bombardier, a world leader in the aerospace transportation industry, who has kept the Evinrude brand alive; literally tens of thousands of today's bass anglers fish from boats powered by Evinrude outboard engines.

Kiekhaefer resigned as president of the company, Kiekhaefer Marine, in 1969, at which time the firm became known as Mercury Marine, the name it carries today. He died October 5, 1983, but the company he started so many years earlier now employs some 4,000 people and has manufacturing facilities not only in Wisconsin but also in Mexico, Japan, Belgium, and China.

In 1960, another company quietly entered the outboard market, but it would be a number of years before its impact was felt in America. The company was Yamaha, who, under the leadership of Genichi Kawakami and with an established reputation in both the music and electronics industries, was looking for a way to utilize idle machinery that had formerly been used to fabricate airplane propellers.

Five years earlier, Yamaha had introduced its first motorized product of any kind, a 125 cc, two-stroke motorcycle, and in 1960 their first outboard, the P-7, which had basically been designed by trial and error by a handful of engineers, quickly became more well-known for its noise and vibration than for its performance. If anything, however, the Japanese engineers listened to their first customers, primarily lobster fishermen off the Japanese coast, and their second engine, the P-3, not only solved the noise and vibration issues, but also pushed the company into the international marketplace.

Those first international customers came from Bangladesh, a country swept by annual floods so severe that boats were more practical even than bicycles for much of the year. In fact, Yamaha even designed a special boat, the P125AK, for the conditions. By 1970, Yamaha had entered the US market with its motorcycles and golf carts, but the first outboards did not reach the market until 1984. In 1975 a 27-year-old Temple University graduate, Phil Dyskow, became the first Yamaha boat dealer in the United States, and under his leadership, the dealership grew to become the largest Yamaha boat dealer outside of Japan.

In 1981, Dyskow joined Yamaha Motor Corporation U.S.A. as one of the first employees tasked with researching and then planning the introduction of Yamaha outboard engines into the US market. Eventually he became vice president of Yamaha Marine, and in 1997, president. Under his management, as the horsepower race continued upward, Yamaha spent much of its R&D time refining its four-stroke technology, which because of various emission regulations, would become the new standard for outboards. Historically, this had meant sacrificing performance for efficiency.

In 2009, however, the company introduced an entirely new generation of lighter, high-performance four stroke outboards, the VMAX SHO family, that easily outdistanced the existing two stroke engines with their better acceleration and fuel economy. By 2010, in just 50 years, Yamaha had produced some nine million outboard engines to a worldwide audience, and pushed the technology curve to its highest point, and no one was happier than America's bass fishermen.

In the beginning, once they shut down their outboards, most bass fishermen moved their boats into casting positions by sculling, sitting at the bow, and quietly figure-eighting a small paddle. Not only was it tiring, it also detracted from fishing. That led, in 1934, to the development of small electric-powered engines known as trolling motors. The first one was invented in 1934 by North Dakota fisherman O. G. Schmidt, who attached the starter motor from a Model A Ford to a flexible shaft and added a propeller. His little company was located near the border with Minnesota, so he named the new operation Minn Kota, which today remains a major manufacturer of trolling motors. Virtually every bass boat on the water today includes a bow-mounted trolling motor.

Initially, the Minn Kota trolling motors were operated entirely by hand, both for power as well as for steering. Like sculling paddles, this took an angler's attention away from fishing. That's how another fisherman, G. H. Harris of Jackson, Mississippi, felt after one of his many outings to nearby Ross Barnett Reservoir, so in 1951 he developed and patented a foot-controlled trolling motor he named the Motor Guide. Like Minn Kota, Motor Guide (now owned by the Zebco Corporation) has become a world leader in trolling motors. Features like rack and pinion steering, variable speeds, and retractable mounting systems are all standard today.

One additional item, the depth finder, or sonar unit, was also developed during this period, and it provides another clear indication of how strongly bass fishing was impacting the American culture. The man who started the electronic fish-finding revolution was an Oklahoma vegetable farmer and former US Navy flight instructor named Carl Lowrance. Like so many others who developed specific products simply to help themselves become better bass fishermen, Lowrance and his sons Darrell and Arlen had realized through their underwater diving experiences that bass preferred certain types of habitat not visible from the surface; they wanted something to help them find that habitat.

Since the end of World War II, fishermen had been trying to adapt military sonar units for this purpose, but none had proven satisfactory. Lowrance and his sons solved the problems, introducing the Fish Lo-K-Tor in 1959, which immediately became known as the "little green box."

It was a portable unit and incorporated a rotating neon light that showed not only the bottom contour but also everything between the boat and the bottom, including fish. It was boxy-looking, and it was painted green.

Many of the fishermen competing with Wood that week at Smith Lake had Fish Lo-K-Tors, since the unit's instant popularity had led Lowrance to steadily incorporate a long list of improvements. Not only was it becoming more and more accurate at depicting objects, it could now do so while a boat was moving at full speed. Within a very short time, no bass boat was considered complete without some type of depth finder, and by 1975 well over 100 firms were making them, taking advantage of both transistor and Lowrance technologies. By 1983, Lowrance itself could report just under $30 million in sales, which climbed to $45 million in 1987.

Today, sonar units by Lowrance and others are considered as basic to bass fishing as rods and reels, and many anglers equip their boats with two and even three separate units, located both at the driver's console as well as at the bow where they can be studied while either navigating or actually casting to different targets. The units now provide much more information, such as water temperature, side imaging, and GPS systems that show the boat's position on a lake. Different species of fish can be identified, and when fishing in deeper water, an accomplished angler can drop his lure to individual bass he sees on the depth finder screen, then watch them approaching that lure and striking. It's as if he's taking part in a live video game. By 1996, Lowrance sales had climbed to nearly $95 million.

Because not all bass boats, outboard engines, trolling motors, trailers, and other accessories were available from a single location, fishermen had to purchase them separately and then pay once again to have someone, most often the boat dealer, install them to create a workable fishing machine out of the different parts. Everything changed in 1978, when Bass Pro Shops (BPS) expanded its already successful fishing tackle business, based in Springfield, Missouri, to include boats.

All Bass Pro Shops founder Johnny Morris did was begin offering his aluminum Bass Tracker boats as a complete, ready-to-fish package, including boat, motor, custom-designed trailer, trolling motor, and sonar electronics. He single-handedly created one-stop shopping for bass boats. Not only that, prices were published nationally and the boats were available at that price at dealerships throughout the United States. It totally revolutionized boat buying, and quickly become the industry-wide standard.

Bass Tracker boats are still being sold the same way today, with total sales now well above 400,000.

Bass Pro Shops entered the fiberglass bass boat business ten years later, when it purchased a small Tennessee boat company named Nitro, a well-engineered craft being made by experienced builder Alan Stinson, a former boat racer for Paul Allison. Veteran tournament fisherman and Toledo Bend guide Tommy Martin led Bass Pro to Nitro. Morris had instructed Martin to look for a small fiberglass boat company to purchase, and Martin had known Stinson from his days with Skeeter; a few years earlier Stinson had designed the famous Skeeter Wrangler.

Martin was impressed with Stinson's new boat and Morris bought the company shortly thereafter. He held his first Nitro dealer meeting in 1989 in San Diego, where Martin gave test rides in the Pacific Ocean. Bass Pro Shops has not only kept the Nitro brand, but also steadily improved it each year, and Martin has been using one ever since, as well. From the beginning, Morris sold Nitro boats as packages, too.

By the mid-1980s as many as 80,000 bass boats were being built and sold annually, an industry valued in the billions of dollars. Today, top-of-the-line models sell for more than $60,000, and Nitro, Allison, Ranger, Skeeter, and other bass boats have been sold to anglers as far away as Africa, Asia, South America, Canada, and Mexico. Even by the late 1970s, Wood had shipped Rangers to fishermen in Hong Kong and Istanbul, locations he'd heard about but wasn't sure he could find on a map.

He looks at the new boats now in use by young bass anglers and only shakes his head in wonderment. At the same time, many of those same fishermen, who weren't even born when Wood fished that Smith Lake tournament back in 1967, sure are glad he was there.

Chapter Twenty

Dale Calhoun: "Shipping Stump-Jumpers Was Harder Than Building Them"

Dale Calhoun was the fourth generation of his family to build the famous cypress "stump-jumper" boats on Reelfoot Lake. The boats could float in just 10 inches of water, and slide easily over the lake's submerged stumps. Originally powered by oars, Calhoun later added small inboard-mounted lawn mower engines.

Long before there were Ranger and Triton bass boats, and nearly a century before Holmes Thurmond built his first Skeeter, bass fishermen in northwestern Tennessee were fishing the shallow, stump-filled waters of Reelfoot Lake in boats named, appropriately enough, stump-jumpers. The boats evolved, surprisingly, through necessity so area fishermen and hunters could take advantage of a lake that had been formed by an earthquake only a few decades earlier.

That earthquake, actually a series of quakes, started on December 16, 1811, and continued for three months, centered in northwest Tennessee and southeast Missouri. The hardest jolt occurred just before dawn on February 7, 1812, and was felt from Canada to Venezuela. The wreckage that night included an entire forest of cypress and oak that lay shattered and broken across a 15,000-acre depression where the land actually sank. Some say the Mississippi River flowed backward that day, filling the 14-mile long depression; at any rate, the result was a new lake that came to be named Reelfoot. It averaged only about five feet deep, but it was filled with fish from the river, and before long, the lake also became the winter home for millions of migrating waterfowl.

In the beginning, a number of people tried building stump-jumpers, including a blacksmith named Joseph Marion Calhoun. Sometime around 1860, he put aside his anvil and horseshoes long enough to try his hand at something different, and his new pointed-bow, flat-bottom watercraft gained almost instant acceptance, largely because it could float in ten inches of water and "jump" over the submerged stumps. Soon, Calhoun became a full-time boat builder, the first of four generations of Calhouns who would continue building stump-jumpers for almost 150 years.

Joe Calhoun's son Boone was the next generation. He grew up in the shop and continued building stump-jumpers until he passed the tradition to his son Bill Calhoun, who taught his son, Dale, how to make them. Fashioned out of local cypress planks fitted around a white oak frame, the basic design of the boat remained essentially unchanged this entire time. When Dale's father Bill took over the business, a 15 ½-foot stump-jumper sold for $10; today, they're more than $2,500. Dale once traded a boat for a Model 12 Winchester shotgun, but as the business grew, he rarely had time to enjoy it.

Born July 24, 1935, Dale, like his father and grandfather before him, grew up making stump-jumpers. He made his first one by himself when he was 14, completing the job from start to finish over a weekend to surprise his father, who had taken his grandfather to a cotton-picking contest over in Arkansas. Later, as his skill increased, he and his father could turn out three stump-jumpers a day, and they needed to, since the demand was that great. By the mid-1970s there were between 5,000 and 10,000 Calhoun-made stump-jumpers on Reelfoot alone, to say nothing of boats Dale had shipped to other states. Some went to Canada, one was sailed across Lake Michigan, and another was in use by game and fish officials in Cuba before Castro's takeover.

At one time, Dale made stump-jumpers out of mahogany, buying the wood in New Orleans because it was cheaper than cypress. When prices for mahogany rose too high, he changed back to cypress, which he bought from local sawmills around Reelfoot. He inspected every board for quality, but there were never any formal blueprints for a boat; the planks were nailed around a framework of oak ribs in lengths ranging from 13 ½ to 17 ½ feet, and some of the tools he used were the same ones used by his grandfather more than 100 years earlier.

Until 1938, all the Reelfoot stump-jumpers were oar-powered, but not by the usual oars. In 1884, an Illinois visitor to Reelfoot, Fred Allen, invented a double-hinged oar that propelled the boat forward, not backward as common oars do. This was a major step forward in stump-jumper evolution because it not only allowed the user to see where he was going instead of having to continually look over his shoulder, it also produced all the power of a full stroke with half the effort. After Allen's death in 1959, Dale purchased the patent rights, and not only continued to equip all his stump-jumpers with the oars, but shipped them separately all over the world for use on other boats.

In 1938, however, the stump-jumpers took another step forward when a local fisherman named Homer Cannon installed a ¾-horsepower gasoline engine from a Maytag washing machine on his boat. His was the first motorboat ever on Reelfoot, and folks around the lake immediately named him High Speed Homer. Dale's father Bill put one on their stump-jumper, mounting the little engine behind the rear seat and attaching a long drive shaft through the hull. A sheet metal plate under the transom protected the propeller and helped the boat slide over stumps, while a hand-operated rudder provided steering.

Early on, Calhoun had to take the engine out of his boat and reinstall it in the family washing machine on clothes washing days, so eventually they began installing three-horsepower Briggs & Stratton engines in the stump-jumpers. The engines cost $29 each factory-direct, but when the price increased to $32, Calhoun was afraid they'd have to quit using them because they were so expensive. Over the years, of course, the engines increased to as much as $185 and the eight-horsepower models Dale started using were $769 each.

The only problem with cypress-made Calhoun stump-jumpers was their durability; the boats rarely required any real maintenance. In the 1950s he began applying liquid fiberglass to waterproof them, and Dale once replaced the white oak ribs in one customer's boat, which they figured was at least 50 years old. Before it was lost in a fire, Dale had found another stump-jumper made by his grandfather that was over a hundred years old. Dale's stump-jumpers do survive in different museums, including the Reelfoot Lake State Park Ellington Museum, the US Fish & Wildlife Service Reelfoot Visitor's Center in Walnut Log, the Obion County Museum in Union City, and at the Tennessee Aquarium in Chattanooga.

★ ★ ★

Dale Calhoun grew up making stump-jumpers.

Shipping stump-jumpers was a lot more of a problem than building them. In the early 1960s, for instance, NBC commissioned me to build six special boats to use in a documentary they were making of the Lewis and Clark expedition. Apparently, my boats were the closest thing they could find that looked like canoes of that time. Anyway, I built the boats but then I couldn't find anyone who would ship them to New York, so I ended up loading all six in a trailer and driving up to Radio City Music Hall where I delivered them.

The boats have been used in several movies, too. Sometime back in the 1970s a movie named *Black Water* was filmed at Reelfoot and my boat was featured in it, and in 1998, parts of the movie *U.S. Marshals* starring

Tommy Lee Jones, Robert Downey Jr., and Wesley Snipes was filmed here using my boats. In fact I was one of the boat handlers in the movie.

Being around Hollywood actors and actually having a part in the movie was a thrill, but it didn't compare to the thrill I had in July of that year when the National Endowment for the Arts notified me that I had been nominated to receive a National Heritage Fellowship for my boats. In October I went to Washington where Hillary Clinton, then the First Lady, presented the award to me. The $10,000 prize that went with the award went straight to my wife, of course.

For years I always did my best to support folk arts festivals and projects, and have given boat-building demonstrations not only around here at Reelfoot, but in different cities. I even built a boat once on the Mall in Washington for the Smithsonian.

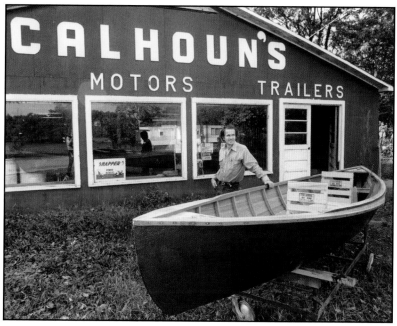

Dale received a National Heritage Fellowship for his boats.

I've had a lot of publicity over the years, mainly, I guess, because I've been able to continue a craft started by my great grandfather, and the boat, of course, is pretty unusual. I've even received letters from people who didn't know my name and simply addressed the envelope to "Boat Builder, Reelfoot Lake, Tennessee." I always keep one or two completed available in my shop for a customer I have in California, who periodically awards one to an employee.

Somehow, people everywhere seem to know what a stump-jumper is.

★ ★ ★

Dale Calhoun died April 6, 2007, of pancreatic cancer. He is buried in Cobb's Chapel Cemetery in Obion County, Tennessee.

Chapter Twenty-One

Paul Allison: "Cupping the First Prop"

Paul Allison, shown here in 1960 piloting a small runabout, spent his career working on ways to improve boat performance. Among his achievements were cupping the first propellers and also creating the first V-bottom boat with a running pad. Photo courtesy of Allison Boats.

Paul Allison wasn't the first member of the Allison family to earn the nickname of "river rat," but he certainly did his part to keep the tradition alive. Virtually every company in the bass boat industry incorporates features first pioneered and developed by Paul or his son Darris. Paul's innovations, including among others, the first engine power trim unit and the first cupped propellers, came directly from his powerboat racing; his first foot throttle may have been nothing more than a big barn door hinge with a screen door spring attached, but it impacted the entire boating community because it allowed the driver of any boat to keep both hands on the steering wheel while underway. Even the world famous unlimited hydroplane, Miss Budweister, copied some of his inventions.

Paul Allison enjoyed bass fishing, but he never built a bass boat. He did build pleasure craft, however, but his real love was boat racing, and he built many of the fastest boats of the era, setting records as the first craft in various classes to top 50 miles per hour (mph), then 60, 70, 80, 90, and 100 mph. Over time, Allison boats became the winningest boat in the world and set more speed records than all other brands combined. The desire to constantly go faster than anyone else on the water, and do it safely, started when he was a young man racing against his buddies on Saturday afternoons across Fort Loudon Reservoir near Knoxville and continued for more than two decades of racing at major boat racing events around the nation.

Among his fondest memories is the six-hour marathon race in Miami's Biscayne Bay in 1962 when he entered three boats. One, a 15-foot flat bottom powered by an 85-horsepower Mercury, finished second overall, just behind a twin-engine catamaran. In the 40 to 50 cubic inch (engine size) class, however, his driver, in a 13-foot boat with a 50-horsepower Mercury, won by 11 laps, or more than 50 miles. After the race, the president and founder of Mercury Marine, Carl Kiekhaefer, asked Allison how he could run so fast, and Allison showed him a cupped propeller blade; Kiekhaefer, wearing a suit and tie, sat down in the sand and water to study and run his hands over the slightly cupped blades, because neither he nor his engineer, Charlie Strang, had ever seen one before. Today, of course, all outboard propellers are cupped to improve their performance.

★ ★ ★

In 1953, my friends and I liked to spend our weekend afternoons trying to outrun each other on Fort Loudon Reservoir not far from Knoxville. We were just boys having fun, and we called it "Saturday racing." I had a little green 25-horsepower Johnson outboard mounted on a small aluminum fishing boat that I'd braced so the hull wouldn't bend, and it would run pretty fast.

I'd even spent $12 for an Oakland-Johnson two-blade bronze racing propeller from Oakland, California, and put it on my engine; it was quite a bit faster than the regular aluminum props that came with the outboards. I gained another mile an hour by cutting down the skeg that protects the propeller, since it reduced water resistance, but it made my boat much harder to steer.

At my home, I had built a new garage for the boat, and it had a concrete ramp of maybe two feet leading into it. When I backed the boat up the ramp and into the garage, I'd always raised the motor but one day I decided to go down to the lake and try out something, and I forgot to raise the motor. As I went down that ramp, the bronze prop rolled on the concrete and made a little curl in each blade.

I thought I'd ruined the propeller. I took it off, put it in my vise, and very carefully tried to straighten each blade. I was afraid I'd break it, but when I thought I'd gotten it straight again, I put it back on and went to the lake.

I picked up about one mile an hour, but I lost rpm doing it. I was going faster, but the engine was working harder, so I jacked the motor up a little bit on the transom and made another run down the lake. I picked up another mile an hour. I hadn't gotten all the curl out of the blade, so I figured that if just a little curl helped that much, maybe more would be even better, so I went home, put the prop back in the vise, and started pecking at the blades with my hammer.

I kept doing that as long as I was gaining speed, and when I lost speed, I took some of the cupping out. On the lake, with my cupped blade, I could outrun everything, even the Mercury outboards that had much more horsepower. That's when I decided to build my first race boat. It was just a little plywood boat and I put my 25-horsepower Johnson on it, then entered it in a 100-mile marathon race being held there on Fort Loudon Lake. With the cupped prop, I outran everybody.

Well, the people I beat found out about my propeller and started bringing their own props to me for cupping. They were driving me crazy. Then one of the propeller companies, Michigan Wheel, learned about it and flew one of their technicians down to see what was going on. I was working at a Knoxville marine dealer's shop getting some boats ready to race when he walked in. He looked at me cupping a prop with my hammer, and thought I'd accidentally bent it on a rock or log.

He'd never seen anything like it, and when I explained cupping to him, he got out a piece of paper, drew a picture of the prop, and measured exactly where I was making the curl. A month or two later, Michigan Wheel started producing and selling cupped propellers. Then Mercury learned about it and started cupping their props, and Outboard Marine Corporation started cupping theirs, too. It's been around ever since. In fact, I'm not sure you can find any propeller, even on the smallest outboards, that isn't cupped today.

★ ★ ★

Now 90 and retired from his company, Allison Boats, Paul Allison still lives in Louisville, Tennessee, not far from the plant or Fort Loudon Reservoir where he first became one of the Allison river rats.

Chapter Twenty-Two

Forrest L. Wood: "Back in Business in 40 Days"

By his own admittance, Forrest Lee Wood never planned to become a boat builder. Before the boats, he'd raised cattle, poured concrete to finish the Bull Shoals Dam, built houses and boat docks, and then become a fishing guide on the very lake he'd helped create. There really was never any plan at all, except trying to make a living. Only later, after several years of successful guiding not only on Bull Shoals and the White River, but also on the Buffalo River and Crooked Creek, did he begin to think how nice it would be if a person could actually make a lifelong career by catching fish.

That was in the mid-1950s. What actually happened is that Wood made a career helping others catch fish, specifically largemouth bass, and he did it by making fishing boats. The boats started as plain, wooden, flat-bottom river boats Wood made in his garage—he needed more boats because his guide business was expanding rapidly—and in time evolved into the finest state-of-the-art fishing machines the world had ever seen.

His company, Ranger Boats—named after the famous Texas Rangers law enforcement agency because they symbolized strength with integrity, qualities Wood himself adhered to—became synonymous with bass fishing around the world. At one time the firm employed more than 600 people in the small Arkansas town of Flippin, and boats were being shipped to every corner of America and to several foreign countries.

Other companies were building boats before Wood started Ranger in 1968, of course, but what set him apart over the years was his long and

Forrest Wood and his wife Nina started the famous Ranger Boats company in Flippin, Arkansas, in 1968, and for decades supported bass fishing at all levels of the sport. Literally tens of thousands of people started bass fishing because of Wood's generous sponsorships.

continued support and involvement in bass fishing at all levels of the sport. Wood had a decades-long association with B.A.S.S., the highest level of competitive tournament fishing, and the company gained much of its reputation through that relationship, but at the very same time Ranger sponsored as many as two dozen other smaller tournament organizations throughout the nation. In essence, Wood and Ranger Boats reached tens of thousands of new fishermen who never could or would fish national competitive tournaments.

Again, in Wood's own words, he was willing to offer a boat sponsorship to just about anybody who came along and looked halfway honest. Not only did that philosophy make Ranger boats more visible on the water, a number of anglers Wood sponsored went on to achieve national prominence and helped spread the Ranger image. Few, if any, other companies in the fishing industry have ever spread their message so effectively, or helped the sport grow as successfully as did Ranger. Today, Forrest Wood and the Ranger Boats brand are virtually impossible to separate, and indeed, Wood still represents the company at various events throughout the country, even though he sold Ranger in 1987.

Such success never entered Wood's mind when he made his first fishing excursions with his father and then with young friends along the banks of the White River. Born June 9, 1932, in Flippin, his earliest fish weren't even bass; they were catfish, often caught on trotlines or limb lines. He was 12 years old when he bought his first rod and reel for $8.88 from a mail-order sporting goods store in Kansas City.

Steady jobs were hard to come by in the rural community, and for two years Wood actually worked on the construction of the Bull Shoals Dam, handling a jackhammer to break rock, driving trucks, placing dynamite—basically doing anything he was asked to do. He was just glad to have a job; even as the new lake began filling while he was still working on the dam, he never thought much about a future career in fishing.

On April 21, 1951, Wood married his high school sweetheart, Nina Kirkland, and together with whatever money they could spare, they began purchasing cattle. Their future then, it seemed, was headed toward ranching, but the cattle business did not do as well as they had hoped, and to pay off the debts they'd incurred, they moved to Kansas City. They stayed 15 months, just long enough to pay off those debts, then returned to Flippin, determined to make a living anyway they could, but never to leave again.

By then, Bull Shoals had filled, a boat dock had been built, and the bass fishing was exceptional. At the same time, the Arkansas Game and Fish Commission began stocking rainbow trout in the White River as a form of mitigation for the change in the river (from warm water to cold) created by the lake. Wood still had not made any serious decisions about a future career, so in 1953 he applied for and received a guide's license and began taking bass fishermen out on the new lake, and trout fishermen on the White River.

It was a job he kept for the next 14 years, and it was the perfect stepping stone into his future as a boat builder. The tall, slender, slow-talking Wood wasn't just a good fishing guide, he was also a good people person; even today, a half-century after he started guiding, people still come up to Wood to describe a float trip or day on the lake they enjoyed with him. Wood had more customers than he could guide himself, so he hired other guides to help him.

That meant he also needed more boats for those guides, and the very first ones were built in his garage. These were narrow, flat-bottom johnboats for use on the river, the same type used today. Then, in 1968 Wood decided to build what he called a lake boat, a slightly larger craft featuring the same flat bottom but incorporating a wider beam to make it more suitable for open water. By hit-and-miss, Wood learned how to cover his creations in fiberglass, which made them stronger and more durable, and certainly, more attractive to other fishermen.

About that same time, Wood and another White River fisherman named Jerry McKinnis, who had first met Wood several years earlier when he'd hired him as a guide, entered their first bass fishing tournament, a team contest held on Greers Ferry Lake, a 30,000-acre Corps of Engineers reservoir south of Flippin near Heber Springs. He and McKinnis won the tournament, but more importantly, when Wood asked any of the competitors if they'd like to buy a boat, one angler did. His name was Dennis Demo, who spent $495 for what would be the very first Ranger boat Wood ever sold; Demo went on to spend years working for Wood as a sales representative.

That was the simple, humble beginning of what would become the largest bass boat manufacturing company in the United States. Later that year in November, Wood entered his first B.A.S.S. tournament, the Dixie Invitational on Lewis Smith Lake in Alabama, and there wasn't any doubt in his mind that he or McKinnis, who also entered, would win. Neither came close to victory, but once again, Wood's new boat drew a lot of attention and he returned to Flippin with several orders.

He admits he didn't know anything about selling; he just asked people if they wanted to buy a boat, and some of them did. He took orders on the backs of business cards and on restaurant napkins, and built each boat to the buyer's specifications, just how he wanted it. In those days, anglers fished out of practically anything that would float, and Wood's Ranger was the first pure fishing boat many of them had ever seen. He moved his building operation out of his garage into the back of a gas station, and built six Rangers that year, but the next year he built 600, and in 1970 sales topped 1,200.

Something else happened at that Smith Lake tournament that also changed the course of bass boat history. Wood met Ray Scott, the founder of the Bass Anglers Sportsman Society, and the two men formed a personal and business friendship that literally put them both on the map. Ranger became the official boat sponsor of B.A.S.S. and remained so for the next 20 years, adding visibility to the boat and credibility to the organization. Both grew together, and together they grew the sport.

Not only did Ranger become the most visible of the B.A.S.S. sponsorships, Wood himself became as equally well-known as the boats he built. He continued to fish B.A.S.S. tournaments, and in 1979 he won the New York Bassmaster Invitational at Thousand Islands, New York, bringing in 15 bass, primarily smallmouth, that weighed 47 pounds, 3 ounces. Wood took a lot of ribbing about winning one of his own boats (the winner of each event was awarded a fully-rigged Ranger), but he admits it was a huge thrill for him to hoist the victory trophy. He qualified for the Bassmaster Classic that year, his second appearance in the championship (he'd also qualified in 1972).

One day, a young man named Mike Whitaker came to Flippin to present a proposal to Wood to sponsor his tournament circuit, Operation Bass, which Whitaker had designed and created to give "weekend" anglers a chance to compete in a series of regional tournaments and qualify for their own national championship event, the All American. Wood agreed, and thus the Ranger brand spread even deeper across the bass fishing landscape.

In 1987, Wood sold Ranger to the Southland Corporation, owners of the 7-Eleven chain of quick-stop stores. It was a decision he and Nina agonized over for well over a year, finally deciding the sale would benefit more people than it would harm. In 1992, Ranger was acquired by Genmar Holdings, a Minneapolis-based pleasure boat company controlled by Irwin Jacobs, who enjoyed fishing almost as much as he enjoyed making money; between 1986 and 1988, Jacobs had been on Forbes's list of the 400 richest Americans.

In 1996, Jacobs purchased and reorganized the Operation Bass tournament organization Wood and Ranger had continued to sponsor, renaming it the FLW Tour. The "FLW," of course, are the initials of Forrest Lee Wood. Jacobs brought the Walmart Corporation in as the FLW Tour's title sponsor, offered the highest cash prizes in the sport, and in the process created another top-level professional tournament circuit that continues to grow and thrive today. In 2008, more than $2.5 million was awarded to contestants in the Forrest Wood Cup, the organization's three-day championship tournament.

Although his own role at Ranger Boats has gradually diminished over the years, recognition for his contributions to the sport have not. He has been inducted into the International Boating Hall of Fame, the Professional Bass Fishing Hall of Fame, the National Freshwater Fishing Hall of Fame, the Arkansas Business Hall of Fame, Legends of the Outdoors Hall of Fame, and in 1988 he received the American Sportfishing Association's Lifetime Achievement Award.

★ ★ ★

On the night of May 4, 1971, Roland Martin, Nina, and I were eating dinner together at our home in Flippin. Roland had won an earlier Bassmaster event and was not only a close personal friend but also one of our earliest sponsored professional anglers. As we sat at the table that evening, we noticed smoke not far away, so because Flippin is such a small town, we jumped in a vehicle and drove out to see what was on fire. The chances are, I would probably know what or whose place was burning, and perhaps Roland and I could help.

Well, in a couple of minutes I certainly did know whose place was burning. It was mine; Ranger Boats was engulfed in smoke and flames. Barrels of resin were exploding like bombs, sending fireballs hundreds of feet in the sky. My first thought was whether or not any of the about 60 employees we had were in the building, but fortunately, none were. All had already gotten out safely.

My second thought was to salvage whatever I could from my office, specifically orders for new boats. Roland and I smashed a window, climbed inside, and dragged my desk over and through the window. There were 60 orders for new boats, and we saved them. By then, the rest of the building and everything in it were destroyed, and we didn't have any insurance.

We didn't know we were supposed to be out of business. I immediately started looking around for another building to buy, and a place to borrow money to buy it. We found both. I put the desk under a tree for shade, hung a telephone on a limb, and started calling those 60 people whose boat orders Roland and I had saved, assuring them we intended to fill their order but that it would take a little longer. Not one person cancelled his order, and thanks to the efforts of a lot of wonderful people, we were back in business full-time in 40 days.

★ ★ ★

Forrest and Nina Wood still live in Flippin, Arkansas, where they divide their time between looking after their cattle and making special appearances for Ranger Boats and for the sport of bass fishing.

Chapter Twenty-Three

Earl Bentz: "The Accident That Changed an Industry"

Earl Bentz has been actively involved in the boating industry since the age of 14. After a highly successful powerboat racing career, he began working at Hydra-Sports Boats, then in 1982 started his own company, Stratos, followed in 1996 by Triton Boats. Under his guidance both Stratos and Triton became leaders in the bass boat industry.

For more than 40 years, fishermen throughout America have been thankful Earl Bentz decided not to be a veterinarian. That's where he was headed as a student at Clemson University in 1970 when he dropped out to instead pursue some type of career in the marine industry. He didn't know exactly what he wanted to do, but what he did know was that he had a deep passion for speed and boating performance.

That passion eventually translated into two of the most successful bass boat companies in history, Stratos and Triton.

Utilizing his lifelong experiences both in the industry and as a sports-man himself, Bentz brought innovative hull and transom designs into the market that quickly took Stratos to the top of the sales charts. After selling that company and starting Triton Boats, he took that brand to the top, as well, making them the most popular and successful bass boats in the world in a matter of months. In both, Bentz redefined the meaning of high performance; his boats were faster, smoother, and handled better in rough water than any of his competitors, many of whom soon began copying his designs.

The passion had really started years before, on the day his father gave him his first boat and outboard motor. Bentz was five years old at the time, and lived on the water in Charleston, South Carolina. His father had promised him the boat when he was strong enough to pull-start the outboard, a five-horsepower Evinrude.

It didn't take the future boat builder long to figure out how to accom-plish that. All he had to do was stand on the engine cowling, grasp the starter rope firmly in both hands, and fall over backward into the boat. On the day he showed his father that he could indeed start the engine, he ran the outboard for 20 minutes to warm it and insure it would restart imme-diately on his first fall, and when it did, his father gave him the boat. Soon, he and his cousin, who had a boat with a 7½-horsepower outboard, had tied the two engines together on Bentz's boat so they could go waterskiing.

One of Bentz's uncles, D. F. Jenkins, owned Jenk's Marine, a marine repair shop in Charleston, and in 1966 when he was 14, Bentz began working for him. Packing wheel bearings and scraping barnacles off hulls wasn't a very glamorous way to spend a summer, but there were benefits, namely helping his uncle prepare the boat he was racing on weekends. The boat had a V-bottom hull and would reach 60 to 65 miles an hour, and Jenkins allowed his young nephew to test-drive the boat on the Intra-coastal Waterway not far from Charleston.

When he was 16, his uncle bought Bentz his own race boat, a Galaxy with a tunnel hull and powered by a 115 Johnson. He was just a senior in high school, and depending on how they set up the boat, it could reach speeds of up to 100 mph. They were extremely successful, and when he entered Clemson, Bentz continued to race, driving home each weekend to pilot his own boat or help his uncle. That's when, after a couple of years of 400-mile weekend commutes, Bentz gave up any thoughts of becom-ing a vet.

One day in 1973, the proverbial magical phone call came in. It was from Mercury Marine, wanting to talk to Bentz about becoming one of their drivers on the Mercury racing team with full factory support. He and his uncle had been receiving partial support from its rival, Outboard Marine Corporation, the makers of Evinrude and Johnson outboards, but the relationship had become strained after OMC had sent them a special propeller Bentz had then used to beat OMC's full-time factory team driver, after which they promptly requested he return the prop. Bentz agreed to meet with Gary Garbrecht, Mercury's director of racing, and Jim Mertin, director of competition. That's when the accident that changed the bass boat industry happened, on Alabama's Lake Eufaula not far from the state park.

★ ★ ★

The American Power Boat Association national championship races were being held on Lake Eufaula in August, and Gary, Jim, and I had spoken that very morning and scheduled a meeting in Phenix City, north of the lake, later in the evening. I was curious to see what their reaction would be, since I was competing against their drivers and my boat was probably 10 miles an hour faster than anyone else's.

I was in the back of the pack at the start of my three-lap heat race, and on the first lap I probably passed 10 boats. Then I hit a rogue wave from a spectator boat that may have been as much as half a mile away. It sent a three-foot roller through the race course and I hit it at 115 miles an hour. The boat came up and flew level, but I'd been fighting air in my power trim line all weekend so when I let off the throttle, the nose of the boat snapped up when it landed in the water. The steering wheel hit me in the face, broke my jaw, and knocked me out. The battery broke loose and smashed into my ribs, and the impact of hitting the water broke my back in three places.

Medical personnel transferred me to Dothan, Alabama, but I don't remember much about my first week there. What I do remember is learning that another driver was killed and 16 others were taken to area hospitals, a lot of which was due to hitting spectator boat wakes as I had done.

The following week, Jim Merkel called me and asked if I was still planning to race. I said yes, and he told me they still wanted me to race for them. That October, still wearing a back brace from the accident, I moved to Oshkosh, Wisconsin, and joined the Mercury team. Two months later, against doctor's orders and still wearing the back brace, I won the Gator Bowl Regatta in Jacksonville, the third year in a row I'd won it.

As bad as the accident was, it was really the turning point in my life. At that time, Mercury had an annual racing budget of $2 million, and my association with them not only moved me up to the next level in racing, it also unintentionally moved me into the bass boat business.

That's because during the energy crisis of 1973–74, the Mercury factory racing team and others, were banned from competing. Mercury offered me my choice of their top equipment, however, I wanted to continue racing, so I picked out a boat and all the racing gear I could haul back to Charleston and started working again in my uncle's marine dealership. Together, we continued racing around the country.

In 1975 I received another of those special telephone calls that changes your life. It wasn't from Mercury, but it came because of Mercury. The caller was Joe Reeves, owner of Hydra-Sports Boats near Nashville.

Here, Earl Bentz is leading the Six Hours of Paris powerboat race in October, 1980. He is driving an experimental 3.5-liter Mercury outboard delivering about 500 horsepower. His expertise in powerboat handling and engine performance were important factors in his creation of highly successful bass boats.

I had never heard of Joe Reeves and had no idea who he was, but he had heard about my racing and wanted me to come to work for him. He was especially interested in building smaller boats using a new material named Kevlar, so in June 1975, I moved to Nashville and began working for him. Later that year, Mercury re-assembled their national racing team, so I competed with them for seven months of the year, racing all over the United States and in Europe, and built bass boats for Joe Reeves the rest of the time.

At Hydra-Sports, Reeves showed me the manufacturing side of the marine business. He taught me engineering and design, lamination, customer relations, everything. With Mercury I was racing the unlimited outboards that didn't run on gasoline, but rather, on a mixture of alcohol and nitrous oxide. It was all top secret with experimental equipment that would eventually find its way to the transom of a bass boat.

For instance, in 1975 there were no V-6 outboards on boats, except in our racing. The V-6 had actually been developed two years earlier in 1973, and in 1974 I ran the Six Hours of Paris race with fuel-injected V-6 engines but no one knew what they were. Then, on one of my trips up to Oskosh, the engineers showed me V-6 outboards they were running on 22-foot boats; they were producing 175 horsepower, and I told the engineers they needed to have those engines on bass boats. By now I knew from my work at Hydra-Sports that bass boats would be the market of the future.

The engineers told me to bring them a bass boat, which I did, a 17 ½-foot model rated for a 115 outboard. We bolted a V-6 to it and I ran it down the Fox River. After we changed the gear case on the engine, the boat handled perfectly at 74 miles an hour. I emphasized again to the engineers to get ready, and in 1976 they finally, and somewhat reluctantly, introduced the engine. This was the outboard that became Mercury's famous Black Max, and that year, 80% of their sales went to the bass boat market. Mercury was stunned, but from that point on, they started developing equipment specifically for the bass boat market and they have been ever since.

In March 1981, I ran my last powerboat race. By then the factory teams had pulled in their budgets and the heyday of big racing teams was coming to a close. I was 29, I had won two world championships, and I was getting married, so I decided it was time to finally go to work. Hydra-Sports was also losing money, and Reeves had not only made me vice president and general manager, he'd also made a deal to sell me the company if I could get it out of the red and keep it in the black for three years.

I was able to do that, but then Joe decided he didn't want to sell after all, so we parted on good terms and in 1982 I started my own company, Stratos. The Stratos line of bass boats was very successful, and in 1987 I sold the company to Outboard Marine Corporation, the very firm I'd left to begin racing with Mercury. They were buying boat companies and for nine wonderful years I served with them as president of both their Fish and Aluminum Divisions. When I resigned in 1996, OMC owned not only Stratos, but also Lowe, Grumman, Hydra-Sports, Quest, Sea Nymph, and Sun Cruiser pontoon boats.

I still wanted to own my own company again, so that's when I started Triton Boats, and as with Stratos, I was able to take advantage of the huge growth in the sport of bass fishing. Triton became the top-selling bass boat in the United States and stayed on top for years. In 2005 I sold Triton to the Brunswick Corporation, so once more, I have had the opportunity to be on the inside of the industry looking out, and I'm still enjoying it.

The success I've enjoyed has been due to the people I have worked with over the years at Hydra-Sports, Stratos, OMC, Triton, and Mercury, but the real deal-changer in my life was probably when my uncle offered me that first summer job in his dealership when I was 14 and gave me my first taste of the marine industry. Without a doubt, however, that boating accident in August 1973 and the loyalty Mercury exhibited afterward was the turning point that truly opened the door for me into the bass boat business. Hydra-Sports would never have telephoned and given me that job if they hadn't heard about my racing.

★ ★ ★

Today, Earl Bentz divides his time between his home in Stuart, Florida, where he regularly fishes inshore and offshore waters, and Nashville, Tennessee.

Chapter Twenty-Four

Bill Huntley: "I Told Ray His Program Would Never Sell"

For someone who grew up in Lawrenceburg, Tennessee, just a few long casts from some of the finest smallmouth bass fishing in America, it was probably inevitable that William F. "Bill" Huntley become a bass fisherman himself. He did, and since the mid–1960s his name has been synonymous with trophy smallmouth fishing on the Tennessee River, particularly Pickwick Lake where he has caught literally truckloads of smallmouths over six pounds.

In 1967, even as he held down a full-time job selling medical supplies, he and his wife Pat started the Bumble Bee Bait Company, making spinnerbaits and jigs at night at the kitchen table. He was the first to use ball bearing swivels in spinnerbaits so he could fish them slower and still get fast blade rotation, and he created the special deeply cupped Alabama blade that smallmouth couldn't resist. He did a lot of night fishing, and when word got out of some of his enormous catches, like five smallmouth over five pounds each, his reputation and his lure business quickly grew. It did not take him long to realize he could actually make a living making fishing lures, even though he was working 18-hour days to do it, and he kept his sales reps busy.

Bill Huntley, the CEO of T-H Marine, was able to make his boating supply company a worldwide success because he himself is an avid bass fisherman and spends thousands of hours in a bass boat each year.

The main business of those reps, however, was actually representing the marine parts and accessories industry, and through them Huntley had a good look at that business. At the same time, because he was also spending a great deal of time in a boat himself, he naturally began to pay a lot of attention to boat and motor performance. In the early 1970s he recognized he somehow had to position his outboard farther behind the transom to keep water on the prop. He found a piece of structural aluminum, cut it to size with a hacksaw, drilled some holes, and bolted his outboard to it.

It may not have actually been the first jackplate, but it was close. Huntley knew he'd never seen one before he made his, but being the possible inventor of one of bass fishing's most standard engine/boat items didn't really interest him. What did interest him was how much more efficiently his boat ran.

That was just the beginning. In 1983 he sold Bumble Bee Baits and that same year he became the third employee of a Madison, Alabama-based company, T-H Marine, which had been in business then about a year. It had been started by Charlie Nix and John Baker, and occupied one 20 by 30 foot basement room. Their only product at that time was a power trim control switch for outboards that mounted on the throttle/gear shift handle. In fact, the company name T-H came from "trim handle." Being too broke and not having a full knowledge of the marine business, Nix and Baker did not get a patent on the trim switch, and before long every engine manufacturer copied their idea, which has been a standard feature ever since.

Because he was not only an experienced bass fisherman but also an expert boater, Huntley's role from the start was to develop and sell new products primarily for use on bass boats. When he joined T-H Marine, they were actually supporting their marine endeavors by fabricating aluminum frames and chassis parts for computers, but that soon began to change. Huntley's first product, and the second for the company, was a foot-operated trolling motor control switch, which T-H still sells. Then he brought out the foot-operated throttle named the Hot Foot, which was immediately a success and put T-H on the marketing map. More than a million have since been sold.

Huntley's philosophy was simple: he saw a lot of ideas that could be put on boats that bass fishermen would like, so that's where he took T-H Marine. In those days, when a boat was sent to a dealer, there really was nothing on it, no steering wheel, probably not a seat, maybe not even a console. All those had to be added by the dealer before he could sell it. What Huntley tried to do was build items the boat builders themselves could incorporate in the boat before it went to a dealer.

For example, one of T-H Marine's products is a simple aluminum cup holder. Huntley likes to drink coffee while he's fishing, especially at night for smallmouths, and on one particular fishing trip while looking for a place to put his cup, he realized a cup holder could be one of T-H Marine's products, which it now is. That's how many of the company's products came about; Huntley always thought about things a bass fisherman would like in his boat. In one year alone, T-H introduced 52 new products.

Drain covers and plugs, battery trays and boxes, deck tie-down straps for fishing rods, trailer backing lights, and entire aeration systems have all come from Bill Huntley. Even that jackplate he designed so many years ago has been continually refined and improved so that it is now standard equipment on many fresh and saltwater craft.

Today, virtually every boat made in North America, from bass boats to yachts, has some T-H products on it, and over the years Huntley made it his mission to personally visit the majority of those manufacturers; over the years he has become one of the most well-known and highly respected individuals in the entire boating and fishing industry.

T-H Marine, the little firm that started in a single basement room, today is the largest producer of accessories for the marine industry in the United States, and on some days the company ships as many as 125,000 items around the world.

★ ★ ★

It's been a delightful surprise to me. All we do is build items that might make life a little more fun for a fisherman or boat owner. As bass boating grew and evolved, I was privileged to work with some of the original boat builders who kept pushing the sport forward. That opened up a lot of room for new ideas, and because I was a bass fisherman myself, I always thought about improvements from a fisherman's point of view.

We've got over a thousand items in our catalog now, but really, one of my favorites has always been the Hot Foot, because not only does it make driving a boat at high speed much easier, it also makes it much safer.

I got the idea back about 1975 or 1976 when I was attending a lot of boat races. In those days we were running 80-horsepower motors on boats probably designed for 20, and I'm sure we'd have put a 150 on our boats if one had been available. Nevertheless, all of us began to think about safety and keeping both hands on the steering wheel at the speeds we were reaching, and today's Hot Foot is almost exactly the same as the original we introduced more than three decades ago.

We have been active in designing aeration systems, too, including for saltwater, and we actually design specific systems for individual boats. We go to a manufacturer's plant and assist them in creating a system that works best for them. Our success in this area is probably one of the things we're most proud of, and it's an ongoing project. Our Oxygen Generator System, which literally separates oxygen from the air and pumps it directly into the livewell, is something I modified for boats from my days in the medical field.

Bill Huntley knows what bass fishermen need in their boats because he has been a serious bass fisherman himself for dozens of years. Here he demonstrates one of his innovations, a new livewell oxygen system designed to help keep fish alive under the most stressful situations.

When we were testing the Oxygen Generator System, I made a special redfishing trip to Venice, Louisiana, in June when the air temperature was 102. We put 14 redfish weighing between 9 and 12 pounds into one livewell, and that afternoon when we finished fishing we released all 14 reds, completely healthy and lively. That told me our aeration system could also be an important addition to the bass market, where the penalty incurred for weighing in a dead largemouth might cost an angler $50,000 or more.

T-H makes a lot of trivial things, too, like a rub rail end cap. It's not too exciting, but if you don't have a cap to put over the rub rail where they cut it off, all you have is an ugly looking cut-off rub rail. We sell millions of them.

Over time we constructed a new building with about 40,000 square feet and we later added 65,000 additional square feet. Today we still own that building but we have since bought a new plant with 40,000 square feet and added 40,000 more.

We grew at a fairly steady pace and in 1994 when Charlie and John wanted to retire, I bought the company from them. We were able to double the business the first year and quadruple it the next year. From then until 2000 the growth was phenomenal. I had met many of my customers like Forrest Wood, Earl Bentz, and the late Joe Reeves of Hydra-Sports through bass fishing, and we've all grown together.

Bass fishing has been a phenomenon I never imagined. At a boat and tackle show back in the late 1960s, the late Bob Steber, then outdoor editor of the Nashville *Tennessean* newspaper, introduced me to Ray Scott. Ray offered me the chance to be the tenth charter member of a fishing club he was starting, the Bass Anglers Sportsman Society, but I declined and told him he could never sell that program because bass fishing would never become that popular.

★ ★ ★

Now 80, Bill Huntley has turned over the management of T-H Marine to his son Jeff. He still maintains an office in the company, but tries to spend more of his time, naturally, in a bass boat where, while casting for his beloved smallmouth, he still thinks of new products for T-H Marine to produce.

THE PROS

Chapter Twenty-Five

Casting for Green Gold

Ray Scott, left, hands Rick Clunn the winner's check in the 1976 Bassmaster Classic at Lake Guntersville, Alabama. It was the first of Clunn's four Classic victories over the years, and, ironically, the first major tournament win in his storied career.

A professional level of competition exists for practically every sport in America, and bass fishing is no exception. Across the nation, a small number of anglers compete regularly against each other in tournaments for hundreds of thousands of dollars in prize money in three- and four-day events on reservoirs across the nation; the one who brings in the heaviest accumulated weight wins, and all the bass weighed in are released back into the lake.

While many regional and local organizations conduct smaller one- and two-day contests in which fishermen compete for cash and merchandise prizes, there are two primary organizations that today provide the highest level of bass fishing competition through multi-tournament circuits offering the most lucrative prizes. These are the Bass Anglers Sportsman Society (B.A.S.S.), formed by Alabama fisherman Ray Scott in 1967; and FLW Outdoors, started in 1996 by Minnesota businessman Irwin L. Jacobs.

Although the overall number of full-time professional fishermen in either organization is extremely small when compared to the total number of bass anglers throughout the nation, these anglers have become the sport's most visible ambassadors, and their well-publicized tournaments have been the primary vehicles pushing the sport forward over the years. Through competition, these pros have not only developed new techniques casual fishermen can use to catch more bass, they have been instrumental in the continued development of new and improved equipment, including but certainly not limited to rods, reels, lures, boats, and outboard engines.

Just as importantly, they have increased the overall knowledge of the largemouth bass itself; spurred further scientific research by different institutions; influenced improved reservoir management practices; helped establish national boating safety regulations; and increased national awareness of environmental issues affecting water quality in which bass (and other species) are found. Congress created the Environmental Protection Agency (EPA) after years of national pollution lawsuits filed by bass fishermen.

As in many sports, these accomplishments are frequently lost behind the headlines of who wins a particular tournament and how many fish he caught. Such was the case, for example, when the first national B.A.S.S. tournament on New York's Saint Lawrence River was conducted in September 1977. An angler named Jim Rogers won the three-day event with a total of 56 pounds, 2 ounces, and he received a lot of good publicity for his accomplishment.

Afterward, New York fisheries management personnel admitted they had never realized just how spectacular the largemouth bass fishery in the Saint Lawrence was. Until the pros came to the river for their event, the river was known exclusively for its smallmouth bass fishing, conducted primarily by guides in big cabin cruisers and using live bait, and that's how the state had been managing it.

The result is that the entire Saint Lawrence River region is still benefiting economically today, more than three decades later, by the influx of thousands of largemouth bass fishermen, many bringing their families, who come from all parts of the nation to enjoy their sport in one of the Northeast's most scenic areas. There is no way to calculate the actual dollar value of that first 1977 bass tournament, except to say it is still growing.

During another tournament on Florida's Lake Tohopekaliga, in which professional angler Dean Rojas set two records, a one-day catch of five bass weighing 45 pounds, 2 ounces, and an overall four-day tournament weight record (since broken) of 108 pounds, 12 ounces, the Kissimmee Area Chamber of Commerce reported bass anglers from as far away as New Jersey and Pennsylvania booking trips to fish the lake before the event had even been completed. They were watching the event unfold day-by-day on the Internet.

Bass tournaments have been conducted for more than half a century, but it was not until June 1967 when B.A.S.S. founder Ray Scott conducted his first tournament on Beaver Lake in Arkansas and paid the winner of that event, Stan Sloan of Nashville, $2,000, that tournaments took on a new appearance. Until Scott's Beaver Lake event, bass tournaments had commonly been plagued by cheating and scandals and the sport's overall image could hardly have been lower. Scott quickly created a set of strict guidelines, and more importantly, enforced them.

Still, it took more than a single event to create truly professional bass anglers, especially considering that contestants were paying *him* to fish *his* tournaments, a concept unheard of in most sports. The true birth of the professional fisherman occurred on October 22, 1971, when Scott handed Arkansas angler Bobby Murray a check for $10,000 for three days of bass fishing on Lake Mead. That event was Scott's first Bassmaster Classic, a type of championship he formulated for the top-ranked 24 fishermen who had competed in his events that year.

He provided them with an expenses-paid trip to Las Vegas, as well as furnished identical boats to use, but it was a winner-take-all tournament. After seeing Murray's check—$10,000 was a lot of money in those days, especially for just going fishing—many of the competitors realized they could actually cast for cash and get paid to fish.

Today's pros do, indeed, get paid to fish, and the money does not come strictly from winning. In fact, if their incomes were limited only to tournament prize money, many would actually lose money over the course of an 8- to 12-event season because of the high level of competition. Instead, the majority are paid monthly retainer fees by various sponsors, primarily by companies within the bass fishing industry, who hire the anglers to promote their products.

They do this through tournament exposure as well as in public appearances, seminars, articles, television programs, and other efforts. A number of fishermen earn retainers totaling well over $100,000 annually; quite a few receive vehicles to use by different manufacturers; and the majority of today's full-time pros are contracted by boat and outboard engine companies.

Their influence on the overall bass fishing public cannot be overestimated; during the 2008 economic depression in which America's major automakers were threatened with collapse, for example, Chevrolet never dropped its major sponsorship of professional bass fishing in the FLW because that exposure continued to produce such positive results. Another major FLW bass fishing sponsor, the National Guard, was spending more than $10 million annually in the sport because it had seen enlistments increase dramatically. Other nonfishing-related sponsors, including Walmart and Goodwill Industries, also report increased customer interest due to their involvement with professional bass fishing. Walmart's title sponsorship of the Forrest L. Wood (FLW) Tour, in fact, was the first national sponsorship of any kind for the world's largest retailer.

Exposure comes from many sources, a testament of the sport's increasingly long reach to the public. Such notable publications as the *Wall Street Journal*, *USA Today*, *Sports Illustrated*, *Forbes*, and others have featured major stories about either the pros or their sport. Television has been just as active, and today events are regularly aired by ESPN, the Outdoor Channel, the NBC Sports Network, and other cable outlets.

The highlight of any fishing season has become the year-end championship. For the FLW Tour, this is the Forrest Wood Cup tournament, and for B.A.S.S. it is the Bassmaster Classic, held annually since Murray's 1971 victory at Lake Mead. Instead of taking home $10,000 as Murray did, however, today's Classic winner takes home $500,000. The three-day event itself is believed to generate as much as $20 million for the host city. It has become a high-stakes game of casting for green gold, and cities bid heavily for the right to hold the Classic.

For the pro who wins a Classic, the $500,000 prize is only the beginning. Most winners quickly begin a year-long schedule of appearances and seminars, filming, and interviews. With such widespread television coverage, they are now recognized in airports, restaurants, and shops. Classic winners have thrown out first pitches at major league baseball games, been grand marshals at parades and NASCAR auto races, received keys to different cities, and been invited to the White House.

Even with the sport's long and storied history, today there still is a rite of passage all fishermen must endure if they hope to have a career as a professional bass tournament angler. It's the first day of competition in the very first truly professional event they enter, and while most freely admit to being extremely nervous fishing against the very pros they may have idolized for years, the majority of these new anglers know they must persevere if they ever hope to gain some of the more lucrative sponsorships.

The first tournament day experience of Arkansas angler Larry Nixon provides an example. Nixon's first-ever competition day took place on January 19, 1977, on Florida's St. Johns River, long recognized for its warm weather and trophy bass. For weeks Nixon, then 27, had been dreaming of how he was going to catch a ten-pound bass there and put his name into the record books, and, in fact, he had made a bet with one of his cohorts as to who would catch the first ten-pounder.

The trouble was, it was snowing that first morning of competition and the rod locker on Nixon's boat had frozen shut. In a panic, he tried to thaw the lock by pouring hot coffee all over it. Later that morning, his boat had mechanical problems and neither he nor his partner caught a single bass the entire day. Nixon did not have any money to rent a motel room, so he slept in his truck, and limited himself to one meal, usually a hamburger, a day.

Still, the young Arkansas angler survived, and today, at age 64, he continues to be a threat to win any event he enters. He not only went on to become one of the first full-time professional bass fisherman to win more than $3 million in prize money, he remains one of the sport's most highly respected spokesmen.

Although tournament days may be delayed or cancelled by bad weather such as fog, high winds that create dangerous boating conditions, floods, or the possibility of tornadoes, pros like Nixon are accustomed to competing under conditions that would keep a casual fisherman indoors. North Carolina pro Guy Eaker, who retired at the conclusion of the 2010

Larry Nixon's professional debut in January 1977 was not a memorable one, but the Arkansas angler persevered and today he is considered one of the finest bass fishermen in the world. He has won the Bassmaster Classic, two B.A.S.S. Angler of the Year titles, and more than $3 million in prizes.

Bassmaster Season after more than 25 years of full-time competition, can remember a tournament on Alabama's Lake Eufaula during which it was raining so hard he could barely see to cast. Still, he did manage to hook a big bass in the nine-pound range, but when he called for his partner to grab the net, his partner couldn't hear him in the storm and the fish escaped, costing Eaker the tournament win.

Another veteran bass pro, Ron Shuffield of Arkansas, won a national tournament on Grand Lake in Oklahoma during a week in which air temperatures rarely rose above 20 degrees. Still, in three days, Shuffield weighed in more than 49 pounds of fish, probably because he was able to stay warm while on the water. His attire included insulated underwear, a regular cotton/polyester shirt and jeans, a down-filled jacket, a snow-mobile suit, gloves, and a toboggan. The same can't be said for his reel, which was freezing every second or third cast.

Today there are not only foreign anglers who come to America to compete, but also international competitions in Europe, Africa, and other nations. Most are based on the rules established by B.A.S.S. and FLW Outdoors, and while none have achieved the status of either the Bassmaster Classic or the Forrest Wood Cup, these international events certainly promote and continue the spread of the sport to an ever-widening audience.

Without question, one of the foremost conservation ethics all the tournament pros have been instrumental in spreading to the general public over the years has been the concept of catch-and-release, in which the bass caught in a tournament are released after being weighed. This was one of Ray Scott's ideas, after he'd watched trout fishermen release their catches, and he first tried it in 1972 at a B.A.S.S event in Florida, where it became a huge success. Because the pros were initially penalized two ounces for bringing in a deceased bass, the anglers themselves made greater efforts to keep their catch alive during the day.

Today, the catch-and-release concept is followed not only in all professional-level tournaments, but by rank-and-file bass fishermen everywhere, including those just out for a quiet day of relaxation. Even though the largemouth bass provides excellent table fare, the fish is rarely eaten. Releasing the fish safely and healthily has literally become as important as catching them; even trophy-class bass in the 15- to 20-pound range, are released now after weighing and photos.

Studies have shown that while there may be some instances of delayed mortality to the fish, dependent largely on weather conditions, the majority of bass do survive and many are frequently caught another time at a later date. Some, in fact, have been caught multiple times, even just a day apart in the same tournament.

Overall, there can be no question that tournament bass fishing, particularly at the highest levels, has truly helped shape bass fishing as a sport and provide its identity. Bass fishing, of course, was a sport long before 1967 when Scott held his first tournament, but it had remained small for decades, and the industry itself was all but nonexistent and certainly without any definable goal. Tournament competition provided the spark that ignited the sport, created its first recognizable personalities, and moved bass fishing into mainstream America.

Chapter Twenty-Six

Scott Suggs: "I Dreamed I'd Hold Up Two Big Bass"

In 2007, when Arkansas bass pro Scott Suggs won the Forrest Wood Cup tournament on Lake Ouachita, he became the first bass angler to win $1 million in a single tournament. He still competes regularly in FLW Tour events. Photo courtesy of FLW Outdoors.

On July 24, 1996, when Minneapolis businessman Irwin L. Jacobs purchased a small Gilbertsville, Kentucky-based fishing tournament organization, only Jacobs himself could envision where he wanted to take the sport of bass fishing. Not only did he see the demand among anglers for a second truly professional level of tournament competition (B.A.S.S. had been conducting its tournaments since 1967) with high cash prizes, he also understood that the entire bass fishing community—not just the tournament pros—represented a huge consumer audience numbering in the tens of millions that manufacturers could reach through those tournaments.

He renamed his newly purchased organization FLW Outdoors,

and initiated the FLW Tour that same year, a series of tournaments for the nation's best tournament pros. In 1997, Jacobs signed Walmart as the title sponsor of these tournaments, which in turn led to the direct involvement of more than four dozen major corporations, including many non-fishing firms like Procter & Gamble and Kellogg's, into bass fishing.

The money these sponsorships provided had never before been seen in professional tournaments. In 1997, Jacobs paid out $3.1 million in FLW Tour prize money; a year later that figure had climbed to $3.65 million for just seven events. South Carolina pro Davy Hite, the winner of the Forrest Wood Cup, that year, the FLW's season-ending championship, collected $250,000, the largest individual prize ever awarded in bass fishing.

Jacobs wasn't finished, however. In 1999, the FLW Tour payout increased to $3.97 million over seven events, and in 2000 the number jumped to $4.45 million. Three years later, FLW Tour pros were fishing for $5.76 million, including $500,000 to the winner of the 2003 Forrest Wood Cup. By the following year the FLW Tour pros were gunning for $6.8 million in prizes.

With prize money like that, bass anglers from throughout the United States and several foreign countries flocked to the FLW Tour, including an Arkansas fisherman named Scott Suggs. Born in Little Rock on May 27, 1966, Suggs grew up in a fishing and hunting environment in which his father started taking him to the lake or the forest as early as age two. By the time Suggs was in high school, he was taking his coaches and teachers bass fishing, and in 2006, after a decade of fishing both B.A.S.S. and FLW events, he joined the FLW Tour full-time.

At the conclusion of that 2006 season, FLW Tour officials announced the 2007 Forrest Wood Cup championship would be held at Lake Ouachita. Suggs couldn't believe it. Ouachita was the very lake he and his father had been fishing for decades and he knew it better than anyone. Irwin Jacobs also announced the amount of the prize he would award the winner: $1 million.

Both were strong enticements for Suggs during the 2007 Tour season, but he still had to qualify for the Cup. He opened with very respectable finishes of 27th, 45th, and 5th in the first three events, but then the wheels slowly started coming off. He finished 63rd at Beaver Lake in the fourth event of the season, followed by an even worse 165th place finish on the Potomac River.

Heading into the final qualifying tournament of the year at Lake St. Clair and the Detroit River, Suggs needed a good finish but not a great one, to qualify, but on the first day of competition he brought in only nine pounds. He'd been concentrating on smallmouth bass but high winds had turned his water dingy and the fish had stopped biting. He was a nervous wreck, because that meant he had to make a good catch the next day or he'd be heading home to watch the Cup from the sidelines.

That second day, the fish did cooperate and by 9:45 a.m. he had nearly 17 pounds in the livewell, enough to guarantee his place in the championship, but he had made a long run down the Detroit River and he still had to make it back to the weigh-in. The wind was howling, so even with hours of fishing time still remaining, Suggs decided to head back in. On the way, he submarined a wave; his boat filled nearly to the gunnels with water, and his glasses had been knocked off so he could barely see, but somehow he made it back in time and qualified for the Cup.

★ ★ ★

That year, the Forrest Wood Cup was held in August, so I knew the bass on Ouachita would be suspended in deep, flooded cedar trees that most of the contenders wouldn't find. I knew where those cedars were because I'd fished them for years, so I didn't even go to the lake to practice when all the others were out there. There was no off-limits time then, so some of the pros started practicing as much as two weeks before the tournament began.

They started phoning me, too, because the fishing was tough, just like I knew it would be. Finally, a week before the tournament started, I borrowed a friend's boat, put on a big straw hat, and started my practice. The first place I stopped, about 1:30 p.m. in the afternoon, I caught a 3 ½-pounder suspended in the cedars just like I thought. I ran to another place I knew and caught a four-pounder there, and when I brought that fish to the surface, 25 other bass came up with it. For the next two hours I ran to different spots, and by 3:30 that first afternoon I quit practice because I knew exactly where and how I was going to fish the entire tournament. I went back to the home on the lake I was renting and spent the rest of the week swimming and relaxing with my family. I even went walleye fishing.

I rechecked my spots two days before the tournament was set to start, and the bass were still there, so I called the friend whose boat I'd borrowed and told him to bring me mine. No one had recognized me at all in his boat, but mine was a wrapped model and well known, so on the last practice day I spent my time fishing places I had no intention of going to during the tournament. I knew everyone would be watching me.

The first morning I ran straight to the first spot I had visited during my practice day a week earlier and caught a four-pounder and a three-pounder on back-to-back casts. On my second spot, I had a hit on my first cast with a big spinnerbait and just like before, as I brought the bass to the surface, I could see maybe a hundred bass down below in the clear water. I boated my first fish, made another cast and caught another and didn't even unhook it. I just threw the rod and bass in the bottom of the boat, picked up another and made another cast.

I was a little surprised at the weigh-in that first day that I was only in third place, but I wasn't concerned. In most tournaments, the fishing becomes progressively more difficult each day as the bass seem to get more and more spooky and lure-shy. Even after the next day when I still wasn't leading, I wasn't concerned. After that second day, all but the top ten fishermen were eliminated and our weights were put back to zero. In essence, it now boiled down to a two-day tournament between just the ten of us.

Things did get tougher the third day, and I brought in just about 11 pounds, but that was enough to lead. I even had a cushion of nearly 5 pounds over the second place angler, so I felt really good. The thought of winning a million dollars really wasn't on my mind. Rather, it was just the idea of *winning* a major championship like the Forrest Wood Cup, beating so many truly great bass fishermen, that was on my mind.

The final morning, I ran to my best spot that had produced some fish each of the previous three days, but a local striped bass guide was anchored right where I wanted to fish. I made a few half-hearted casts, but didn't get a bite. I ran to my second spot and as I got closer I saw a boat there, too, surrounded by diving flags. I didn't even stop.

Now, I did start to get worried. My third spot was identified by a single tree still standing out of the water, but as I approached I could tell it didn't look right. Then I realized someone was in the water holding on to the tree. It was a knee-boarder, and his buddies were out in a ski boat running all around, creating waves, and totally destroying the place for fishing.

By now, it was nine o'clock and I hadn't made more than half a dozen casts, much less caught a fish, but at my next stop no one was around.

I checked my depth finder, dropped out two marker buoys for references, and eased back to cast. Before I could make my first cast, however, a ski boat roared by and another knee-boarder fell off not ten feet from my buoy. As I stood there speechless, the ski boat pulled around four different times trying to pick up the knee-boarder; they were making so much commotion my buoys were rolling over.

Finally, after running back up the lake, I was able to make my first honest effort of the day to fish, and I caught a tiny 13 ½-inch bass. It was legal, and I dropped it into the livewell. I left and fished several other places but without any success. I was really beginning to believe it just wasn't meant for me to win this tournament.

I moved to a place I had not fished in years, but when I had fished it, I usually caught a big bass. I changed my style of fishing entirely, switching from a spinnerbait to a ten-inch plastic worm, and after a few casts with the worm I set the hook on a solid fish. When I reached for the net, it got all tangled in my shoes and legs, but at last I got that bass into the boat. It weighed right at 5 pounds, and suddenly, with that fish I realized the second place angler now had to catch about 11 pounds to beat me.

I started to calm down and figure out what I needed to do. There was still a lot of time left to fish, and I certainly knew of plenty of places to go. I spent the rest of the afternoon visiting those places, and never had another strike.

Scott Suggs was the first bass angler to win $1 million in a single tournament.

With just a few minutes left before weigh-in, I headed to a spot I'd been saving all week. It was a big bay right outside the off-limits area near the weigh-in, and I'd always caught some fish there. When I arrived, however, the shoreline was completely lined with ski boats, party barges, and other bass boats, all of them waiting for me to come to weigh-in.

All those people, who were cheering and yelling for me, shook me up a little, but I lined up on my reference points and threw out the big worm. I had a hit almost immediately, and the cheering got even louder, and when I played the fish around the side of the boat I could see it was another solid five-pounder. That bass would absolutely seal the win for me, but when it opened its mouth, my worm just floated out. I had never even hooked it.

There were only two minutes left before I had to weigh in. I'd had a total of three strikes all day, and after losing that bass I felt sure I'd lost the tournament.

Standing in the weigh-in line, I remembered both a phone call and a dream I had had the night before. The call was from a fellow competitor who hadn't made the top ten, David Walker, who reminded me that if conditions seemed tough for me, they would certainly be tough for everyone, and he was exactly right. Even though I weighed in just over six pounds that day, I won by more than four pounds. Becoming the first bass fisherman to win $1 million in a single tournament did not sink in until later, when the calls for interviews started coming in from all over the world.

In my dream I was standing victorious on the stage holding up two big bass. I only got to hold up one, but thankfully, it was enough.

★ ★ ★

Scott Suggs still competes regularly on the FLW Tour, and nearly won a second $1 million in the 2009 Forrest Wood Cup. He and his family live in Alexander, Arkansas.

Chapter Twenty-Seven

Bill Dance:
"We Gotta Move
That Log"

Bill Dance, fishing here with Dr. Loren Hill, has often been described as "America's Favorite Fisherman," due to his long career as a successful tournament angler and television personality. He has taught literally millions of people how to fish through his television shows, videos, and magazine articles.

It's a warm, sunny weekend morning in Memphis in 1950, and at a city bus stop a 10-year-old, a fishing rod in his hand and his pockets crammed with worms and dough balls, waits for the bus to take him to Chickasaw Gardens, a housing development that includes a lake filled with bluegill and catfish where he will spend the entire day fishing from the bank.

Now it's more than 60 years later, and the boy has not only grown into manhood but also into the most famous bass angler in the world. His name is Bill Dance, and he's still fishing. Each week, millions of people watch him fish on television while others study his videos, read stories by him or about him, or see him in person at fishing promotions. For more than three decades he has been America's leading ambassador for the sport.

Born in Memphis, Tennessee, on October 7, 1940, Dance started fishing even before he discovered the bluegills at Chickasaw Gardens. Spending summers with his grandparents in Lynchburg, Tennessee, all he had to do was walk out their front door, cross a meadow, and he could be wading, swimming, or fishing in Mulberry Creek. Fishing-wise, he had a fly rod he loaded with grasshoppers or crawfish, and every once in awhile he'd catch a smallmouth weighing as much as four pounds. Mulberry Creek, Dance says, is why he still enjoys fishing moving water more than any other type of fishing.

As he grew older, Dance graduated to Horseshoe Lake, a Mississippi River oxbow 40 miles from Memphis. His grandmother would pack a lunch and drop him at Luke Clayton's boat dock and leave him all day, and Clayton let him use a flat-bottom boat Dance would scull around the pier pilings and cypress trees. This is where he learned the basics of both shallow cover and deepwater structure fishing. His first artificial lure was a topwater Arbogast Jitterbug he bought for 75 cents.

Eventually, he bought an outboard engine and his own flat-bottom boat and began fishing Pickwick Lake and the Tennessee River. In June 1967, Dance fished Ray Scott's first professional tournament, the All-American, and finished second by less than two pounds behind winner Stan Sloan. Because he was the first to reach his fishing spot the first day of competition there, Dance is credited with catching the first bass (on his first cast) in a B.A.S.S. competition. He also finished second in his next two events, a BSFA tournament conducted by Glen Andrews at Kentucky Lake, and Ray Scott's Dixie Invitational in October at Lewis Smith Lake in Alabama.

Then he won at Ross Barnett, Sam Rayburn, and back at Smith Lake. He was a furniture and hardware salesman at this time, but after returning home from a tournament one day in 1968, he found telephone messages from three of the most prominent lure companies in the nation waiting for him. He went to work for Nick Crème and Crème Lure Co., because plastic worm fishing had become his favorite technique, and for the next two years he not only continued to fish tournaments but also promote bass fishing in general through his association with Crème.

Then he joined Charles Spence, who offered him half ownership of Spence's fledgling company, Strike King Lures, but this association lasted less than a year before Dance gave his ownership share back to Spence. A week later Cotton Cordell called and offered him a job doing the very same thing he'd been doing for Crème, and he accepted. Not long afterward, Cordell suggested getting into television, and before Dance could refuse, Cordell handed him a camera and told him to get started; just that quickly Dance became producer, editor, cameraman, and star of his own show.

There was one problem, however. Dance's first filming effort, produced at Sam Rayburn Reservoir in Texas, was rejected by two of the three television stations in Memphis. At last, the third, an ABC affiliate, did take it, and Dance was off and running in what would become his ultimate career path. He began by doing 52 half-hour shows, not only honing his presentation but also his fishing skills. Gradually, the number of markets increased, and he left Cordell and syndicated his own program through Telesports, Inc.

Eventually he moved to CineSport, which produced not only his *Bill Dance Outdoors* program but also fishing programs for fellow tournament anglers Tom Mann, Roland Martin, Rayo Breckinridge, and Mark Sosin. It was the heyday of outdoors programming for television, and Dance's reputation, combined with his continuing success in competitive bass fishing tournaments, soared. When syndication became too expensive, he moved his show to The Nashville Network (TNN) and started his own production company back with Charles Spence, named Strike King Productions.

When Spence sold Strike King to Ray Murski in November 1995, Dance bought his show back so he had full ownership, and moved from TNN to the Outdoor Life Channel, which later changed its name to Versus, and which is now the NBC Sports Network. Although his schedule has slowed somewhat in recent years—at one time Dance was giving more than 50 promotions and traveling over 75,000 miles annually—he remains an active angler and television personality. His busy schedule forced him to retire from competitive tournament fishing at the end of the 1980 season; he finished with 7 national Bassmaster titles, 8 seconds, 6 thirds, and 21 other top-ten finishes, as well as 3 Bassmaster Angler of the Year titles.

★ ★ ★

In the early tournaments it wasn't the other tournament fishermen who would watch you fishing and then come back and claim the spot for themselves, but rather, local anglers. We didn't have GPS systems in those days, but because they already knew the lake, it was easier for locals to return to your exact spot, especially if you were fishing some type of visible cover.

One year, Carl Dyess and I were practicing together for an upcoming tournament on Lake Eufaula in Alabama. We motored back into Pataula Creek, one of the lake's better-known tributaries, where we found a big log sticking out of the sand right on an inside bend of the creek channel in about 12 feet of water. The log looked so good we eased up into casting distance, and when I flipped a plastic worm over to it, I got an immediate strike. I set the hook and reeled in a bass of nearly five pounds.

Carl flipped a worm in and caught another bass the same size, and when I bent my hook over and flipped again, I got our third strike in three casts. I couldn't resist, and flipped in once more, and had still another hit. We knew we'd found a spot that was loaded with bass, but two local boats had seen us catching those fish.

"We gotta move that log so they can't find this place," exclaimed Carl, and I agreed. I pulled out a compass and took two degree readings to triangulate the spot exactly, then we looped a rope around the log and started to pull it away. It actually moved, so we eased slowly down the creek pulling that log behind us. Whenever another boat would come by, we'd stop so the log would sink out of view and pretend we were fiddling with our tackle or something in the boat.

We kept pulling the log until we'd moved it about 75 yards and came to another bend in the creek that looked just like the one we'd left. It really was perfect, too. There was a 12-foot ledge that dropped into the channel, so we eased up and dropped the log so it stood up just like it had before.

"That spot sure looks good," I mentioned to Carl. "I wonder if there are any bass on it?" Carl just looked at me. We both had the same thought, so we eased back and made three casts to our "new" log, and caught three bass.

"We gotta move it again," said Carl.

So we re-tied our rope around the log and dragged it another 50 yards farther down the creek, but this time we dropped it on a straight section of the creek, not a bend with a channel break. Then we left Pataula Creek and fished in White Oak Creek for awhile, then returned to Pataula. Another boat was already fishing the log we'd just dropped there.

During another Eufaula tournament, I was practicing with Jerry McKinnis, and we found a log where he caught a nine-pounder and I caught a seven on our first two casts, but again, a local boat had seen us. Jerry wanted to move that log, too, so nobody would recognize his spot, but when we tried to pull it free, it wouldn't budge. We nearly sunk our boat trying because the entire stern went under as we pulled. We went over to Chewalla Marina and borrowed a saw, but the log was actually underwater and after an hour of trying to saw it in half we'd barely gotten a quarter of an inch through it, so we gave up. Jerry went back to it several times during the tournament, but never caught another bass there.

We were dead serious about moving those logs so nobody would find our fishing holes, but we still had a lot of fun at those early tournaments, too. Doug Odom, who fished B.A.S.S. events in 1976 and 1977, was about the same size as me, and one year at a tournament at West Point Lake in Georgia he caught a huge snapping turtle. He didn't know which room I was in at the Holiday Inn so he put on sunglasses and an orange and white Tennessee baseball cap like I always wear and told the front desk clerk he'd accidentally left his room key in the room. The clerk immediately gave him the key to my room.

Odom put the snapping turtle in my bathtub, then slipped back outside to wait for me to come in off the water. After awhile he called my room from a pay phone just to see how I was doing. The turtle had bitten a broom handle into two pieces when I tried to move it; I still work up a sweat just thinking about it.

I got him back, though. I put a duck in his boat livewell one night. The next morning when he went through the checkout line to start fishing, he had to open his livewell for inspection and when he did the duck flew out. It startled the checkout girl so much she fell off the pier into the lake.

Tom Mann and Billy Westmorland got me once, too. At a tournament they signed my name to a week's worth of motel room tickets, meal receipts, lures they'd bought, and even gas receipts at the boat dock, so when I tried to check out I had a bill for more than $3,000. They timed it so they were right beside me and couldn't stop laughing the whole time.

★ ★ ★

Bill Dance and his wife of 53 years, Dianne, live near Memphis. When he's not traveling or filming *Bill Dance Outdoors,* he still finds time occasionally to fish Horseshoe Lake where he first learned many of the basics of bass fishing more than 60 years ago.

Chapter Twenty-Eight

Dee Thomas: "That's How Flipping Started"

California angler Dee Thomas changed bass fishing forever by introducing the technique of flipping, now a standard presentation used by anglers everywhere. In flipping, lures are not cast, but rather, flipped underhand, through the use of a long rod, which Thomas also helped design. Flipping allows the quiet presentation of a lure into heavy cover in shallow water.

For a fisherman who did not catch his first bass until he was 19 years old, California angler Dee Thomas has more than made up for lost time in the years since. He's won more than a dozen major tournaments and championships, but more importantly, Thomas introduced the lure presentation technique of flipping to the bass fishing world. Criticized and protested at the tournaments he won with the then-unheard of technique, today flipping is one of the most widely accepted and commonly used fishing presentations in the sport, and rods, reels, lines, and lures have been developed specifically for flipping.

Ironically, that first bass, which he caught in 1957 in Whiskey Slough in the California Delta and weighed just over four pounds, came on a black/orange Bomber crankbait. Thomas caught it on his first and only cast of the day—he'd been allowed to accompany two other bass fishermen only if he agreed to row their boat—and he made the cast while the two were taking a lunch break on shore. It was the only fish anyone caught that day, and it turned out to be one of the most important bass anyone has ever caught, because it turned Dee Thomas into a bass fisherman for life.

From then on he fished with the two gentlemen frequently, eventually buying his first boat, a 12-foot aluminum model he skulled by hand for years. Clear Lake, located north of San Francisco, became one his favorite haunts, and one afternoon after he'd fished all day but caught only a single bass, he watched two men load their boat in preparation for fishing. The two men, O. C. Magee and Claude Davis, put two 20-foot fiberglass poles in the boat, and Thomas, who had never seen anything like them, waited at the ramp until they returned at dark just to see how the two men had fared.

Magee and Davis were among the first, if not the first bass fishermen to use the technique of "tule dipping" in California, simply holding the long poles out over the shoreline tule vegetation and dropping their jigs into open holes in the vegetation, or even behind them where big bass were hiding. That evening, when Thomas met them, the two brought in ten bass weighing between 35 and 40 pounds.

The two men showed their young fan—Thomas was 20 years old at the time—how the poles were rigged with just 12 feet of heavy line and how, when a bass hit, the fish was pulled to boat, since the rods had no reels. Thomas couldn't find any poles like theirs, but he did purchase a 14-foot cane pole and rigged it with heavy line just like that used by

Magee and Davis. He could skull his little aluminum boat with his right hand while he held the long pole in his left and braced it under his rib cage. He found some ⅜-ounce jigheads with long-shank hooks, put skirts on them, and added black Pedigo E-6 trailers as his lures.

This became his total bass fishing outfit for the next seven or eight years, and he never bothered with a tacklebox, since he could put everything he needed for a day of fishing—a few extra jigs and trailers—in his pockets. He never bothered with fresh line, either, because bass never broke it. His personal best day using the cane pole and jig combination was ten bass weighing 69 ½ pounds on certified scales at California's Lake Folsom, where he dropped the jig around the lake's big slabs of granite.

Clear Lake remained his favorite lake, however, and he and Chet Anderson, who became his frequent fishing companion, and who had a 12-foot aluminum boat, as well, would stack their boats in the bed of one of their pickups and whoever had fewer bass at the end of the day would have to buy dinner on the way home. In all the years they fished this way, Thomas only had to buy dinner one time. They expanded their range to include lakes all over California, including one-day trips all the way up to Lake Shasta and back. If bass weren't biting on one lake, they'd pack up and try another before heading home.

Word of their success spread, of course, and one day in late 1972 or early 1973 (Thomas isn't sure of the date) Wayne Cummings and Jerry Abney, the founders of the fishing organization Western Bass, called and invited them to compete in one of their tournaments. It was a team tournament at Lake Berryessa he and Anderson had fished often, so they decided to enter.

It was the first tournament Thomas ever fished in his life. He was 34, and all he had was his 12-foot tule dipping pole and the aluminum johnboat. There were 30 to 40 other contestants, all of whom had regular bass boats and the best bait-casting tackle of the time. Thomas and Anderson only caught seven bass the first day, the largest weighing just over four pounds, and Thomas wasn't enjoying the experience at all. In fact, after weighing in their bass, they left, heading to Clear Lake to fish the next day.

As it turned out, the fishing was not up to their standards at Clear Lake, either, so they returned home early the next afternoon. About six p.m. someone knocked at Thomas's door and handed him two trophies; he and Anderson, with only their long poles and aluminum boat, had only fished one day of the two-day event, but had not only won the tournament but taken big fish honors, as well.

They decided to fish the next Western Bass tournament, at Lake Don Pedro, but the other contestants objected, emphasizing they had to put reels on their poles. With that, Anderson dropped out of the tournament scene, but Thomas soon teamed with another angler, Frank Hauk, who would also become a longtime fishing partner. Hauk telephoned Alabama rod maker Lew Childre who provided them with 12-foot poles called Hawger Sticks, and they were designed to hold a reel. Thomas and Hauk took their new rods to Don Pedro and finished 14th, but at the next tournament, at Lake San Antonio, the two won by a margin of nearly ten pounds. He and Hauk sat in fifth place after the first day but Thomas was so upset and frustrated he never went to bed that night. The next day, he fished with a vengeance, but with their win came even more arguments against their unorthodox equipment.

Basically, their poles were considered too long and seemingly gave Thomas and Hauk an unfair advantage. They wouldn't be allowed to compete again unless they used shorter rods. Thomas went into his workshop and pulled a seven-foot, six-inch rod he'd used for striped bass from a rack and asked Cummings if that one would be acceptable. It was, and that's how the standard rod length for what was to become the flipping presentation was established and is still used around the world today.

★ ★ ★

I put a reel on that 7 ½-foot rod and went out to practice, and the first thing you know, I started reaching up for line and pitching my lure underneath little bushes and logs, swinging the rod in a pendulum and controlling the line with my hand. Pretty quickly, I was putting my lure farther out there with that rod than I had been with my longer 12-foot rod. If I'd been allowed to stay with that 12-foot pole, I'd have quit tournament fishing a long, long time ago, but when they forced me to use the shorter rod, it opened up a new way to fish.

We were now permitted to fish the Western Bass event, being held at Lake Nacimiento, and the first day we didn't catch a lot of bass, but the second day Hauk and I had a good catch but then we swamped our boat and lost those fish. Two skiers helped us to the shore, and after about

30 minutes I finally got our outboard restarted. Then we went out and caught another limit of fish and won the tournament.

The next tournament was at Lake Oroville. Lew Childre had been sponsoring us because we had been using his rods, but I gave that sponsorship entirely to Houk. It was only $100 a month. In the meantime, I had been contacted by Dave Myers, then the head of public relations for the Fenwick rod company, and in 1973 Fenwick began sponsoring me, a relationship that lasted until 1993, a full 20 years.

One day we were fishing together on Lake McClure, and Dave asked me about a name for the technique I had been using. Hell, I said, all we're doing is flipping jigs into the brush.

"Then that's what we'll call it," Myers decided.

It was a natural. I was using a Ranger boat made in Flippin, Arkansas, and flipping lures into the bushes. That's how the name for the presentation was decided. Just like that, probably in less than two minutes.

Myers wanted Fenwick to develop a rod for flipping, and we went through 30 or 40 prototypes before we decided on a design I liked. They had made another I really liked, and it was perfect, with a big, stout butt and a really fast tip, but one day in the boat Dave broke every one I had, just so I couldn't use them. He said he could never sell them.

Anyway, I won the Lake Oroville tournament, finished second at Don Pedro, fifth at Lake Mead, and won flipping gin clear water at Pine Flat Reservoir near Fresno. That's where I won the first boat ever given away in a bass tournament on the West Coast. Then Myers suggested we try a B.A.S.S. tournament in the Southeast, and we picked the Louisiana Invitational on Toledo Bend in March 1975.

I showed up and was totally starstruck. I met all the fishermen I had been reading about, including Roland Martin, Bill Dance, everybody, and I was pretty intimidated. Dave had come down a few days early and spoken to B.A.S.S. founder Ray Scott and his tournament director, Harold Sharp, about my longer rod. Ray laughed and said it was fine, and when Harold learned the longer length of 7 ½ feet was allowed in California, he agreed, too. That's how the 7 ½-foot length rule was originally set in B.A.S.S. competition although now longer rods are permitted.

I didn't do well at Toledo Bend. I was scared of all the stumps and trees in the water. It was like nothing I'd ever seen at home. I finished so far down in the standings nobody even knew I was there. A local Texas guide named Marvin Baker won with 61 pounds, 6 ounces. Dave and

I stayed around until after the awards were presented, then went up to speak to Ray before we left. Ray thanked me for coming, and said I was welcome to bring some of our California money back to the South anytime. He said it jokingly but with his straight face, and it made me so mad I couldn't even speak to Myers for three states as we drove home.

Finally, I asked if I could try another one, but I wanted to choose the lake. It happened that the next event on the schedule was the Arkansas Invitational on Bull Shoals the very next month, and that's what we decided I'd fish. When we got there it was snowing and cold, but we entered the special one-day fly fishing tournament Ray was conducting prior to the regular tournament. I couldn't even find my rod in the boat because it was covered with snow. I caught one short bass that day, and during the three regular practice days I only caught one legal bass.

The first tournament day, my lucky draw was a fisherman who had not been on the lake at all during practice, and because I had caught one fish, he let me do whatever I wanted. I went straight back to the little creek by the Bull Shoals Dam where I'd caught that one fish. I planned to put the trolling motor down there and just fish my way up the shoreline back to the weigh-in. I had on a hair jig and 25-pound test line. That day I lost four bass over five pounds, but put seven keepers in the boat. I figured the bite had turned on for everyone and that I'd be way down in the field, but as it turned out, I was in second place.

The next day I drew one of the fishermen I'd drawn at Toledo Bend. He was a big guy and tough, the kind who could eat grizzly bears for breakfast, but he hadn't caught a fish the first day, so he let me choose the fishing spot. In fact, he told me if I'd take him to the fish, he'd show me how to catch them. Sure enough, at my little creek by the dam, I never got a bite, so I made a long, long run up the lake. I found a marina and stopped for gas; my boat would hold 18 gallons but I think I put 19 gallons in.

At my first spot I hooked a five-pounder on my first flip, but it straightened my hook. I moved away from the bank and tied on a heavier ⅝-ounce bucktail jig. I scraped away all the bucktail and put on a two-inch white worm, then went right back to the same spot I'd just lost that five-pounder. I caught five bass up to five pounds on my first five flips. My grizzly eater in the back of the boat was going crazy because he couldn't catch any. When I had four more keepers in the livewell, he said he was going to protest me for not leaving him any water to fish.

I didn't say a word, but I just went to the back of the boat where he was standing and flipped my jig by another bush, and caught a keeper bass. I put it in the livewell, and he never said another word to me. At the weigh-in I had an eight- or nine-pound lead, and even though I only caught one bass the next day, I won the tournament with a little over 36 pounds.

I won less than $5,000 there, but it was really the most prestigious event I ever won. The media started writing about my flipping technique and Dave Myers and Fenwick promoted it, too. That was more than 35 years ago, and that's how it started. The equipment today is much improved over what I had, but the actual flipping technique itself is exactly the same.

★ ★ ★

Today, Dee Thomas and Terry, his wife of more than 40 years, still live in Brentwood near the California Delta, and while he has retired from competitive fishing, he still enjoys getting on the water with his long rods, especially if he can show a newcomer how to flip.

Chapter Twenty-Nine

Rick Clunn: "A Special Lure for a Special Tournament"

In the sport of professional bass tournament fishing, no one can match the extraordinary achievements of Rick Clunn, 67, of Ava, Missouri. He has won four Bassmaster Classic world championships, including back-to-back titles in 1976–77; ten other BASS national titles; the BASS Angler of the Year; the Red Man All-American; two U.S. Opens; several Forrest L. Wood tournament circuit titles; and more than $3 million in prize money.

A native Oklahoman, Clunn began bass fishing as a youngster, following behind as his father waded different Oklahoma streams. Later, after moving to the Houston area where he began working for the Exxon Corporation as a computer programmer, he joined a local bass club and began honing his angling skills on both Sam Rayburn and Toledo Bend reservoirs.

He resigned from Exxon in 1972 to follow his dream of becoming a professional bass tournament angler, and started guiding on Lake Conroe north of Houston. His first national tournament win was also his first Bassmaster Classic victory, at Lake Guntersville, Alabama, in 1976.

Rick Clunn not only won four Bassmaster Classic world championships, he designed a lure specifically for the conditions on the James River where the 1990 Classic was held, and used it to win the event.

Until that win, Clunn had not performed particularly well in national competition and few had ever heard of him. On the second morning of that Classic, however, when he boated four bass weighing nearly 25 pounds in less than ten minutes, the Clunn Legend began, and it has been growing steadily ever since. His catch at Guntersville of 59 pounds, 15 ounces was the heaviest Classic winning catch ever recorded, but Clunn himself shattered that record in 1984 when he won with 75 pounds, 9 ounces.

Acknowledged as a power fisherman who relies heavily on crankbaits and spinnerbaits for his fish, Clunn has designed a number of lures over the years. He is even more well-known for his analytical approach to fishing that emphasizes a thorough understanding of both bass and baitfish behavior under specific circumstances as well as his own personal attention to detail.

★ ★ ★

During practice for the 1988 Bassmaster Classic on the James River in Richmond I had located a lot of bass around cypress trees in the mouths of several creeks, but actually, I did not completely figure them out until the first day of competition. They were hitting my RC-3 crankbait, but on low tide the lure was actually running too deep. That first day I lost three bass in the four- to five-pound range in succession.

That's what really got me. Those are what I call "momentum" fish that truly can determine the outcome of a tournament. I would hook the fish in one to two feet of water, and when the fish turned to run away, I would see that the back hook of the lure was always only hooked on the outside of the head or gill plate, and when the fish turned, that hook would simply pop loose.

It took me several days after the tournament to understand what was taking place. I tried to visualize everything that had happened, and at last I realized my lure was actually diving too deep for the water I was fishing; the bass were forced to attack it from the top instead of from the side or bottom as they normally do. I could feel them pick up the lure but from that angle the hooks were never inside their mouths. I eventually finished 18th in the tournament.

The type of lure selection and action of the lure were correct, but the RC-3 was running too deep, probably actually burrowing slightly into the soft bottom. One possible solution was to use much heavier line to keep the crankbait higher, but this would change the lure's action entirely. I could hold my rod higher, but that would impede my hook setting. I could also design another lure similar to the RC-3 but which would not run quite as deep, and that's what I decided to do.

I had designed the RC-3 crankbait I used in the Classic several years earlier, and I really liked it. It was made of cedar and the company, Poe's, had done a good job with it, both in manufacturing and in marketing. This gave me the opportunity to design another lure for them, but when I did begin working on it I had no idea the Classic would be held on the James River again in 1989. Until that year, the Classic did not have a history of back-to-back visits to the same location.

In 1989 when we did return, I did not fish the same spots again, and to this day I do not know why I didn't. I had my new crankbait, the shallow running lure I had named the RC-1, but one of the flaws in my fishing philosophy, I suppose, is that I do not like to return to the same places I have fished before. I was catching bass on the RC-1 in my other areas, but they were not the quality fish I had found the previous year.

On the last day of that Classic I did return to the cypress trees of the previous year and I quickly had about ten bites, but although none of them were big fish, all were well hooked. That gave me a lot of confidence that the lure was the right one to use but it also made me feel kind of foolish that I really had never given those fish much of a chance. I finished tenth.

When I learned we would be returning to the James River for an unprecedented third successive Classic in 1990, I made up my mind I was going to completely dedicate myself to those particular fish around the cypress trees. The first two days of the Classic we had a lot of rain, and combined with the high tide we fished in, I chose the deeper-running RC-3. I actually lost two more nice bass on the lure, one each day, and I realized from those two fish that they still were not completely taking the lure very well. It was just as it had happened two years earlier, but this year after two days of competition I was nearly ten pounds behind the leader.

On the third day we had a strange low tide. It was going out when I arrived at the cypress trees, and it never really came back in, so I fished the shallow running RC-1 almost the entire time. That day I weighed in more than 18 pounds, the heaviest weight of any day during any of the three James River Classics, and won by nearly 7 pounds.

★ ★ ★

Still active as a full-time tournament angler, Rick Clunn lives on a 600-acre farm near Ava, Missouri, with his wife Melissa and sons Sage and River.

Chapter Thirty

Takahiro Omori: "I Slept in My Truck for Three Years"

Japanese angler Takahiro Omori competed in his first American bass tournament in 1992, even though he could speak only a few words of English, and caught only one bass in the three-day event. He slept in his car and ate one meal a day to save money, and in 2004 he won the Bassmaster Classic world championship. He now lives in Texas near Lake Fork and continues to fish competitively.

Born in Tokyo, Japan, in 1970, Takahiro Omori discovered bass fishing when someone put largemouth bass in a pond in a park near his home. He caught his first bass there, a ten-inch fish, on a live nightcrawler, when he was ten years old.

He'd been fishing before that memorable day, catching other local species with his father and also with school friends. After landing his first bass, however, Omori began directing all his fishing efforts toward bass, and in high school he started fishing junior tournaments. After reading about the Bassmaster Classic world championship in the American fishing magazine *Bassmaster*, he decided he wanted to become a full-time bass tournament pro. To do so, however, meant he would have to come to the United States.

After graduating from high school in 1988, it took Omori three years of working odd jobs to finance his first tournament trip to America. Although that first visit was a near disaster, Omori nevertheless persevered in following his dream, enduring incredible hardships along the way that included sleeping in his car and skipping meals in order to save money for fishing.

Gradually his dedication began to pay off, and today Omori has become a very successful full-time tournament pro. He fished 19 national events in 2003, including his second Bassmaster Classic appearance, and in 2004 he won the Classic world championship, after which sponsors gave him a hero's tour back through Japan where he was greeted by thousands of cheering fans. Omori is also well on his way to becoming an American citizen. He took classes at Texas Wesleyan University in Dallas to learn to speak English better, and he has bought a home near Alba, Texas, just a short distance from the launching ramps at Lake Fork.

★ ★ ★

It took me three years to save enough money to come to fish in the United States. My first American bass tournament was at Sam Rayburn Reservoir in Texas in March 1992. I had tried to fish B.A.S.S. tournaments the year before, but they were already filled. So when I finally made my first trip to the United States I was able to fish two tournaments, Rayburn and then Lake Guntersville in Alabama 40 days later.

I brought all my best fishing tackle and flew from Tokyo to Dallas. I had no idea where Sam Rayburn was in relation to Dallas (approximately

300 miles), I spoke no English, but I rented a car and drove away. That's how bad I wanted to be a bass fisherman.

Japanese bass fisherman Takahiro Omori.

Bass fishing has become very popular in Japan, and all the serious fishermen want to come to America for the challenge of competing against the best anglers and on the big lakes. It is hard for American fishermen to understand how strong those dreams are among foreign anglers because they grow up with the lakes all around them. Most of us in Japan grow up in big cities.

In Japan we drive on the left side of the highway, so I started driving on the left as I pulled out of D–FW International Airport. I was driving 45 mph, too, and pretty soon I had about five cars bunched up behind me, although I couldn't understand why. Finally, a guy on a motorcycle drove up beside me and gave me the finger, and so I started changing lanes until I realized I had been driving in the passing lane.

My flight had arrived in the evening so sometime later that night I pulled into a parking lot to sleep. I was going to be in the United States for 40 days and I had to save as much money as possible. It took me two days to reach Sam Rayburn, and I don't remember how many times I got lost.

When I arrived at the boat ramp and looked at the lake, all I could see was water. It was larger than any lake I'd ever seen, larger than I'd imagined. Early the next morning when tournament practice started, I stood at the boat ramp and I asked every fisherman who came by if he would take me fishing. At last one man agreed to take me, and that day I caught two bass, my first American fish. I was thrilled.

The next day I went to the official tournament registration and I met Gary Yamamoto, who was also competing. He spoke a little Japanese and tournament officials asked him to be an interpreter, and he took me fishing the next day. I had actually met him during a fishing promotion he made in Japan, but of course he didn't remember me. Gary was renting a house at the lake for the tournament and he invited me to stay with him that week.

In the tournament I finished in 304th place out of 325 fishermen. I caught one bass I could weigh on the last day. I was in culture shock. Seeing the fish-catching skills of the American anglers and the way they could drive boats on the big lakes, I knew immediately I had a lot to learn and would drastically have to improve if I was going to survive.

The week after Sam Rayburn I came to Lake Fork because I had heard so much about it in Japan. Lake Fork is one of the most famous lakes in the United States because of all the trophy bass it has, so Japanese fishermen dream of coming there just for the chance to catch a big fish. There are very few large lakes in Japan, and certainly not many of them have a big bass population like Lake Fork.

Because I did not know anyone, spoke very limited English, and did not have a boat, I just walked and fished from the shore, and in a week I caught three 8-pounders. I thought every lake in America had big fish like that, because they had caught them that way at Rayburn, too. Shaw Grigsby had won the tournament with a total of more than 60 pounds.

At Lake Guntersville I finished 280th. I was still sleeping in my car in the parking lots; during that first 40-day trip to the United States I only spent two nights in a motel and I only ate one meal a day.

After Guntersville I went back to Japan to work and tried to earn money to come back and fish the tournaments again. I met Masake Shimono, another Japanese angler who also planned to come to the United States, and he had a sponsorship deal that would get him a truck and a boat. Masake and I teamed up; my job was to keep his truck and boat clean, and take him to the airports so he could just fly to each lake, and I drove his truck. We kept this partnership for three years. I still slept in the truck each night, but now I could go to a lake and practice every day in his boat, even though I fished the tournaments as a non-boater.

I stayed in the United States for six months on that second trip. That year I finished in eighth place at Lake Eufaula, Alabama, getting my first check in American fishing. The last day of that tournament I caught four bass that weighed 20 pounds, including an 8-pound, 12-ounce fish that won big bass of the tournament. That fish is still the biggest bass I've ever weighed in during a tournament. I was the first Japanese to ever earn a check in a B.A.S.S. event.

Little by little I was learning English, but not as well as I really needed to. At Grand Lake in Oklahoma the next year, Masake and I were both disqualified because in practice we were fishing near two local anglers on the bank and they started talking to us about where to find fish. Neither of us understood enough English to know what they were saying, but other tournament anglers heard it and told us it was illegal to get local information like that.

Takahiro Omori was the first Japanese fisher to ever earn a check in a B.A.S.S. event.

That made me even more determined to become a tournament pro and make a living fishing American bass tournaments. At last, in 1996 I won a Bassmaster Central Invitational tournament at Lake of the Ozarks in Missouri, but one of the best tournaments I ever had was in 2001 when I won the B.A.S.S. Central Invitational on Sam Rayburn. It was my tenth year of American bass fishing, and my tenth tournament on Rayburn.

It was really special and very emotional because the first time I fished there I didn't know what to do at all. After I won Rayburn, I won a national FLW tournament on Lake Martin in Alabama. In 40 days I won

$200,000. It wasn't like the first 40 days I had spent in the United States 10 years before.

★ ★ ★

Takahiro Omori still lives in Emory, Texas, and competes in both Bass-master and FLW Tour events each season. In his two decades as an American bass pro, he has won six national events, including the 2004 Bassmaster Classic, and pocketed more than $2 million in prize money.

THE BUSINESS

Chapter Thirty-One

The Business
of Bass

———

As the outdoor editor of the Tulsa Tribune, *Bob Cobb was instrumental in helping generate interest in Ray Scott's first professional tournament in 1967 at Beaver Lake. In 1970, he became the first editor of* Bassmaster, *the official publication of B.A.S.S., and built it into the nation's premier fishing publication. Photo courtesy of B.A.S.S.*

Texas angler Ron Speed has a lifetime of bass fishing memories. After all, the former high school football coach picked his school assignments by their proximity to good bass lakes. Thus, it surprises some that he usually recalls an early spring day in 1974 when he wasn't even on the water as one that stands out the most. That's when he had 17 charter flights full of bass fishermen heading to three different Mexican lakes at the same time.

The three lakes were Guerrero, Palmito, and Don Martin, each of which were producing one-day catches of at least 100 bass per day per angler and many of them in the three- to five-pound class. Speed had established fishing camps at all of them. He knew how easy it was to catch bass fishing fever since he'd had it for years. Late one night in 1969 he had caught it worse than ever.

It was during the Christmas holidays, and Speed, who was teaching and coaching at Hemphill High School in Hemphill, Texas, just a long cast away from Toledo Bend Reservoir, received a midnight telephone call from a friend who told him he'd just found the best bass lake in the world, an obscure 11,000-acre body of water named Lake Dominguez where ten-pounders were waiting in line to strike spinnerbaits and plastic worms. Speed had never heard of Lake Dominguez, but within hours he and five friends were pulling their boats down the highway to find it, 1,860 miles away across the border in Mexico.

They hardly caught any bass at all, and nothing close to a ten-pounder, but practically by accident Speed met an American named Charlie Wright who lived at the lake and convinced him the fishing there really was good. Wright also convinced Speed he should consider sending other American bass anglers down; they could even stay at Wright's home. Several months later, Speed packed his first 20 clients on a chartered DC-3 and sent them to Wright. They caught more bass than they'd ever caught in their lives, and with that, Speed was out of the teaching and coaching profession and into the outfitting business.

Palmito was normally booked a full year in advance, even though the trail to the water was so steep and treacherous anglers rode burros back and forth while a horse pulled a homemade sled piled high with their fishing tackle. At Guerrero, Speed had been forced to construct a second lodge because his first one, La Retama, which he'd opened in May 1973, could not accommodate the demand.

Speed is the man who opened Mexican bass fishing for American anglers, and between 1973 and 1976, he sent more than 20,000 avid bass fishermen to Guerrero alone. With Guerrero, bass fishing truly became an international sport for the first time, a fact not lost on Mexican fisheries' personnel. As a result of Speed's work, they began attempting to limit commercial netting on the lake, the first time sport fishing had ever received such a helping hand in that country.

Speed's success—his company, Ron Speed's Adventures, based in Malakoff, Texas, continues to send fishermen to Mexico as well as to South America for peacock bass—was only a hint of how large the sport of bass fishing would grow over the next decade. Today, bass fishing is estimated to be a $40 to $50 billion business, if not more, and while high-level professional tournament competitions held by the two largest fishing organizations, B.A.S.S. and FLW Outdoors, receive much of the attention, the sport has a much longer range.

Consider, for example, that today more people fish than play golf and tennis combined. The American Sportfishing Association suggests that if fishing were ranked as a corporation, it would sit among the top 50 on the Fortune 500 list of American corporations, based on total sales. That would put it ahead of giants like Microsoft. This isn't all just because of the popularity of bass fishing, but a lot of it is.

Bass fishing is now an accepted collegiate sport, with roughly 300 colleges and universities in more than 30 states sponsoring teams that compete in nationally televised championships; among them are such notable institutions as Cornell, Texas A&M, Nebraska, Georgia, and Virginia Tech. The National Guard, a primary sponsor of college fishing programs like these, saw its enlistment rate increase dramatically once it became involved.

Other major corporations have used bass fishing to reach their customers, as well, including such giants as Chevrolet, Toyota, Walmart, Folgers, Anheuser-Busch, Wrangler, Purina, and even Skippy Peanut Butter. In bass fishing, they have found a relatively inexpensive way to reach a huge consumer base that may total as many as 30 million active participants, the majority of whom fit their demographics very well. Over the years, those consumers have exhibited strong brand loyalty to their sport's sponsors, too; afterall, every bass boat owner needs a vehicle to pull his rig, so why shouldn't it be a Chevrolet or Toyota?

Walmart, the world's largest retailer, entered the sport in 1996 when Minnesota businessman Irwin Jacobs purchased the Kentucky-based fishing organization known as Operation Bass. Jacobs, already the successful owner of Genmar, a group of recreational boat manufacturing companies, including Forrest Wood's Ranger Boats, was looking for a way to sell more boats, and he knew bass tournaments were one way to do it. He quickly expanded the Operation Bass format by renaming his company FLW Outdoors and creating the FLW Tour (both named after Wood), and through Walmart's sponsorship increased tournament payouts dramatically. Today, in addition to Walmart, FLW Outdoors has more than three dozen major sponsors, produces nearly 250 fishing tournaments annually throughout the United States (not all for largemouth bass), and offers almost $40 million in prize money.

In addition, there are also interactive CD-ROM computer games about bass fishing, and songs describing bass fishing are released regularly by Nashville recording artists. Fantasy fishing leagues attract tens of thousands of players, many of whom have never held a rod and reel in their hands, for cash prizes that have reached as high as $1 million. And while Ron Speed continues to send bass fishermen to far-flung locations, he now has plenty of competition from similar outfitters.

While Speed was building his fishing/travel company, another bass fisherman in Springfield, Missouri, who had been competing in some of the early professional tournaments, recognized the potential public demand for the very same lures and tackle he and his fellow pros used in those tournaments. In 1971, fresh out of Drury College with a business degree, the young fisherman took out a loan for $10,000 and used it to purchase a trailer full of more fishing lures. Then he began reselling them from the eight feet of shelf space his father provided him in one of his liquor stores. The fisherman's name was John L. Morris, and he called his little business Bass Pro Shops.

Soon Morris was selling lures not only off the shelf, but taking telephone orders, as well. That led to a mail-order business; he purchased mailing lists containing more than 10,000 names in nearly two dozen states and sent each one a 180-page catalog describing more than 1,200 separate items. In time, the catalog would grow to more than 400 pages, and the mailing list would expand to four million customers around the world.

In 1981, just ten years after starting on that eight feet of shelf space donated by his father, Morris opened his first showroom, Outdoor World, adjacent to his original catalog business. Here, his customers could see lures working in an indoor pond, test their shooting skills at rifle, handgun, and archery ranges, and simply absorb the atmosphere of a 300,000-square-foot emporium devoted entirely to outdoor recreation. Today, there are more than 60 Bass Pro Shops Outdoor World showrooms throughout the United States.

Even B.A.S.S., the original company founded by Ray Scott in 1967 that started the sport on its popularity climb, increased in value beyond Scott's wildest dreams. In July 1986 Scott sold the firm to his then vice president, Helen Sevier, who had partnered with the financial company Jemison Investments of Birmingham. The price was reported to be in the $12 to possibly as high as $18 million range. Fifteen years later, in 2001, Sevier sold B.A.S.S. to the sports television company ESPN, a division of the Walt Disney Corporation, for a price often rumored to be as high as $40 million. In late 2010, ESPN sold B.A.S.S. to three individual investors for an undisclosed amount.

Bass fishing had been on television in one form or another for years, starting with the personality-driven programs produced by an angler named Roscoe Vernon Gaddis, whose weekly program, *The Flying Fisherman,* began its initial 13-week trial run in 1963 on station WOR-TV in New York. Gaddis had acquired the nickname "Gadabout" in 1938 as the host of his radio fishing show in Schenectady, New York, and it stayed with him throughout his television career. Eventually, Gadabout Gaddis was airing on 73 stations nationwide with 20 million viewers, and while he did not limit himself to bass, he certainly included them from time to time.

The Gaddis program was far different from today's fishing shows in that it was filmed entirely without any audio. Sound effects, as well as his own informal—and totally unscripted—narrative were added later in the studio. His trademark was the opening scene of him flying into some remote fishing spot in his own airplane (he'd earned his pilot's license in 1952), and while he occasionally offered lures for sale on his program, it was not a promotional advertisement. Rather, the lures, usually a package of six spinners selling for a dollar, were used to judge viewer response to his program.

Virgil Ward's first experience in television began in 1963, as a co-host with Bud Inman, of an outdoor show sponsored by the Missouri Conservation Commission. This led then to Ward's national syndicated *Championship Fishing* television show, which he hosted for the next 25 years. In 21 of those years, the show was rated as the top fishing show on the air.

In 1985, B.A.S.S. began airing its own television program, *The Bassmasters,* on The Nashville Network (TNN), offering a mix of the company's own tournament results along with technique features of the tournament winners. It was a delicate balance, with most of the serious work done in the editing room. On-the-water fishing coverage has seldom been viewer-friendly because the sport itself is so unpredictable and repetitive.

It's an even more delicate balance today, complicated not only by market saturation but also by a much more sophisticated market. In 1985 few channels were available or willing to air fishing programs. Today, TNN is no longer around, but it has been replaced by the Outdoor Channel, NBC Sports Network, Sportsman's Channel, Pursuit Channel, the World Fishing Network, and others, all of which offer 24/7 fishing, hunting, and outdoors-oriented programming. The top production companies today are forced to use different cameras in six or more boats during competitive events, as well as film from helicopters and on shore, and create supplementary fill-in features weeks in advance.

There are literally dozens of bass fishing programs airing, not only giving viewers a wide choice of what to watch, but at the same time

Bass fishing has been on television for several decades, and has been a major factor in the overall growth of the sport. In major competitions, television cameramen ride in the boats with leading anglers to film every catch.

diluting the audiences for all of them. The ESPN sports group, once a leader in this type of programming, was still airing *The Bassmasters* as of 2013, but little else in that field, as it returned to its core sports of football, baseball, and basketball.

Bass fishing popularity also benefited greatly from the print media, which, in many cases, quickly recognized the growing interest in the sport as well as the new base of revenue available from the sport's advertisers. No other species, not catfish, not trout, not pike, ever produced a devoted fan base or its own supportive industry as fast as the largemouth bass.

Outdoor writers for newspapers and magazines had, of course, been penning bass fishing stories for years, but seldom did the fish or its fishermen ever receive top billing. That changed in 1969 when an Oklahoma writer named Bob Cobb became the editor of a magazine named *Bassmaster*, a publication Ray Scott had started to provide specific bass fishing information anglers would find nowhere else. It was designed to become one of the benefits of joining Scott's Bass Anglers Sportsman Society; what it became under Cobb's editorship was a flagship in the entire publishing world.

Cobb began producing the first truly successful "vertical" fishing magazine, meaning that every story related to the same subject, in this case, bass fishing. More than 40 years later, *Bassmaster* is still considered one of the most successful vertical magazines of all time, with a circulation at one time of more than 550,000, and still publishing nothing but bass-related articles.

Just as importantly, as bass fishing continued to grow in popularity, other older, long-established publishing houses, *Field & Stream* and *Sports Afield* among them, began devoting more and more magazine space, even complete issues, to the sport. *Bassmaster* was not available on newsstands, but these other publications were, and they exposed the sport to a brand new audience. Jason Lucas, the fishing editor of *Sports Afield*, had published his first book on bass fishing, *Lucas on Bass Fishing*, back in 1947, and as the sport really became of age in the 1970s, a whole new generation of readers discovered him. Other magazines, far outside the realm of fishing, such as *Forbes*, *Sports Illustrated*, and *USA Today*, to name just a few, have also reported on the sport and its popularity.

Outdoor writers from different publications were also invited, all expenses-paid, to attend the annual Bassmaster Classic tournament. The scribes took turns riding with the pros during actual competition days, then spent evenings visiting with them during catered dinners. The resulting stories from these weeklong events reached literally millions of readers nationwide for months following the tournament, and produced clipping scrapbooks two to three inches thick. Not only that, it produced writer/angler friendships that resulted in even more bass fishing stories for years to come.

Today, the Internet has changed much about how bass fishing is reported. There are still many, many written features about professional fishing techniques, but when the words "bass fishing" are entered into a search engine like Google, more than 23 million responses are noted. Just as the proliferation of cable television channels diluted the television fishing market, the Internet has done the same to print media. Many fishing publications (as well as those covering other fields) no longer exist. Indeed, the growing use of videos on the Internet has even diluted the television marketplace.

Still, 23 million responses to the search words "bass fishing" mean the sport is still alive and well. And yes, somewhere in that listing you'll find Ron Speed's name promoting those trips to Mexico.

Chapter Thirty-Two

Bob Cobb:
"It All Started
in a Pickle Box"

Bob Cobb, Ray Scott's first editor of Bassmaster Magazine, *was also an enthusiastic bass fisherman himself, and often fished with Scott not only on lakes in the United States but also in Mexico and Canada.* Photo courtesy of B.A.S.S.

As Bob Cobb tells the story, he couldn't help but love bass fishing so he never considered writing about it as work. Even through the years as he guided a fledgling fishing magazine named *Bassmaster* into the nation's premier fishing publication with a circulation of over 500,000, Cobb never lost his enthusiasm or his sense of wonder at learning how others caught largemouth bass. Indeed, Cobb, as much as anyone, helped make the largemouth the most popular fish species in the nation.

Born October 3, 1935, in Blanco, Oklahoma, as a child he walked behind his father as he fished Brushy, Wild Horse, and other creeks in Pittsburg County. His father was a school teacher and knew the best creeks in the county, and they'd get out early to pick grasshoppers off the sunflower stems, put them in a mayonnaise jar for safekeeping, then fish them on a flyrod for bass.

Later the family moved to McAlester, where in high school Cobb began writing the sports report each Saturday for the special page the *McAlester News Capital* daily paper devoted to high school news. In 1958 he earned a degree in journalism from the University of Oklahoma, and soon afterward became a staff writer in the sports department for the *News Capital*.

Sitting at the typewriter one day, he heard high heels clicking across the floor, and looking up, saw a beautiful brunette looking for the society editor. She was Barbara Foster, and in early 2012 they celebrated their 50th wedding anniversary; Cobb gives Barbara full credit for guiding and encouraging him to take the crucial step—leaving family, friends, and a secure job to take a chance on another man's dream—that forever shaped the sport of American bass fishing.

By 1966 Cobb had moved to Tulsa and worked himself into the job of outdoor editor for the *Tulsa Tribune*. One April day he received a notice describing a press meeting in Springdale, Arkansas, about "the greatest thing that ever happened in fishing." It was Ray Scott's announcement about a bass fishing tournament he planned to conduct at Beaver Lake.

Cobb attended the press conference, and after everyone else left, he and Scott talked for another three hours. The tournament was to be held in June, and Scott needed entries. Cobb wrote a story about their meeting, and not long afterward, Scott telephoned to say that he still wasn't getting any entries from Tulsa. He did, however, have an idea about how to get them, but he needed Cobb's help.

The idea was to create a rivalry between bass fishermen in Memphis and Tulsa, and start it with a challenge issued by Memphis bass fisherman Clyde A. Harbin that Cobb printed in the *Tribune*. The next day Cobb's telephone rang. The call was from a Tulsa bass fisherman willing to accept the challenge, Don G. Butler, who would go on to become one of the sport's legends over the following years.

Cobb and Butler quickly organized a group of anglers named the Tulsa Bass Club. As enthusiasm grew, Zebco, already a well-known manufacturer of bass fishing rods and reels, contributed green jackets to the dozen or so club members to wear during the tournament.

The agreement between Tulsa and Memphis was that each member of the winning team would get to go to the losing team's tackle boxes and pick any lure the angler wanted, regardless of value. The three-day tournament, named the All-American by Scott, was won by Nashville fisherman Stan Sloan, but the Tulsa-Memphis rivalry was touch-and-go until the night before the final day of competition. That's when the Tulsa fishermen, who were leading their rivals after two days, decided to have their celebration early. The Memphis fishermen, by contrast, went to bed early, fished hard on Sunday, and won.

Scott realized after that initial Beaver Lake tournament that he had the nucleus of a fishing organization, and in January 1968 he returned to Tulsa to ask those fishermen to help him organize nationally. He already had his organization named, the Bass Anglers Sportsman Society, or B.A.S.S.

Scott and Cobb stayed in contact as B.A.S.S. began conducting other tournaments. Cobb had gone to work for Zebco as head of their public relations department, so Scott started talking to Barbara about getting them to Montgomery so Cobb could use his editorial skills to produce a new magazine Scott wanted to start sending his growing membership.

Barbara talked to her mother about the move. Her answer was that if they didn't try it, they would always wonder if they could have done it. So, in January 1970 Cobb and his family packed their car and headed into an editorial adventure he could not have imagined in his wildest dreams.

★ ★ ★

The front door to the B.A.S.S. offices wasn't easy to find. It was really the back door to the building in an alley. Across the street was a building with tombstones out in front—a monument company—and I hoped it wasn't a bad omen for things to come.

When Barbara and I finally did get inside, Ray met us in the hallway. At that time, B.A.S.S. headquarters consisted of Ray's office, a secretary's alcove, a hallway, and an empty room, which would become my office. An architectural firm had previously occupied the office, so there were cabinets around the wall, and below them a waist-high table where they spread their drawings. There was no other furniture.

Ray had rented a Royal typewriter, which sat on the table, and for a chair he had put in a Pro Throne with a permanent base—the kind of seats that were just then becoming popular on bass boats. At least I could raise and lower it as I needed.

There was also a large cardboard box labeled Whitfield Pickles on the table by the typewriter. In the weeks ahead, I was to become not only totally familiar with the box, but the pickle company itself, a Montgomery-based firm that packed pickles from 1924 until 1978. The slogan on the box read, "Picked to the peak of perfection by particular pickle picking people."

Ray pointed to the pickle box. "That's the file for *Bassmaster*," he said. "I've got to answer a phone call. Good luck." Then he walked out. Just like that, I inherited a magazine, the entire contents of which were in one fairly small pickle box.

I felt like I had just stepped off the wing of an airplane without a parachute, but in truth, the feeling did not last long. As I started going through the box, glancing at handwritten stories by bass anglers, not professional writers, I realized I was looking at pure poetry. Ray had done a pretty good job of soliciting his B.A.S.S. membership to contribute to the new magazine, and I immediately decided I didn't want to rewrite it. I wanted to use their exact words.

The concept of what we were doing at *Bassmaster*—getting avid, self-taught bass fishermen who'd kept their fishing techniques secret for years to share those secrets—was totally new, but somehow it worked. Every issue became a treasure trove of information as more and more fishermen began sending me their pencil-written tricks. It was an education in itself to see how dedicated the readership was. The encyclopedia of bass fishing was just developing, and we were the ones writing it.

Bob Cobb helped promote Ray Scott's first professional bass tournament in 1967 at Beaver Lake in Arkansas, and later became the first editor of Bassmaster Magazine, *during which time he helped spread the popularity of the sport by having tournament pros tell their techniques for catching fish.* Photo courtesy of B.A.S.S.

In the first issue I produced, which was not the first true issue of *Bassmaster,* I probably wrote four or five stories, just to fill out pages. We had a four-color cover, which was a picture of me because it was the only color picture we had. Inside, we had a hodge-podge of typefaces, and not much else. Somehow, we filled up 48 pages.

In the beginning, we had four issues a year. I started a Guide Directory of B.A.S.S. members who were guides on different lakes so readers could contact them for specific information. I had another section I named Mail Call, and printed letters from readers. One early letter, from a Mrs. R. A. Reid of Chattanooga, was particularly inspiring. It said:

> Dear Sirs: My husband recently joined B.A.S.S. His last trip gave him extra pleasure because when he came to the camp with his stringer filled, a not-so-successful would-be bass fisherman commented to his companion, 'No wonder. Look at that emblem on his jacket. It's a B.A.S.S. emblem.'

After awhile we established an editorial budget, and as we increased the number of issues, we also increased the number of advertisers. I got an art director, and gradually we began receiving submissions from professional writers and photographers. Tournaments rapidly grew in importance because we were starting to create the first bass fishing "heroes," and readers demanded more and more information about their successful fishing techniques. That demand, in turn, spurred the industry to create new products. Everything fed on itself.

Bassmaster was, and still is, what's known as a "vertical" publication, in that every article relates to the same subject. Over the years *Bassmaster* became one of the most successful magazines of this type ever produced, and I credit it all to the fishermen themselves, who never hesitated to tell their fishing secrets to the rest of the nation's anglers.

It was fun and it was exciting, and even today I still have a hard time realizing it all started in a pickle box.

★ ★ ★

After moving from the editor's chair at *Bassmaster,* Cobb produced *The Bassmasters* television show for B.A.S.S. until his retirement. He and Barbara still live in Montgomery, Alabama.

Chapter Thirty-Three

J. L. "Mac" McBride: "Catching Bass and Talking about Them"

Beginning in the early 1950s and continuing for more than two decades, J. L. "Mac" McBride taught tens of thousands of eager fishermen the finer points of bass fishing through his seminars and personal appearances across 11 states. An excellent angler himself, McBride was one of the first, if not the first, fisherman to present these types of seminars, representing companies like Fenwick, Shakespeare, and Stembridge. Photo courtesy of Jenny Young.

Public speaking doesn't come easily for most, even when they can talk about their favorite subjects, but J. L. "Mac" McBride was always an exception. When he talked about his favorite subject, which was bass fishing, people everywhere listened, and in time he was so much in demand as a speaker that a typical week in his schedule often included as many as six separate seminars in two states, and all in front of packed audiences and record crowds.

This was in the early 1950s, more than a decade before the real bass fishing boom began, and many consider McBride the father of modern fishing seminars. He could talk about bass fishing because he himself was a fisherman. Born January 26, 1922, in Farmersville, Texas, his earliest memories of fishing revolved around Lake Dallas (now Lake Lewisville, north of the city of Dallas). That's when, at age six, his father would tie a rope around their waists and then they'd walk and fish around the shoreline. There were fishing seasons in those days, and Mac and his father would often go the night before opening day on May 1 and camp at the water's edge.

In 1940, he went to work as a printer for the *Dallas Morning News*, but soon afterward World War II intervened, and Mac joined the United States Coast Guard (USCG) where he served on a USCG cutter patrolling for enemy submarines. The highlights of his military service, Mac often laughed later, did not come from sinking enemy subs but rather, from catching fish to feed the cutter's crew. He didn't actually catch them, but rather, found excuses periodically to roll off one or two depth charges ("tin cans" as they were known during the war) with fuses set for just 25 feet. The shallow explosions brought hundreds of fish of all species to the surface, which the crew quickly dipped up and ate for several days.

Returning to this job at the *News* in 1946, he also took a part-time job at LB Mercantile, a sporting goods store near his home. He took his pay in fishing tackle, and soon became close friends with Neal Bond, a sales representative for the Shakespeare Company whose products Mac was selling in the store. In 1950 Bond invited him to operate the Shakespeare tackle booth at the Dallas Boat and Tackle Show, and just that easily his career as a bass fisherman, public speaker, and tackle representative began.

There weren't many bass clubs in those days, but everyone it seemed, including local Kiwanis and Lions Club organizations, made McBride a regular guest at their functions. Of course, his topic was always bass fishing, either relating one of his own personal experiences or detailing a new technique. One day in 1964 a man named Bill Stembridge came to the Shakespeare booth at the Dallas show and asked him to do speaking engagements throughout Texas to promote the new plastic worms, named Fliptails, Stembridge was making. McBride flew to Houston and did a presentation on worm fishing to a bass club, and shortly afterward, the Jim Gieseke Company, which represented and sold Stembridge's Fliptail worms, began sending him out for even more speaking tours.

By this time, Mac had enough seniority at the *Dallas Morning News* to have an annual three-week vacation, and he was using it all to give bass fishing presentations. Because Stembridge also worked for Delta Airlines, he'd simply send Mac tickets and off he'd fly. Because the bass boom had started in earnest, McBride easily fueled the excitement everywhere he went by adding trick casting demonstrations to his lectures.

Who couldn't fail to get excited watching this easy-talking, non-assuming Texas pro nonchalantly dropping plastic worms into a cup underneath a chair cast after cast? Radio and television loved him and promoted him at every opportunity; by the time he retired in 1982, Mac McBride had made more than 700 bass club appearances and hundreds of additional talks at sports shows and store promotions in 11 states.

Traditional outlets like Walmart, Kmart, and Bass Pro Shops were only a few of the places he spoke; other locations were as varied as Tom Thumb and TGY grocery stores, Gibson's Department Stores, and even the Dallas Press Club.

He taught tens of thousands of people the basics of bass fishing techniques, and as his popularity and reputation grew, he was often called to speak before civic groups, probably the first bass fisherman ever to do so. He helped design the very first Flipping rods for the Fenwick Corp. with California flipping expert Dee Thomas and taught this new technique throughout Texas and the South. Stories describing his bass fishing techniques appeared in dozens of newspapers and national magazines and on ABC NBC, and PBS affiliate television stations throughout Texas and Oklahoma.

McBride's expertise with underwater sonar helped Texas Parks and Wildlife Department officers locate fish traps used by poachers; and his work with the Izaak Walton League in promoting the catch-and-release fishing ethic helped the League earn a commendation from then President Gerald R. Ford. He taught fishing classes at Dallas-area high schools; regularly donated fishing tackle to the Boy Scouts of America;

and provided fishing experiences for orphan children of the Presbyterian Home in Waxahatchie, Texas.

Along the way, of course, McBride also found time to go bass fishing, competing in both the 1965 and 1966 World Series of Sport Fishing tournaments. These were multi-day events first organized by *Sports Illustrated* photographer Hy Peskin, and drew dozens of entrants from around the United States as well as several foreign countries. They are considered the forerunner of today's modern bass tournaments. McBride was also a charter member of the Bass Anglers Sportsman Society and during his career he competed in 22 national B.A.S.S. tournaments, finishing in the top 20 each time. He received a Distinguished Angler's Award from *Sports Afield* magazine in 1968; a Certificate of Angling Achievement from the Garcia Corp., also in 1968; and in 1972 the Fenwick Master Fisherman Award.

★ ★ ★

Like every bass fisherman, I was always anxious to fish new lakes, particularly those that other fishermen hadn't heard of, and in 1966 I learned about a place named Valley Lake, or sometimes called Lake Savoy because it was located near Savoy, Texas. It was owned by the Texas Power and Light Company and was only 1,100 acres in size, much smaller than Lake Texoma or Sam Rayburn where I had been fishing for years.

Anyway, one day I drove up from Dallas to take a look, and learned that the company did allow fishing, but only from the shore. I walked around the shore, and found a narrow stretch of water hidden by cattails that couldn't be seen from the headquarters building, so I decided to come back again and fish it from a float tube. I actually fished the lake for two years that way, and even took friends with me occasionally.

I caught quite a few bass, but nothing really big, even though the lake looked like it should hold big bass. Then one day, I sneaked into the water with a portable Lowrance depth finder. As I paddled around in my tube, I held the transducer under water with one hand and the screen in my other hand where I could see the bottom configuration. I found a drop off right at the edge of the cattails where the water fell sharply from 3 down to 16 feet; it was exactly the type of cover and depth change I'd been looking for.

Since Savoy was a power plant lake in which warm water was discharged back into the lake, I knew the very best fishing would take place during the winter months, so on February 18, 1968, I took two fishing friends with me to see if my steep ledge by the cattails really held any bass. The water was so cold my friends decided it wasn't worth the effort, but I eased in with my float tube, and almost agreed with them, too. It seemed like only a few minutes before my legs had turned numb.

I had a heavy nine-foot saltwater flyrod with a black jig tied on so I didn't do any casting. I just stuck the pole out toward the cattails and let the jig fall straight down to the very edge of the drop. I'd drawn a basic map from my depth finder study and memorized how the bottom looked, and once my jig touched the bottom, I'd just shake it.

I'd never caught a bass weighing 10 pounds or more, but in two hours I had three of them weighing 10-8, 10-7, and 10 even. I caught fifteen bass that day, and besides the three 10-pounders, I had two more weighing 9-9 and 8-2. Those five weighed 48 pounds, 10 ounces, which was the heaviest five bass catch ever weighed in Texas.

When I got out of the water, I couldn't walk back to my truck. I had to lie on my back and pump my legs like I was riding an imaginary bicycle until I could restore the circulation. We took the five heaviest fish to the *Dallas Morning News* office where the photographers took photographs that were not only published in the *News,* but also distributed nationwide by the Associated Press.

The sad thing is that the very next year Texas Power and Light Company poisoned the cattails, and I never fished it again after that. It was just a special day, and I was very lucky to be there. It certainly gave me plenty to talk about at all the seminars and speaking engagements I was doing then.

★ ★ ★

J. L. McBride died December 2, 2004, in Richardson, Texas.

Chapter Thirty-Four

Charlie Brewer: "Doing Nothing to Catch Bass"

Charlie Brewer was one of the earliest proponents of using light tackle and smaller lures to catch more bass, and developed his famous Do Nothing Slider Fishing system in the late 1960s. His original techniques have since expanded into the broader concept known as finesse fishing.

One warm summer afternoon in 1967 or 1968, a television repairman in Lawrenceburg, Tennessee, looked up from his work to see several boys walking down the street with their fishing rods and carrying a very nice stringer of bass. A lifelong fisherman himself, the repairman stepped outside to admire the catch and ask how the boys caught them.

What they showed him was like nothing the repairman had ever used before, or even thought about using: very light, limber rods and extremely small lures. For years he'd been fishing with stiff, heavier rods and big lures like Dalton Specials, River Runts, and Hellbenders, along with 12-inch plastic worms he molded himself on the kitchen stove, but catching bass this way had been getting more and more difficult each year as pressure on his favorite lakes increased.

The repairman listened to what the youngsters told him. He cut down a flyrod to about five feet to get the limber action, and he kept shortening his plastic worms until he settled on four inches. And he started catching bass again, more bass, in fact, than he'd ever caught before.

The repairman's name was Charlie Brewer, and what gradually evolved out of that fateful afternoon conversation was the first true concept of what is today known as finesse fishing, the use of extremely light action rods, very small lures, and light lines. It is one of the most popular and effective styles of bass fishing in the world today, and is practiced by many of the sport's top professional anglers.

Brewer named his technique the Slider System because of the special jigheads he created, and his presentation became known as the Do Nothing method, because all a fisherman had to do to catch bass was cast and reel the lure back very slowly, in essence, doing nothing special to attract a bass. It wasn't about the lure itself—Brewer's little plastic worms certainly did not resemble baitfish—but rather, about imitating how the baitfish acted in the water, which was generally slow and without any excessive action.

Born May 16, 1920, in Lawrenceburg, Brewer grew up in an area filled with creek and pond fishing opportunities in Lawrence and Wayne Counties, and he and his father fished them regularly. Although they were a short distance from the Tennessee River, only one of the big lakes that would play a prominent role in Brewer's later life, Wilson Reservoir, had been constructed, and Brewer and his father often visited one of Wilson's primary tributaries, Shoal Creek.

As a teenager, Brewer became extremely interested in ham radio, the amateur radio system that allowed individuals to communicate with other amateur enthusiasts all over the world. Brewer built his own radio out of junkyard parts, only purchasing one item, a vacuum tube, to make it work. In the summer of 1941 when he enlisted in the US Navy, and because of his ham radio experience he became a radioman. After the Japanese attack on Pearl Harbor, he dived into the sunken ships to salvage whatever radio equipment he could find, and later he was sent to the South Pacific, but not before he'd purchased a heavy action rod and reel to test the area's fishing.

After the war, Brewer returned to Lawrenceburg and opened Brewer's Radio & TV, selling and repairing the very first television sets in the area. At night, he'd turn on a television set in the shop's window, and townspeople would park on the street and watch, just like a drive-in movie. He was still fishing as much as possible, too, and many evenings were spent with other fishermen sitting around a backyard table whittling lures and trying to figure out how to catch more bass. He had an oar-powered Thompson wooden boat by then, too, but before every fishing trip he still had to fill the boat with water so the wood would swell and it wouldn't leak as badly.

Brewer had always been one to put his heart and soul into any endeavor he tried, and once he spoke to the youngsters that afternoon on the street, he also began studying not just bass but also the baitfish they fed upon. Those baitfish, he noticed, barely wiggled as they swam along, so the best way to make his retrieve mimic them was really to do nothing except reel his lure slowly without shaking or twitching it. That's how the Do Nothing presentation originated and got its name.

Those baitfish, he realized, just seemed to slide through the water. All he really had to do was control his speed of retrieve and the depth of his retrieve, so Brewer began experimenting with jighead designs that would let him do that while still maintaining the subtle, do-nothing action. The result was his flat, soft leadhead that could be flattened even more, or clipped with pliers to reduce weight, and thus, the Slider system was born.

For some time, Brewer had been thinking of trying to sell his new fishing tackle, which at that time consisted only of his leadhead hooks and four-inch worms, and in 1970 when he did, he named his business the Crazy Head Lure Company, because those jigheads looked like nothing any fishermen had ever seen before. Everything was done on the kitchen table, and luckily, Brewer also kept his radio and television repair shop open, because for all of that first year, he sold only $1,100 worth of tackle.

It was a hard sell, but if nothing else, Brewer was a born and determined salesman. He purchased booth space at the annual boat show in Nashville, talked area tackle reps into carrying his Crazy Head hooks and worms, and started giving seminars and fishing trips to anyone who would listen. There were interviews and even television appearances that helped spread Brewer's light tackle message, and once, after catching a big smallmouth on Wilson Lake, he telephoned a Birmingham-based photographer to come up for photos, but acceptance certainly did not happen overnight.

Then Brewer received what he considered one of the biggest publicity and marketing breaks of his life. He had sent George Pazik, the editor of a magazine named *Fishing Facts*, a photo of a seven-pound, two-ounce smallmouth bass he'd caught on his Slider, to see if Pazik would publish it. The editor wrote back and asked Brewer to write the story of that catch and his tackle, which he did. Brewer then went on to become a regular contributor to the magazine, in exchange for free advertising space.

Fishing Facts had actually been started as a four-page tip sheet named *Fishing News* by a promoter named Bill Binkelman in 1963, and it quickly became one of the most popular publications of its type. Even though it was only designed to sell fishing tackle to customers of Binkelman's sporting goods department in a retail store, within two years the *Fishing News* was being sent out to more than 40 states. Binkelman hired Pazik in 1966, and four years later Pazik took over as editor, and changed the publication into a magazine he renamed *Fishing Facts*.

Brewer, literally by chance and without any formal training as a writer, thus joined a fishing publication that would eventually share his light tackle expertise and spread the Slider name to hundreds of thousands of avid readers over the next few years. His byline joined others who would also become giants in the fishing industry, most notably Al and Ron Lindner of Brainerd, Minnesota, who themselves would go on to create their own highly successful publishing and television business with a multi-species fishing magazine named *In-Fisherman*. The Lindners would eventually develop new lures and techniques to expand fishing knowledge around the world, and Al would even win one of Ray Scott's professional B.A.S.S. tournaments, the 1977 Virginia Invitational.

The more Brewer did, the more people called him, and the easier it became to sell his finesse fishing concept. It wasn't hard to teach the concept because it was so simple, and practically without fail after a single day on the water, Brewer would have his pupil convinced of the ease of

Doing Nothing to catch bass. The pupil then helped spread the word even further. Although he had started his operation on the kitchen table, Brewer soon had to add a backyard workshop to handle the business. When he needed still more room, he moved back into his old radio and television store, and later had to build a special warehouse as Slider popularity continued to grow. While smallmouth bass were his favorite, Brewer quickly began designing additional tackle for largemouths, as well, and then for crappie.

In 1984, Brewer sold the company to his son Charlie Brewer Jr., and his wife Linda, who changed the name to Charlie Brewer's Slider Company. They have owned the firm ever since, and while they have added many new products, they continue to sell many of the very same items Brewer developed more than half a century ago.

★ ★ ★

One hot August day, I was smallmouth fishing on Pickwick Lake with one of my buddies, Inky Gilmore, and I had a surprise opportunity to promote Slider fishing to four strangers, even though we never saw them on the water. It was calm and bright, and the water was crystal clear, so overall, conditions could hardly have been worse for smallmouth fishing. Inky and I hadn't even launched our boat until two o'clock that afternoon.

We spooled on four-pound test line and trimmed our Slider heads down so they weighed almost nothing, maybe $\frac{1}{16}$ ounce or less. Then we started throwing toward a deep bluff wall where the Tennessee River channel swung in very close. Overall, we caught 13 beautiful smallmouth, 4 of them topping four pounds, broke off a couple, and released several smaller bass.

About dark we headed back to the ramp, and started talking to four fishermen who'd just spent the entire day on the lake without boating a single fish. They'd been in two modern bass boats with all the newest rods, reels, and tackle, but, I quickly noticed, all of it was big stuff like I used to use. There wasn't any finesse-type gear in their boat at all.

I gave them a complete rundown of our Slider tackle, and told them exactly how Inky and I had fished it. They listened politely, and with a real look of surprise. One of them even said that when he caught his first four-pound smallmouth, he was going to put it on the wall, but he sure wasn't going to catch it with Mickey Mouse equipment like Inky and I were using.

Well, Inky and I left those four fishermen there on the ramp, but *two years* later I got a call from them. I remembered them immediately. They'd talked it over and discussed what Inky and I had told them, then swallowed their pride and bought a bunch of Slider tackle afterall. They were calling to say they'd never caught so many smallmouth, nor had as much fun doing it.

Of course, getting calls like that were always very gratifying, and I received a lot of them. One cold day down in Hemphill, Texas, I was able to show some of the guides on Toledo Bend how effective Slider fishing is, even in cold weather, and once they tried it, I'm sure they passed it on to their clients, and maybe some of those clients passed it on to a few of their friends. To me, that was always the most effective way to market Sliders. In the beginning, it was really a foreign idea to most bass fishermen, but I could always remember my own experiences that were exactly the same.

★ ★ ★

Charlie Brewer died on April 7, 2000, after seeing his Sliders sold all over the world. In 1986 he was inducted into the Living Legends of American Sportfishing Hall of Fame, and in 1998 into the Freshwater Fishing Hall of Fame.

Chapter Thirty-Five

Jimmy Houston: "I Just Wanted to Build a Golf Driving Range"

Jimmy Houston turned his early fishing tournament success into a line of successful businesses, including television shows, six boat dealerships, and a travel agency. His television show, Jimmy Houston Outdoors, has been on the air for more than 35 years.

In today's bass fishing world, no one epitomizes the image of business success more than an angler in Cookson, Oklahoma, named Jimmy Houston. Although he has competed very successfully in both Bassmaster and FLW events since 1968, Houston is far more well known through his long-running television programs, his boat dealerships, his best-selling books, and his public appearances around the nation. He is easily one of the most well-known figures in the history of bass fishing.

Many have described this blond, mop-haired, always-smiling fisherman as a natural showman, and they're probably right, but what has really separated Houston from his peers is that he not only has a keen understanding of the business world but also a driving desire to succeed in that world. Long before he pulls the trigger on a potential business arrangement, he and his wife Chris study it from all angles specifically to see if it will make money.

Early on, Houston recognized how the fishing public liked to be entertained, and he has spent decades working very hard to provide that entertainment and creating his own image. He listens to what his fans like and don't like, and he adjusts accordingly. His habit of kissing largemouth bass before releasing them back into the water, for example, has become one of his trademarks, and is now emulated by young fishermen all over America. Houston has no idea why or exactly when he first kissed a fish, but now he does it regularly. He has fished and laughed with presidents and congressmen, and celebrities from Hollywood to Nashville beg to be on his shows.

And, of course, he is a superb bass fisherman. He has won 10 national tournaments, including Hy Peskin's final World Series of Sport Fishing in 1968, competed in 15 Bassmaster Classic world championships, and won 2 B.A.S.S. Angler of the Year titles, in 1976 and a decade later again in 1986. He began competing on the FLW Tour in 2003 and in just six years amassed winnings of more than $400,000, fishing against anglers less than half his age.

Born July 28, 1944, in San Marcos, Texas where his father was stationed in the Air Force, Houston actually grew up in Moore, Oklahoma, where the family relocated after World War II. He doesn't remember the first time he went fishing or the first fish he ever caught, but it was early in life because both uncles, his father, and his grandfather were all avid fishermen. Often those fishing trips were on Lake Tenkiller near Tahlequah, and in 1961, during Houston's senior year in high school, his parents bought a resort on Tenkiller where the teenager began fishing and even doing some guiding practically every day.

Houston describes that move as a major turning point in his life, for shortly after his graduation from Tahlequah High School the following spring, the final two days of the World Series of Sport Fishing were held on Tenkiller, and during the week of practice, many of the competitors stayed at the family's resort. At that time, the World Series of Sport Fishing was the biggest fishing event in the United States, the precursor to all the Bassmaster and FLW events of today, during which anglers competed on three different lakes and weighed in not only largemouth but also white bass and crappie.

Houston not only met and became friends with the greatest bass anglers of the day, including 1961 World Series champion Joe Krieger, Virgil Ward, Glen Andrews, and other competitors, but was also invited to go fishing with them. He didn't realize it at the time, but these greats of the sport recognized that the youngster knew Tenkiller better than they did so they used him as a guide. At the same time, they freely shared their fishing knowledge with Houston; Ward taught him worm fishing, and Krieger impressed him so much with his casting skills that Houston vowed he would learn to be that good.

Krieger had a weekly television show in Tulsa, *The Joe Krieger Sportsman Show,* which went on to air for 38 years, and Ward, who won that 1962 World Series tournament, used the victory to help launch his own *Championship Fishing* show. Looking back now, Houston firmly believes those two mentors unknowingly led him into a bass fishing career.

From that point on, Houston fished harder and more often than ever, even during his four years at Northeastern University (now Northeastern Oklahoma State University) where he earned degrees in both economics and political science. During his senior year he won a bass tournament on Fort Gibson Reservoir that qualified him for the Oklahoma State Championship at Keystone Lake, which he also won. He was 22 years old, he'd won money, trophies, and fishing tackle, had his picture in the paper, and thought it was pretty neat.

The win also qualified him for the 1966 World Series of Sport Fishing, in which he had to compete against Ward, Krieger, Andrews, and the very men who had been his mentors just four years earlier. For the event, his father bought him an Abu Garcia Ambassadeur 5000 casting reel, replacing the simple spin-cast reel he'd been using up to that point, and he spent the entire summer learning to use it. Glen Andrews won the World Series that year, but Houston finished sixth; they had taught him well.

One day in 1967, the year Houston graduated from college, a man named Ray Scott, along with Tulsa businessman Don Butler, came to the lodge to discuss a bass tournament Scott wanted to hold on Beaver Lake in Arkansas. Scott had not yet created his organization, the Bass Anglers Sportsman Society, but nonetheless, he still sold Houston's father a $10 membership. Houston did not fish Scott's first tournament (the one regret he has in his entire career), but he did fish Scott's fifth tournament, the Eufaula National, in June 1968.

He was in Tulsa selling life insurance, when he went to visit that same Don Butler, and was surprised to find Butler busy making spinnerbaits and packing tackle to fish a tournament at Lake Eufaula, Alabama, a lake Houston had never heard of. Butler was leaving at daybreak the next morning, and invited Houston to fish the event, too, but Houston refused, saying he didn't have the $125 entry fee.

Butler mentioned that Eufaula had a lot of big bass in it, and then asked if Houston could pay for the motel room, which cost $6 a night in those days. When he said he could, Butler told him the entry fee would be taken care of, and to this day, Houston isn't sure if Butler paid the $125, or if Scott simply waived it just so he could have another body on the water.

That tournament became another of the pivotal events in Houston's life. He did fish the event, actually leading it the first day with 11 bass weighing 52 pounds, 8 ounces (the limit was 15 bass per day then). He didn't know how to fish a three-day event, however. When he arrived at his spot the next day and found several other boats nearby, he simply sat in his boat and waited for three hours until they left, then caught 28 pounds of fish in just 20 minutes. The third day he was so upset and nervous he caught only a single bass, but still finished sixth; John Powell won with 132 pounds.

At that tournament, Houston met Forrest and Nina Wood, who convinced him to buy one of their Ranger bass boats, which he did, the first one in Oklahoma. In time, Houston would himself be selling more than 200 Rangers a year for Wood. For the next seven years, however, Houston devoted himself to his insurance business and fished only one or two of Scott's events each season. It wasn't until 1975 that he fished all six B.A.S.S. events, and finished third, behind Roland Martin and Ricky Green, in the Angler of the Year race. What he realized then was that he really was good enough to compete at that level of the sport.

About this same time, he began making and selling spinnerbaits, the Jimmy Houston Redman, which he sold to Sam Walton when Walton had his first 13 Walmart stores. Houston could hardly make enough of them; the lure came with a single Size 4 Colorado blade and a trailer hook, but it was the chartreuse/blue skirt that attracted his buyers. No one had seen such skirt colors before, and they bought the Redman by the thousands. In the process, the spinnerbait in all its forms, became his signature lure, and remains so today. Eventually, he sold the right to make the lure to Bill Norman, and moved on to other challenges.

He determined to win the Angler of the Year title the next year, 1976, and he devoted practically every waking moment to that goal, a trait that would later serve him well in the business world. That season he won one event, the South Carolina Invitational at Santee Cooper, and placed in the top ten in four of the six B.A.S.S. tournaments. He was competing so hard that if he did not have three or four quality bass in the livewell by nine or ten a.m., he'd get physically sick. Winning the Angler of the Year title was that important to him, to prove to himself he could do it.

As his popularity and reputation continued to grow through the years, Houston turned his business interests to writing. His first book, *The Wit and Wisdom of Jimmy Houston,* self-published in 1984, sold about 20,000 copies. It was followed in 1996 by *Caught Me A Big 'Un,* which also sold well. His *Hooked for Life* (1999), stayed near the top of the bestseller list for Christian books for months; and both his 2001 *The Reel Line* and 2012 *Catch of the Day* volumes remain extremely popular.

Over the four decades he has been in the public eye, no single angler has been as successful business-wise as Houston in meshing his own popularity with that of the sport and evolving as the sport itself has evolved. Today, of the approximately 300 requests he receives annually, Houston still makes over 100 appearances each year, largely because he feels he owes that to the sport that has been so good to him. He continues to produce and host two television shows, *Jimmy Houston Outdoors* (on the air now for 35 years and counting) and *Jimmy Houston's Adventures,* and he still fishes competitively on the FLW Tour. He was inducted into the

National Freshwater Fishing Hall of Fame in 1990, followed in 2002 by induction into the Bass Fishing Hall of Fame.

★ ★ ★

Because of the success I enjoyed in tournament fishing, both in winning the state championship several times as well as in the national events, I was receiving a lot of publicity, and was a guest on a number of television fishing shows. Then, other people started talking to me about hosting my own outdoor show. Well, I didn't care anything about hosting an outdoor show, because my insurance business was doing very well.

Still, I started thinking. It might work, so I began researching it. I spent hours studying the shows already out there, primarily those being done by Bill Dance and Roland Martin, both of whom I'd gotten to know well. I studied their production, what they did right and what I thought they did wrong. I wasn't trying to be a TV star, or even trying to make a living as a television fisherman. I looked at television with no other intention than making money at it.

Decorated angler Jimmy Houston.

I hired a production company and we shot a pilot show in 1977, financing it entirely myself. Then I signed a $103,000 contract for the producers to do a full season and syndicate the show to 30 stations. I limited myself to a potential loss that first year to $50,000; if we lost anymore, I'd get out of the television business, but we actually made a profit. We were syndicated on 32 stations around the country; the biggest mistake we made was naming the show *Bass Fishing America,* which we changed the next season to *Jimmy Houston Outdoors.* I felt like we had to promote myself as the host, and we've kept that name ever since.

The second year, we signed Blakemore Lures (now part of TTI-Blakemore Fishing Group) as a sponsor, even though they did not make any lures specifically for bass, so that let us expand to other species, and Blakemore has remained a sponsor ever since, even though we've never had a written contract. We do it all over the telephone.

In 1978 we sold the insurance agency and I became totally involved in fishing. I competed in the tournaments, I did the television show, and I made personal appearances. By now, my wife Chris had become active in bass fishing herself, competing in the professional women's circuit, Bass'n Gal, and in 1984 she qualified for the Bass'N Gals Classic championship on Elephant Butte Reservoir in New Mexico. Normally, I would try to schedule a hunting trip of some type at the same time and location as her Classics, but that year I couldn't find anything.

A friend told me there was great golf in the area, but I'd never hit a golf ball in my life. Still, he sent me a bag of clubs. After the Classic, I told Chris I wanted to buy some land so I could build my own driving range and learn how to hit a golf ball. She thought I was crazy. Still, I bought 27 acres of land on Lake Tenkiller, and I did build my driving range, but we also opened a big convenience store with eight gas pumps.

Then we built a big boat dealership on that same property, where I sold Ranger and Tracker boats, the two brands that I use. Then we opened another boat dealership in Tulsa. They both worked, so I bought a dealership in Oklahoma City, and another one in McAllister, then opened a new one in Rogers, Arkansas, and another one in Little Rock. In just a couple of years I went from one boat dealership to six, and all I had really wanted was to build a golf driving range.

Then I started a travel agency. I had a twin engine Seneca and was flying about 500 hours a year to make public appearances and shooting the television shows. The advantage, of course, was that on many public appearances and seminars, I could fly there and back in the same day.

The disadvantage was that it got to the point I was spending so much time simply administering to the plane that I began to wonder if it was really worth it. The deciding factor came one night flying back from a show in New Orleans. I'd just put the plane through its annual inspection, but when my pilot punched in Auto Pilot, it didn't work. Then, over Fayetteville, Arkansas, I started smelling something burning. For about 15 minutes none of us knew if we'd make it home or not, but fortunately, we did, and the next day I put the plane up for sale.

That's when I told my daughter Sherrie that if she'd run the travel agency, I'd send her to school to learn the business. That's what she did, and now she books a lot of flight schedules for today's bass tournament pros when they're doing their own personal appearance schedules.

★ ★ ★

Jimmy Houston and his wife, Chris, live in Cookson, Oklahoma, where they can be close to their children, Jamie and Sherrie, and their grandchildren.

Chapter Thirty-Six

Alex Langer: "The Infomercial That Changed Marketing"

Alex Langer changed forever the way fishing tackle is sold when he began selling his Flying Lure through television infomercials in 1991. The lure itself was uniquely weighted so that it would glide backward, and was sold worldwide.

Early on the morning of December 21, 1991, during the short span of 28 minutes and 30 seconds, the entire concept of fishing tackle marketing changed. That day, the very first informative television commercial, known as the infomercial, extolling the virtues of one lure, began airing on the TNN network. That lure was the Flying Lure, and that infomercial turned the fishing industry upside down.

The Flying Lure was the culmination of more than a decade of studious fishing, experimentation, and ingenuity by Boston angler Alex Langer, and his infomercial not only changed how tackle was marketed, it also changed television. Most previous infomercials had been limited to personal health products, coins, or jewelry; today, entire channels are devoted to infomercials 24 hours a day, and practically every conceivable product, from dietary supplements to pocket knives to exercise machines are featured.

Even now, lure companies still follow Langer's model when producing their own infomercials, but none have come close to achieving the same impact. During the four years the Flying Lure program aired— Langer produced a total of three different infomercials that were shown in more than 70 countries—millions upon millions of Flying Lures were sold. In just one year, more people bought the Flying Lure than any other lure in history; wherever he traveled around the world, Langer was instantly recognized and known as the "Lure Man."

Before the infomercials began airing, however, Langer struggled for several years to sell his lure, unique in the fact that with its specially weighted jig head it would glide or "fly" backward—thus the name Flying Lure—when fished on a slack line. Up to that point, basically every lure ever made had been designed to attract bass by moving forward as the angler reeled in line; if he stopped reeling, the lure either sank to the bottom or floated on the surface.

The Flying Lure, a soft plastic bait with a flat body and squid-like tail, was simple enough for beginning anglers to use, and Langer's infomercials emphasized not only how to fish the lure but also included testimonials from average fishermen who enjoyed some of their greatest successes while using the Flying Lure. Underwater film sequences illustrated exactly how the Flying Lure would glide right into the bass hangouts that were all but impossible to reach by normal casting, and of course, showed compelling footage of bass coming out of those hangouts to hit the lure.

Langer, born in Boston in 1957, had started fishing with his grandparents at an early age, but his first love then had been model rocketry. He did not really "discover" bass fishing until he was 14, when, after reading a copy of the then-popular fishing publication *Fishing Facts* he caught his very first bass with a live worm while fishing a lake on Cape Cod.

As with so many other bass fishermen, that 3 ½-pound fish opened a brand new world for the young angler, and model rockets were soon replaced with an assortment of rods, reels, and lures. Langer fished his first bass tournament at age 17, just three years later, and finished 11th after catching the biggest bass (5 ½ pounds) on the first day of the event.

He continued to fish seriously until he entered Tufts University in Boston, followed by more years of study at the University of Massachusetts where he earned a bachelor's degree in business administration. He then completed his master's degree in business administration at Boston University. Langer went to work for a computer software company but resigned after three months and started his own software business. He also started fishing again.

Years earlier, when he was 19, Langer had been completely skunked during a two-day bass tournament on Whitehall Reservoir in which the bass were hiding underneath floating islands. He knew the fish were there but had no way to get a lure to them. He drove home and put together a wild concoction of melted plastic worms, a jighead, and even a small aluminum soda can—the first steps of what would become the Flying Lure. Through college and for several years afterward he gradually but secretly perfected the lure, and eventually succeeded in getting them stocked in a local tackle store.

Still, the public did not beat a path to his door to purchase them. In fact, they slammed the door pretty decisively, until that fateful December morning in 1991.

★ ★ ★

I had taken the Flying Lure to the American Fishing Tackle Manufacturers Association (AFTMA) show in Las Vegas, renting a booth where I could show the Flying Lure to both tackle buyers as well as to the press. I met Don Meissner there, a Watertown, New York-based fisherman whose television program, *Rod & Reel Streamside*, aired on Public Broadcasting System stations. Don was one of the first anglers and members of the press who recognized what the Flying Lure actually did, and he began using and promoting it on his program.

Still, it was a grind because the lure simply was not selling. Then one day in 1989, I received a telephone call from Jim Caldwell, a television host in New York who was also dabbling in producing infomercials. Jim was not a fisherman, but someone had shown him a newspaper story about my lure and he called to ask if I would be interested in producing an infomercial with it.

I said no.

To me at that time, infomercials were get-rich-quick schemes and I did not want to be associated with them. But Caldwell was persistent, and over the next two years he called me perhaps as many as ten more times trying to persuade me to put the Flying Lure in an infomercial. Finally, I agreed to try it. After all, I'd tried marketing the lure every other way I could think of, and nothing had worked.

Caldwell and I went to a company named National Media, meeting with owners Kevin Harrington and John Turchi. National Media produced infomercials, and after viewing our little video clip of fishing with the Flying Lure, they agreed to take on the project, since they already knew Jim and his ability to sell products on television. They gave us a check for $70,000 and told us to go make an infomercial.

We flew to Key West where Jim and I talked about the Flying Lure on the waterfront in a beautiful setting. The last thing I wanted was to be on camera, but Jim knew what he was doing. We added some of Don Meissner's fishing footage, along with a few testimonials we had received. It took about six months to get everything edited, and when it finally aired I didn't even see it. Friends told me they'd seen it, including someone who'd watched it while changing her baby's diapers; I had no idea how it would be received.

Two weeks later Kevin Harrington called, and his exact words were, "The infomercial not only works, it's a stick of dynamite!" Finally, I could stop holding my breath because I knew my struggles were over. Sales took off and then held steady for nearly four years. We did a total of three infomercials, producing a new one each year.

Initially, we went to Mann's Bait Company and its production company, Eufaula Manufacturing Company, in Eufaula, Alabama, and asked them to produce the Flying Lures. They almost threw us out and we really had to work to convince them to make the lures for us, but within a short time, people in Eufaula were coming up and thanking me for giving them the work. I wish I knew how many millions of Flying Lures Eufaula Manufacturing Company produced for us.

In television, I soon learned, if something works, you copy it, and very quickly others began producing infomercials about their own fishing lures. People thought they could take any lure, wrap it into an infomercial, and make millions. At the same time, others would aggressively hunt me down and try to convince me to make an infomercial about their lure.

Finally, in 1997 I sold the patent and all rights to the Flying Lure to National Media. They, in turn, turned it over to a third party who never really knew what it was or how to market it. When they couldn't sell it, they threatened to sue me. We eventually worked out our differences and I received my patent and all production rights back, and at some point, after making some improvements, I'm going to re-introduce the Flying Lure through some new infomercials and on the web.

In retrospect, the life lesson to be learned from the Flying Lure experience is probably that all things happen in their own time. Had I known the success the Flying Lure would have through the infomercials, I certainly wouldn't have wasted my time before Jim convinced me to do the infomercial, but if we had, who knows if it would have worked out the same. Overall, I give Jim Caldwell a lot of credit for the Flying Lure's success. He was certainly the right partner for me at the time.

Fortunately, through it all, I have never lost my love of bass fishing, and I still fish once a week at the very same Whitehall Reservoir that has the floating islands where the whole story started. And yes, I still catch fish there with my Flying Lures.

★ ★ ★

Alex Langer still lives in Boston where he owns and operates several radio stations. He fishes with a completely original 1973 Bassmaster Classic Ranger boat, one of four such Classic boats (1971, 1972, 1973, and 1974) he has purchased over the years.

THE TROPHIES

Chapter Thirty-Seven

The Search for Giants

Mark Davis, a highly successful tournament angler, holds up a trophy largemouth weighing more than 11 pounds he caught during competition at Falcon Lake in Texas. Tournament pros do not catch many fish this size due to their fast-paced style of fishing, in contrast to the slow presentations normally required for trophy bass.

It was a Thursday morning, and it was raining. The weather, however, did not stop George Perry and his friend Jack Page from spending the morning fishing a shallow backwater slough in a wet, wooden rowboat. It was 1932 and during those Depression days in rural Georgia men like Perry and Page weren't fishing for fun; they were fishing for their dinner.

The two men had one rod and reel that had cost $1.33, and they'd spooled the reel with 19 cents worth of line from a mail-order catalog. On the line they'd tied the one lure they brought with them, a metal-lipped floating/diving plug named the Fin Tail Shiner, produced by the Creek Chub Bait Company in Garrett, Indiana.

As the story is told, the two men fished for several hours without drawing a single strike. Then, on one of Perry's casts near a partially submerged log, the day turned into one of the most successful bass fishing trips in history. The bass that hit weighed 22 pounds, 4 ounces, a new world record that would ultimately stand unbroken for the next 77 years. Friends convinced them to weigh it on a local grocer's meat scale, which they did at J.J. Hall & Co. in Helena before Perry and his family ate it that evening.

Over the ensuing 40 or so years, relatively little attention was paid to Perry's record, possibly because the largemouth was not America's favorite fish during that period. The Creek Chub Bait Company, whose annual catalog regularly featured letters and photographs showing big fish caught by satisfied customers, did not mention Perry until years later.

In their 1925 edition however, the company had mentioned a Florida fisherman named Fritz Friebel, who, in May 1923, caught a 20-pound, 2-ounce largemouth bass from Big Fish Lake that had more or less established the world record Perry's fish broke. Friebel never had his fish weighed officially (his son Walter helped him weigh it) but at least he did photograph it. *Field & Stream*, which in 1911 had established its annual Big Fish Contest, had noted Friebel's catch in a 1924 issue, but even they did not recognize Perry's fish until 1934, two years after he caught it.

Keeping track of record fish, particularly largemouth bass, just did not have a very high priority in those days. Some also speculate Creek Chub omitted Perry in their catalog because they instead highlighted another world record set that same year for a much more popular fish, a muskellunge from Lake of the Woods, Ontario, weighing 58 pounds, 4 ounces. Even Friebel had had to share catalog space with other anglers.

From a fisherman's point of view, no one spent a lot of time thinking about breaking Perry's record for the next 41 years, until June 23, 1973, when a California fisherman named David Zimmerlee landed a bass weighing 20 pounds, 15 ounces from Miramar Reservoir near San Diego. Not only did Zimmerlee's fish come just as bass fishing in America was starting its rocketing rise in popularity, but it was also the first bass that officially broke the 20-pound barrier since Perry had caught his, and it was only the third 20-pounder ever recorded, Friebel's being the first. Suddenly, anglers nationwide realized a new world record might be possible, after all.

Nowhere was this fever ignited stronger than in California, and especially in the numerous small lakes in and around San Diego where the larger-growing strain of Florida bass had been stocked since the spring of 1959. The first of those fish came directly from the hatchery in Tallahassee and were released in Miramar, Upper and Lower Otay, Murray, San Vicente, and several other lakes. By 1969, just a decade later, Miramar produced a bass weighing 15 pounds, 4 ounces, and fishermen plying the other lakes had recorded 42 other bass topping 9 pounds.

Because Zimmerlee's bass made national news, anglers from throughout the country rushed to California in hopes of breaking Perry's record, or if not, to at least catch the biggest bass of their lives. Trophy bass fishing was on its way to becoming part of the American culture.

Florida had long been the place most anglers had expected to produce the next world record. This was not because the state regularly turned out "high teen" bass, but rather, due to the state's heavy promotion of its bass fishing opportunities. After all, the Sunshine State offered hundreds of lakes, both manmade and natural, that supported healthy bass populations; the fish living in them had excellent habitat and basically year-round warm weather so they would grow year-round; and most importantly, Florida had the purest strain of the largest-growing subspecies of bass, *Micropterus salmoides floridanus*, that other states were asking for, including California. Florida *had* produced huge bass years before Perry caught his record, reminded the publicists, so there really was no reason another fish that big, or larger, wasn't swimming in one of the state's lakes.

Florida had not—and still has not—produced any 20-pound largemouths since Friebel's fish, but the state's waters could certainly give up bass half that size, which happened with amazing regularity. Even 10-pound bass were heavier than anything most visiting fishermen had ever caught, so this is what the state promoted and thus the reputation of Florida's trophy bass fishing continued to spread. When professional bass guide John McClanahan led one of his clients to a 16-pound largemouth in the spring of 1976, interest—and business—spread even faster, especially when it was learned the McClanahan bass might have weighed as much as 19 pounds had it been caught a few weeks earlier before it had spawned.

The following year, however, 162-acre Miramar produced another bass nearly as heavy as Zimmerlee's, a 19-pound, 2-ounce giant, as well as another bass weighing 18 pounds, 4 ounces. Not far away, Lake San Vicente (1,069 acres) gave up a bass weighing 18 pounds, 9 ounces. Because biologists had determined Zimmerlee's fish to be just 12 years old, it was easy to think another fish just a year or so older could add enough weight to break Perry's record, so trophy fishing fever soared even higher.

Different companies began to offer lucrative prizes to the angler who caught a new world record using one of their rods, reels, lines, or hooks. The Florida-based Big Bass Record Club offered as much as $8 million to any club member whose bass was determined to be a new world record; and in Alabama, the Daiichi/Tru-Turn/X-Point Company of Wetumpka, offered $1 million if the lucky fisherman caught the record bass on one of its hooks.

Then Texas entered the big bass race in 1980 when a fisherman named Jim Kimbell caught a 14.09-pound, 9-ounce bass from Lake Monticello; the state had been stocking Florida largemouths since the early 1970s, and Monticello was one of the original lakes to receive those fish. His fish broke the state record of 13 pounds, 8 ounces, which had stood for 37 years. When Mark Stevenson caught a 17-pound, 10-ounce bass from Lake Fork six years later, the resulting publicity literally started a multimillion-dollar stampede to the 27,000-acre lake that continues today and has attracted bass fishermen from around the world.

Stevenson's bass, which he subsequently named Ethel, was the first 17-pound fish ever caught in Texas, and he caught it in a lake specifically designed and strictly managed by the Texas Parks and Wildlife Department to produce trophy largemouths. He later sold Ethel to Bass Pro Shops in Springfield, Missouri, for $25,000, but not before donating her as the first fish for the Parks and Wildlife Department's new ShareLunker Program.

Realizing not only the difficulty in maintaining a trophy bass fishery but also the long-term economic value of establishing such fisheries throughout the state, the ShareLunker Program was created to allow biologists at the Texas Freshwater Fisheries Center in Athens to spawn large female bass under controlled conditions, then restock those fry into other lakes. Only bass weighing 13 pounds or more are accepted into the program, and after spawning, the original fish is either returned to the angler or to the lake where it was caught.

To a trained geneticist trying to determine which traits might be passed on from one generation to the next, simple spawning and restocking practices might seem very rudimentary, but American bass fishermen have certainly reaped benefits from the program, now more than a quarter-century later. More than a million offspring have been stocked in Texas waters through the ShareLunker program and more than 60 lakes have now produced some 500 bass weighing 13 pounds or more that have been donated.

Major corporations, understanding the nationwide interest in trophy bass fishing—at least 75 of the donated big bass have been caught by visiting anglers from nearly two dozen states—have helped sponsor the Share-Lunker program since its inception, including the Budweiser division of Anheuser-Busch as well as Toyota Motor Company. The Freshwater Fisheries Center, built largely from funds raised by the city of Athens itself, performs additional fisheries research, including helping develop new genetic fingerprinting techniques that make it possible to identify specific ShareLunker bass and their individual offspring that make it easier to determine if there is a specific gene that influences growth differences.

Although Texas can be considered one of the nation's leaders in specific trophy largemouth research, California remains the leader in overall trophy bass production. Of the top 25 biggest bass ever officially weighed, including Perry's 1932 fish and Friebel's 1923 fish, the Golden State can claim 20 of them. California can also claim 9 of the 12 bass over 20 pounds that have been caught. In Texas, Mark Stevenson's 17-pound, 10-ounce bass, Ethel, stood as the state record until 1992 when it was surpassed by an 18.18-pound Lake Fork bass caught by Barry St. Clair, which is still the heaviest bass ever recorded in the state.

California had forever solidified its claim to trophy bass supremacy even more strongly in the years preceding St. Clair's 18-pounder, and in the process put another big bass lake on the map. A veteran big fish hunter named Ray Easley had caught a 21.2-pound bass from Lake Casitas, a beautiful 2,800-acre lake north of Ventura, in March 1980. His catch quickly diverted attention away from the tiny San Diego lakes, but on January 8, 1989, still another California reservoir moved into the spotlight.

This was Castaic, a deep, clear 2,235-acre reservoir just 35 miles north of Los Angeles, where on that cool winter day, Dan Kadota brought a 19.04-pound fish to the scales. It wasn't Kadota's bass that made Castaic famous, but what followed. Barely a year later, on February 4, Leo Torres pushed the Castaic record up to 20.86 pounds, but his mark lasted only a month, before being eclipsed by Robert Crupi, who brought in a 21.01-pounder on March 9.

Truly, a year-class of monster bass had come of age that spring at Castaic. Mark Balloid caught a 19.50-pound bass there in late May, but it barely raised an eyebrow, given what had already been brought to the scales. Zimmerlee's 1973 bass had been pushed into the background, but even Krupi's 21-pounder was only a forecast of what was to come. On March 5, 1991, Michael Arujo weighed in a 21.75-pound fish at Castaic, and a week later, Krupi came in with a 22.01-pounder, just barely missing Perry's world record. The area where he caught his two giants is still known as Krupi's Cove.

California fishermen, of course, had known of the quality of fish swimming in Castaic's waters, but visiting anglers from other states had been discouraged at trying their luck, not only because of the lake's depth and water clarity, but also because of the unusual regulations governing the lake. When the parking lot is full, for instance, the lake is frequently closed to any additional anglers; some of them wait patiently in line for hours, as each time one vehicle leaves the parking area, another is allowed to enter. Another rule many visiting anglers aren't accustomed to is that many California reservoirs, including Castaic, are open only from sunrise to sunset.

Although several more 20-pounders have been caught in California since Krupi weighed his 22.01-pound fish, none have come from Castaic, nor has St. Clair's Texas record from Lake Fork been seriously challenged. Still, the interest in trophy bass fishing has never dimmed, nor has the challenge of breaking Perry's record.

On July 2, 2009, Perry's 77-year-old record was broken, at least in the eyes of purists. A 34-year-old Japanese fisherman, Manabu Kurita, caught a bass weighing 22.3106 pounds while fishing in Lake Biwa in southern Japan. Perry's bass weighed 22.2500 pounds, so while Kurita's bass is technically heavier than Perry's, it did not weigh the full two ounces more as required by the International Game Fish Association, which certifies record fish. Thus, in the record books, Kurita and Perry are listed as dual holders of the world record.

A dedicated angler who had previously caught a Lake Biwa bass topping 18 pounds, Kurita has reported seeing bass swimming there that are much larger than his record largemouth. In April 2010 he had even come to California and fished some of the famous San Diego lakes with well-known trophy bass fishermen to learn new fishing techniques he might use back home on Lake Biwa; and in January 2011 the Yamaha Marine Group, a world leader in the manufacture of outboard engines and owner of the popular Skeeter line of bass fishing boats, began sponsoring him in his attempt to catch one of those larger bass and put his name alone at the top of the world record list.

Chapter Thirty-Eight

Bill Baab: "Searching for George Perry"

George Perry caught his 22-pound, 4-ounce world record largemouth on a rainy June morning in Montgomery Lake, Georgia, a record that stood for more than 75 years. Perry was reluctant to talk about his record catch, and even family members knew little about it. Photo courtesy of Bill Baab.

Early one evening in 1959 after dinner at Bennie's Red Barn on Georgia's St. Simon's Island, a young, still wet-behind-the-ears reporter named Bill Baab met the most famous bass fisherman in the world, George Perry. As a member of a writers group invited to tour part of the state's Golden Isles, the meeting with the man who had caught the world record largemouth bass, 22 pounds, 4 ounces, on June 2, 1932, came as a complete surprise, and as Baab recalls, none of the writers, himself included, asked Perry any truly pertinent questions about the record catch.

That chance meeting was the only time Baab ever saw Perry, but over the next several decades, no one, not even Perry's family, learned more about the man or his fish than the outdoor editor of *The August Chronicle*. As bass fishing began its huge popularity climb in the 1970s and Perry's catch evolved into the most hallowed fishing record of all time, no one conducted more research and did more to fill in the gaps or correct the errors of that fateful June day than Baab.

His book, *Remembering George W. Perry*, (The Whitefish Press, 2010) is not only the most definitive study ever done on Perry, it is itself a remarkable study of determination and often difficult research that covered thousands of miles of travel, dozens of personal interviews, and more than a few major revelations that changed how the world now views the famous catch. It was Perry's own son, George L. (Dazy) Perry, who asked Baab to write the book because he thought Baab knew more about his father than he did.

Born January 29, 1935, in Glenside, Pennsylvania, Baab discovered writing before he really discovered bass fishing. One day in the fifth grade, he was given the assignment in English class to write an essay about one of his favorite books, so he chose *The Adventures of Happy Jack*, a children's story about a squirrel written by Thornton W. Burgess, author of the famous Peter Cottontail stories. Baab won $5.00 for his essay, and while it was the first time he was ever paid for his writing, it didn't exactly set him on the path to a journalism career.

That didn't come until he joined the staff of *The Augusta Chronicle* as a copy clerk in 1955 when he was 20. He'd always been a voracious reader, and during his second year at the *Chronicle* the Sunday editor asked Baab if he'd help write some book reviews, which he did. Then the assistant sports editor asked if he would take football game calls on Friday nights; Baab did that, too, and soon he was writing about high school football. He moved to the State News desk where he wrote features for the farm editor. Then, for the Outdoors Department he started a column, "Boating with Bill Baab," which ran each week.

He left the *Chronicle* in 1960 for brief stints with the Georgia Game and Fish Department and then as the sports editor at the *Thomasville (Ga.) Times Enterprise*, but when the *Augusta Chronicle* called in July 1964 and offered him the job of outdoor editor, he quickly accepted. He remained there until his retirement in January 2000, but even in retirement Baab remains the *Chronicle's* fishing editor.

Throughout the years, he never forgot about George Perry, and in 1983 when he learned the state of Georgia planned to erect a historical marker describing Perry's record bass, Baab began researching the man in earnest. He and his wife Bea traveled to Brunswick where they met Perry's widow Pauline along with several other family members and friends. Later that year, he met Perry's son Dazy, starting a friendship that continues to this day.

In 2007, to celebrate the 75th anniversary of the record catch, a new marker was erected, and because by then Baab had become perhaps the most knowledgeable man in the world about Perry and the fish, Dazy asked him to write the book about his father. That book was published in 2010, culminating more than 25 years of research, but even with its publication, Baab continued to search for answers to lingering questions about Perry, his fish, and especially about Perry's companion that day, Jack Page.

★ ★ ★

Even with my years of studying the history of Perry and the world record bass, I honestly had no idea of where to start this new line of research, because I didn't want to write about the fish, but rather, about the man who caught the fish. Just who was George Perry? I wanted to find out. I had actually been scheduled to interview Perry in 1968, due to increasing interest in the record, but something came up and I wasn't able to make it. Then, on January 23, 1974, he was killed in a plane crash and all chances for any future interviews were lost.

Dazy had never really talked to his father about the fish, but he did have a list of some of his father's friends around the state, people who had grown up with George or flown with him, so I began contacting them, and they often led me to other friends. I, of course, did not know any of them, but once I explained what I was doing, all were excited and really helped me.

Once I began these interviews, and I did all of them personally rather than by telephone, Perry's personality quickly became apparent. Many of his friends did not even know he had caught the fish. He was not interested in talking about it or sharing information about it. Even his wife Pauline knew nothing about it. When I spoke to George's sister Rubye, who was there when he brought the fish home, she only remembered that they ate it.

I was somewhat surprised that Perry went to such extremes to avoid talking about his world record, but I kept reminding myself that in those

Depression days, Perry was a poor farmer living in a house with no electricity or any amenities. He was proud that he caught the fish, but only because of its food value. In fact, he later lost his farm because he didn't make enough money to pay the taxes on it.

The only reason we know about Perry at all today is because one of his fishing friends insisted he weigh the fish and enter it in *Field & Stream* magazine's annual fishing contest, which he did, and which he won. *Field & Stream* was the keeper of fishing world records in those days, and that's how Perry's record was established. The magazine's records of that era have disappeared, so I was never able to actually see them, but Dazy has the certificate showing Perry actually won their contest a second time two years later with a bass weighing 13 pounds, 14 ounces, which likely also came from Montgomery Lake where he caught the record.

Everything I'd read about the actual fishing trip on Montgomery Lake that day mentioned that it was raining and that the ground was too wet to plow, so George went fishing. I contacted the Old Farmer's Almanac Company (Yankee Publishing in Dublin, New Hampshire) and had them check the weather in south Georgia on June 2, 1932, and they confirmed it had been raining that day. Later, I read a local newspaper of June 2 and not only was it raining but a tornado had touched down just north of the lake and destroyed a church. George and his partner Jack Page probably didn't know about the tornado until afterward because they were deep in the swamp and surrounded by tall cypress trees.

I made my first visit to Montgomery Lake in 1983, and again, I didn't know quite what to expect. It's an oxbow of the Ocmulgee River, and during Perry's time whenever the river rose, it overflowed into the lake and actually restocked it. Old-timers whom I later interviewed who had fished the lake told me it was probably a mile to a mile and a half long and perhaps half a mile wide. It was probably a great place to fish, and Perry actually kept his wooden boat pulled up on the bank there.

When I visited the lake, the entrance off the Ocmulgee had long ago silted in and the lake had shrunken to perhaps a quarter mile wide and it was much, much shorter. On a good day it might have been six or eight feet deep, and it was filled with cypress stumps, not trees. No one, not even Perry himself, would likely give it much attention today.

One of the most surprising things I learned really happened by accident. Perry's lure that day had always been described as a Wigglefish, made by the Creek Chub Bait Company. Even Creek Chub believed Perry had used a Wigglefish that day, and in October 1973, they sent one to an outdoor writer who planned to interview Perry for *Bassmaster* magazine. Thankfully, the writer made a tape recording of that interview. When my fellow writer and book author Monte Burch obtained that tape while researching his own trophy bass book, *Sowbelly*, he realized Perry had been recorded naming his lure that day as a Creek Chub Fin Tail Shiner.

Monte immediately contacted me, and when I heard the tape myself, I was amazed. Like everyone else, I had always believed Perry had used a Wigglefish. The lures are distinctly different, however. The Fin Tail Shiner was introduced in 1924 and featured both fins and tail made of rubber. The Wigglefish, by contrast, was actually a jointed lure.

Another thing that surprised me in my research was how beloved a man Perry was. He had learned to fly and loved airplanes, so when the manager's job at the local Brunswick Air Park became available, he applied and was accepted. He loved teaching others, especially young people, how to fly. Even those who just landed there for a short time to refuel have mentioned how well they were treated, and that George always greeted them with a smile on his face. In fact, in every photograph I have of him, or have seen of him, he's smiling. He was definitely a positive type of person.

Of course, everyone, myself included, had always asked whatever happened to Perry's fishing partner that day, Jack Page. If ever a person dropped out of history and disappeared, it seemed to be Page. Even the members of Perry's family with whom I spoke knew absolutely nothing about him.

I personally believe Page and Perry may have had some type of argument that ended their friendship. After all, when he won the two *Field & Stream* fishing contests, Perry collected some nice prizes, including not only a new rod and reel but also a shotgun, camp stove, and other items. As far as we know, he never shared any of this with Page. By the time the fishing community became interested in Page's side of the story, he was gone.

My book about Perry was published in 2010, and in June 2013, on the 81st anniversary of the record catch, I received an e-mail with a photo attachment. The e-mail was not signed, so I had no idea who sent it; all it said was that a friend had told him he needed to send me the picture. When I opened the photo and saw it, I couldn't believe what I was looking at—a photo dated June 2, 1932, showing a young man with a

This photo was sent to Bill Baab, the country's foremost historian on the life of George Perry and his world record catch, by the son of Jack Page, Perry's fishing companion the day Perry caught his 22-pound, 4-ounce record, and shows Perry with the fish. Photo courtesy of Bill Baab.

huge largemouth bass. I am certain that young man is George Perry holding the world record.

I e-mailed the sender a long list of questions. The sender turned out to be Jacob Page, Jack Page's son, and the photo was one of a set of pictures he had recently found in an old abandoned tobacco barn his father had owned in northern Florida. He had never been close to his father, who died in the 1950s, so he knew almost nothing about the record fish or his father's role that day.

I e-mailed back again with more questions and asked for a chance to interview him personally, but the e-mail bounced, as have all others since to that address. Jacob would be in his late 70s now, and he just did not want the publicity or to get involved. After all these years, I was so close to answering the final question of that fateful day, and it slipped away.

Still, the entire experience of searching for George Perry was extremely rewarding to Bea and myself. We met some wonderful, wonderful people, and it was exciting to uncover the personality and life of the man most of us consider the most famous bass fisherman in the world.

★ ★ ★

Bill Baab and his wife of 47 years, Bea, live in Augusta, Georgia, where he continues to write as the fishing editor of *The Augusta Chronicle*, as well as about another longtime hobby, collecting old bottles. And, of course, he's always searching for new information about George Perry.

Chapter Thirty-Nine

Jed Dickerson: "I Didn't Realize How Large She Was"

California big bass expert Jed Dickerson holds "Dottie," a bass that officially weighed 21 pounds, 11 ounces when he caught her in May 2003. Dickerson named her Dottie because of a black mark on one gill plate; she was easily identified when Dickerson's close friend Mac Weakley caught her again in 2006 when she weighed 25 pounds, 1 ounce. Weakley released her because he had foul-hooked the fish. Photo courtesy of Jed Dickerson.

Only in a few instances has a trophy bass been caught, weighed, and released, only to be caught again months or even years later after the fish had gained additional weight and become more impressive. Still more unusual is catching the same bass a third time years later when she weighed even more, and rarest of all is when the fish is caught that third time, she shatters the 74-year-old world record of 22 pounds, 4 ounces.

This is exactly what happened to a trio of California's most skilled and experienced big bass hunters on the nation's most storied trophy lake between the years 2001 and 2006, and a giant bass they named Dottie. No trophy fish has been as well-documented as Dottie, as each angler who caught her carefully recorded her weight and photographed her before she was released. In the end, when Dottie was found floating dead in the water, she was thoroughly analyzed by fisheries' scientists who determined her to be an amazing 17 years old.

Officially, Dottie's story began in 1991, when she was spawned as one of thousands of eggs in a shallow nest in Lake Dixon, a 60-acre lake in Escondido. A water supply lake for the City of San Diego, Dixon was also a local fishing mecca because of its two-story fishery of deep water rainbow trout and shallow water largemouth bass. The lake was already producing bass in the 12- to 15-pound range, but its reputation as the potential home of the next world record was still several years in the future.

In 1991, one of the local fishermen who would eventually play a major role in Dottie's story, Jed Dickerson, wasn't thinking about catching one of the biggest bass in the world. He didn't even live in California then; rather, he was in Melbourne Beach, Florida, and more often than not his thoughts were on surfing. Born November 20, 1972, in Newport Beach, Dickerson's family had moved to Escondido when he was a toddler, and a few years later, after school and on weekends, his parents would drop him at Dixon to spend the day trout fishing. His companions were two other boys who would also eventually play a huge role in Dottie's life, Mac Weakley and Mike Winn.

The boys fished almost exclusively for trout, which were stocked regularly in Dixon by the California Fish and Game Commission, but each spring as the bass began to move into shallow water to spawn, they'd try to catch one, but without any real success.

When he was 16, Dickerson moved to Florida where he continued to fish in both fresh- and saltwater. Even though he had access to numerous small lakes and ponds in the Melbourne Beach area, big bass still eluded him. Five years later, in 1993 when he was 21, Dickerson returned to Escondido, and although his job as a carpet layer kept him busy, he never lost interest in bass fishing, nor did he ever lose touch with Weakley and Winn.

It wasn't until 2001 that he really became seriously interested in bass fishing, and more specifically, in catching big bass. He was on Dixon, fishing for trout with a small Acme Kastmaster Spoon on two-pound test line, when a fish hit. At first Dickerson thought he'd hooked a big trout, but it turned out to be an 11-pound bass. Once he held that fish, and realizing that there were even larger bass all around him in the lake, he became determined to figure out how to catch them.

A short time later that spring, on April 21, an angler named Mike Long caught a bass on a swimbait in Lake Dixon weighing 20 pounds, 12 ounces. Long was already an experienced trophy bass fisherman—he would go on to catch more than 80 bass topping 15 pounds during the next decade—and the 20-pound, 12-ounce giant he caught that day was Dottie.

The fish had a very noticeable black spot under its right gill plate and red markings at the base of her tail. Long, because of his experience in catching and handling big bass, noticed the unusual dark marking, but did not name the fish. He continued to fish—and catch—giant bass in several of the lakes around San Diego, but he never forgot the tell-tale dark spot on the 20-pounder.

One afternoon not long after Long's catch, Dickerson and Mike Winn were fishing on Dixon when they both saw a huge bass swimming by their boat. Dickerson estimated the fish to weigh 15 to 20 pounds, and it just helped fuel the flames for both of them to learn more about catching giants that size. They spent hours talking with another accomplished trophy bass hunter, John Kerr, and after watching Kerr catch a 13-pounder the following spring, Dickerson started fishing Dixon every day. His learning curve was a steep one, however, and the lessons learned did not come easy.

That March, he finally caught an 11-pounder, and on another day, after spending hours casting to a much larger bass and repeatedly catching only the smaller male, Dickerson finally left to go to work. Another fisherman moved in and caught the fish, which weighed 18-11.

His breakthrough finally came on April 24, when he got another chance. It was a cloudy, drizzling day, and he found a big bass that hit before the male could interfere. The bass weighed 15-8, but while it provided a huge shot of confidence, Dickerson's education wasn't over. Later that spring he found a much larger bass that hit but broke free in Dixon's thick milfoil. That fish was so big Dickerson's legs were shaking as he sat in the boat wondering what had just happened.

The year 2003 was a different type of year, as Dixon's truly big bass did not move shallow in March as they normally did. Some 13- and 14-pounders were caught, but although Dickerson fished the lake every day, he did not catch any really big bass until the end of May. That's when the lake entered the most productive big bass period in its history, and Dickerson and Dottie met officially for the first time.

★ ★ ★

On April 17, one of the few days I took off from fishing the lake, Mac caught a 17-pounder, and it got us all excited because up to that point we just weren't seeing any really big bass. Then, I started noticing one particularly big bass in the same area day after day. It wasn't on a bed and it wouldn't hit a lure, but it was huge and I started looking for it every day. I thought it could be a world record.

On May 20 the bass finally showed up on a bed. It was the biggest bass I'd ever seen, and Mac caught it. The fish weighed 19 pounds, and even though by then I'd seen a lot of big fish, it was hard to believe a bass could get much larger. A few days later Mac told me he and Mike had seen another bass even bigger, but I was skeptical. On May 27 I went out and caught a 10-pounder, and the next day I was fishing for a 12-pounder when all of a sudden the fish spooked and came to the surface right in front of me. Following it was a bass that looked big enough to eat the 12-pounder. It was absolutely huge.

The next morning, I returned to that spot but there wasn't a fish around. I eased around a corner, and found a big fish, a minimum of 17 pounds, ready to spawn in three feet of water. That fish was probably the smartest, wariest bass I've ever seen, because the instant my jig would hit the water, she'd disappear and not come back for an hour or longer. I'd just leave my lure there and wait, but I never caught that fish, and neither did anyone else that year.

By now, Mac and I were fishing several different lakes looking for big bass, and on May 30 on Lake Poway I caught a 12-pounder, and called Mac and Mike, who were fishing on Dixon. They were seeing a lot of activity, so I left Poway and went over to Dixon that afternoon. I got a rental boat and hadn't gone 10 feet when I saw a big fish down in the weeds, lit up like a green pumpkin. It was a big bass, but when I made a cast, it swam away.

I waited for it to return, but when it didn't come back, I pulled up my anchors and eased away to look for another fish. Then, I changed my mind and eased back to the same spot. The big bass had returned, but again, when I cast, she took off. This time, however, when she did, I saw a small male bass in a hole in the milfoil start butting her, as if to drive her to his nest. I'd seen him before, and there had never been a female on his nest.

Early the next morning, Mack, Mike, and I were all on the water the moment the lake opened, and I went straight to the nest with the little male. It was a five foot by five foot hole in the grass about 20 feet deep that you'd never notice if you didn't know what to look for, and there in the middle of it was the giant bass. It was a gray, cloudy day with a slight southwest wind so the fish was hard to see, but even so, to me she didn't look as big as Mac's 19-pounder.

I didn't want to drop my anchors so I let the wind drift me by the hole. I pitched out a swimbait as I drifted by, and the bass swam away, but then I saw her charging back like a freight train, but she didn't take the

Lake Dixon in San Diego, California, where Jed Dickerson caught his giant bass.

bait. I made several more drifts the same way without any hits. Finally, on my fifth drift, she went nose-down on the swimbait and took it, and I set the hook as hard as I could. She went right through the milfoil, and I just kept cranking my reel. The fish came to the surface and right to the boat and I just scooped her up. I didn't realize how large she was because I was still thinking of Mac's big bass a few days earlier, but when they came up to see the fish, they knew instantly that it was larger.

We put the fish on the scales immediately, and Mac and several others said the scales went down to 22 pounds, 7 ounces, which would be a new world record, but it took a game warden more than an hour to get to the lake to make the weight official, and during that time the fish lost some of her eggs and some of her stomach content. When we finally did get an official weight, it was recorded at 21 pounds, 11 ounces, just 9 ounces under the world record. I honestly don't know if she was a world record when we weighed her the first time.

I put her on a stringer and tied her to a pier piling on the dock, but the fish got all tangled up, and Mike Winn stripped down to his shorts, dived in, and untied her. In all the excitement, we saw the dark marking by her right gill plate, and that's when we named her Dottie. Mike Long also identified her as the same fish he'd caught two years earlier when she weighed 20-12. After photos, I released her back into Dixon.

On March 20, 2006, nearly three years later, Mac caught Dottie again, and this time she weighed 25 pounds, 1 ounce, enough to shatter George Perry's record of 22-4. The problem was, Mac had accidentally foul-hooked the fish below the dorsal fin. Both Mike and I urged him to submit the fish to the IGFA for official world record certification, but instead, Mac released her without ever applying to the IGFA. To me, his fish is the world record bass.

After that, we knew the next time Dottie was caught, she would be the world record, and people from all over the world flocked to Dixon to try to catch her. I went every day for four months during the spring spawning season for the next two years, and saw her only once more, swimming with two smaller males.

On Friday, May 8, 2008, I had just left the water when I received a phone call from Jim Dayberry, one of the Ranger supervisors at Lake Dixon, who told me they'd just found Dottie floating on the surface. I met them at the dock and immediately identified her with the dark markings below her gill plate. She weighed 19 pounds then, and appeared to have just completed spawning, so she left us with the possibility there may well be another world record fish swimming in Dixon in a few years. I'm actually glad no one ever caught her again.

★ ★ ★

Jed Dickerson still fishes Lake Dixon but not with the enthusiasm of the decade he spent chasing the possible world record. In fact, if he sees someone on the water struggling to catch a big bass, he goes out to help them. He and his family live in Carlsbad, California.

Chapter Forty

Dean Rojas: "I was So Excited I Could Hardly Breathe"

*Professional tournament fisherman Dean Rojas sold peanuts and popcorn at
professional baseball and football games in San Diego before becoming one of
America's most successful anglers. Like so many others, he caught his first bass at
an early age and was hooked.*

In the world of trophy bass fishing, emphasis has always been placed on the weight of one individual fish, and early on in the sport, 10 pounds became the standard by which trophies were measured. Some lakes always produced more bass in double-digit sizes than others, including individual fish actually topping 20 pounds and flirting with the world record weight of 22 pounds, 4 ounces. A handful of anglers with regular access to these particular lakes, most notably in southern California and including highly skilled fishermen like Bill Murphy, Mike Long, Jed Dickerson, Mac Weakley, Bob Crupi, and others, became dedicated trophy bass fishermen specializing in catching giant fish.

Rarely, however, are really big bass caught during tournament competition, and the reasons are easy to understand. Pure trophy bass fishing is almost a world of make-believe, because of the variables involved. It is almost always slow, deliberate fishing, in which anglers may remain in one spot for hours waiting for a single bite. Timing and weather conditions are critical, and experienced trophy hunters choose their days on the water with care. In essence, they're only after one fish.

By contrast, tournament fishing is fast-paced, with the immediate goal of catching a five fish limit of bass, regardless of size, usually taking top priority. The fishermen might move often and sometimes visit as many as 20 different spots a day. Most importantly, however, tournament pros fish regardless of the weather conditions and wherever the competitions are being held. They do not get to choose the lakes or the time of year to fish them.

Of course, some big bass are caught in tournament competition, as witnessed by Mark Tyler's 14-pound, 9-ounce bass from the California Delta during a 1999 Bassmaster tournament, or the 13-9 fish Mark Menendez caught during another Bassmaster event at Richland Chambers Lake in Texas in 1997. During the 2008 Bassmaster Elite season, the pros visited Falcon Reservoir, then considered the top bass fishery in America, and they came at exactly the right time. Scott Campbell brought in the largest bass of the event, 13 pounds, 2 ounces, and more than ten pros brought in four-day catches topping 100 pounds.

Nonetheless, tournaments like the one held at Falcon in which all the stars were aligned perfectly, are unusual. That's just part of what makes the 2001 Bassmaster Top 150 tournament on Florida's Kissimmee Chain of Lakes stand out in fishing history. Tournament winner Dean Rojas brought 108 pounds, 12 ounces to the scales during the four-day contest, making him the first angler ever to break the 100-pound mark for a four-day, five-bass limit tournament in history. Years earlier, during the 1969 Bass-master Alabama National on Lake Eufaula, Blake Honeycutt won with a total of 138 pounds, 6 ounces, but Honeycutt enjoyed a 15-bass per day limit then, so the two totals can hardly be compared.

Although Rojas's tournament weight record has since been broken, another record he set during that event still stands, and it remains one of the most remarkable records in bass fishing. On the first competition day, Rojas brought in five bass weighing 45 pounds, 2 ounces, a nearly unbelievable average of 9 pounds per fish. Many bass fishermen spend their lives without catching one bass weighing 9 pounds, and Rojas brought in five that averaged that much in a single, fog-shortened tournament day. Had he been able to spend a full day on the water and not had to return to the weigh-in stage at three p.m., he would almost certainly have had an even heavier weight.

Some who know Rojas well think he may have been born to set that record, for few young men make a career choice as early as age 14 that they want to become professional tournament bass fishermen. Even fewer succeed. Rojas didn't catch his first bass until he was ten years old but it was from Lake Chollas in San Diego, the city where the world's biggest bass were being caught at the time, so the stars were already starting to align. Born July 31, 1971, in Mineola, New York, his family had moved to the San Diego area when Rojas was three, and Chollas was a children's-only lake a short bicycle ride from his home.

He and his brothers fished there initially for bluegills with their cheese-baited hooks, but Rojas saw others catching bass occasionally, so he became determined to catch one himself. When he did finally catch one, a ten-incher, he, like so many other future fishing stars, was absolutely hooked. He started talking to other kids to learn how they caught their bass, he read fishing magazines and watched bass fishing videos to learn even more, and he began to think that catching bass for a living, the way the tournament pros he watched on television were doing, wouldn't be a bad way to make a living.

When he was 15, he started working at what was later named Qual-comm Stadium, selling peanuts and cotton candy at San Diego Padres baseball games. He worked nights so he could fish all day; in 1993, at age 22 and still determined to be a tournament bass fisherman, he started guiding on the famous San Diego trophy bass lakes, including Dixon, Miramar, Hodges, and others. He'd attended college for two years, primarily to satisfy his parents, but dropped out because he knew he needed to be on the water. A thousand people told him he could never do it, but Rojas was determined to take the chance.

In 1996 he won an Anglers Choice tournament, and two years later won the Anglers Choice National Championship event. In 1997, when the Bass Anglers Sportsman Society began conducting tournaments in the Western states, Rojas began competing with them, and in 1999 he won their Western Division Angler of the Year title. That qualified him for the Bassmaster Top 150 events, the sport's top level of competition, as well as for the Bassmaster Classic world championship. The stars were aligning even more.

★ ★ ★

By 2001, I had fished the Kissimmee Chain of Lakes twice, but had not done particularly well. As our practice started, I remembered the 2000 tournament when winner Shaw Grigsby had won by sight fishing for bass on their spawning beds at Lake Tohopekaliga, one of the lakes in the chain. In the clear water lakes in San Diego where I'd guided, sight fishing for bass had become one of my favorite ways to catch them, so I made up my mind to look for shallow water bass on Lake Toho.

On the first practice day, however, while I could see clearings and spawning beds along the shoreline, there weren't any bass. The water temperature was right, and the weather was calm, but I never had a bite. Worse, some other anglers reported later they were really catching a lot of fish farther offshore.

The second practice day I started throwing a topwater lure and felt a little better after I had caught about ten pounds. On the final day I took one of my sponsors out to a different lake, Kissimmee, but he needed to come in at noon, so after I dropped him back at the dock, I decided to re-check the shoreline where I'd seen the empty beds two days earlier. It was a perfect blue-sky day without any wind, and when I reached the first bed, it wasn't empty anymore. A huge green fish hovered right in the middle of it. I continued down the bank a little farther and saw another bass about nine pounds; all of the clearings I'd seen earlier had big fish on them.

I saw another boat coming, so I turned around, and spotted still another huge bass in a nest surrounded by lily pads. I couldn't stand it any longer, and tossed a plastic worm in to the fish, and she charged right

Dean Rojas of Lake Havasu City, Arizona.
caught his first bass at age 10, and by age 14
had made up his mind to become a professional
bass tournament angler. He later worked nights
to earn money to be able to fish during the
day. Today he is considered one of the best
bass fishermen in the world.

at it. As I pulled the lure out of the water, she even chased it, as if daring me to throw it back. On my third cast, she hit it, and I shook her off; she was a giant.

I went on down the shore, then turned around again and went back to that bed. The bass was still on it, so I went about a hundred yards past her, pulled into the shore and picked up a big rock that I carried back down the bank to mark the bed. The forecast called for fog the next morning, so I wanted to make certain I could find her again. I put a little grass and sticks around it so it wouldn't look so obvious to someone else.

The next morning as the tournament began, it was foggy, and I don't remember how long we were held up before we were allowed to leave. We did not have GPS units on our boats in those days, but I knew the area, so I motored out pretty slow. All I had to do was make sure I drove the boat in a straight line, and eventually I'd reach the other side of the lake where I needed to go. In the fog I couldn't see anything, but suddenly I saw a wall of tules in front of me; I didn't know where I was or whether to turn right or left, so I went right.

It was seven a.m., and once I turned right I began to recognize where I needed to go, and in a few minutes I saw my rock marking the bed of the big bass. I tossed in the worm again, but I knew it wasn't the lure to use, because I couldn't see it. I had to know where my lure was, but even as I pulled the worm out, out, the big bass chased it again. I picked up a white lizard and pitched it in, and the bass raced over to look at it. I hopped it once and she took it, but when I set the hook I missed her. Then, another boat came by, the same boat I'd seen in practice, but it went on by me.

I re-checked the lure and made certain my hook was perfectly placed. I knew it was going to happen on my next cast. I flipped the lizard in and the fish ate it instantly. This time when I set the hook, I knew I had her, and that I had to get her out of the lily pads as quickly as possible. The fight lasted maybe five seconds, and my amateur partner that day, Dan Wilmer, netted her. That bass weighed 10 pounds, 12 ounces, and I knew there were other fish around me that weighed nearly as much. I was so excited I could hardly breathe.

The other boat had gone to an area where I'd found three more bass in the nine-pound range practically side-by-side, and I saw that angler catch two of them as I neared the area. He didn't see the third fish, however, and it hit my lizard instantly. It weighed an even nine pounds. It was 7:45, and I already had almost 20 pounds in the livewell with just those two fish. I started moving around and caught two small three-pounders. Then I found another bed with a 6 ½-pounder on it; I fished for her for 15 minutes but when she finally hit, I lost her in the weeds.

While I was re-checking my line, the boat I'd watched earlier came by and stopped. The angler said he had 27 pounds in the livewell and was calling it a day. I congratulated him on a great catch, and he left. It was 11 o'clock and to me, conditions were perfect. I left the area I'd been fishing and went to another spot in Toho named Shingle Creek. I pulled up on the point at the mouth of the creek and saw a hole in the vegetation. I eased up quietly to it, and saw a ten-pounder right in the middle of the bed. It was just sitting there, not moving.

I dropped my white lizard right on top of her, and she hit. She just ate it, but I knew I had to get control of her immediately. The bass went straight into the grass, and I literally winched bass, grass, and everything else to the surface where my partner scooped it all up with the net and dumped it on the boat deck. I started sifting through the grass, not truly sure I even had the fish because I couldn't see anything but grass. Then I saw it; that bass weighed an even 10 pounds, which gave me a total of about 35 pounds. There wasn't any more room in my livewell.

I found another bed a hundred feet away, this one containing one four-pound male and three females, the largest about eight pounds. The bed was about four feet in diameter and in just two feet of water with no grass around. It took 15 minutes of repeatedly pitching the lizard into the nest, but finally I got the biggest female so excited she hit it, and I got her into the boat and culled one of the smaller bass. Now it was one p.m., and I had to be in at three p.m. I had about 40 pounds now.

I knew the one-day catch record was 33 pounds, 10 ounces, but that hardly entered my mind. What I wanted desperately to do was win the tournament. A win at this level would give me personal validation as a tournament pro, something I'd been dreaming about since I was 14.

I continued down the creek, passing up four-pounders I could see, something I'd never before done in my life. I finally found a larger fish about seven pounds, but try as I might, I could not get her to bite, so I left her and went farther into the creek. Then I saw another boat coming toward me, so I turned around and started looking for the seven-pounder again, but I couldn't find the bed. I zig-zagged back and forth but couldn't see anything. I finally gave up and was ready to leave, but then, when I bent down to pull up the trolling motor, I saw the fish.

As quietly as I could, I eased the trolling motor back into the water, and moved a little closer to start casting. I was afraid the bass would feel me breathing. I worked on her for 20 minutes and finally got her to hit the lizard, but she bit it in half and I missed her. When I pitched in a new one, she hit again immediately. With that fish, I culled the second three-pounder I'd caught earlier.

That was my last bass of the day. On the scales, the total weight came to 45 pounds, 2 ounces, which even stunned me. My five fish weighed 10-13, 10-0, 9-0, 8-2, and 7-3, an average of 9 pounds per bass. For the next three days, I fished the same general area, only moving a little farther off the bank. I caught 35-10 the second day, but as clouds and wind moved in the final two days, my catches dropped to 15-8 and finally 13-3, for a four-day total of 108-12 and my first Top 150 victory.

Afterward, I was still more excited about my tournament win than the actual record catch, or the fact I was the first to break the 100-pound mark in a five-bass per day event, but when Anheuser-Busch offered a $1 million prize to any angler who broke that record that season, it began to sink in. I also learned later that by the second day of the tournament, the Kissimmee Area Chamber of Commerce started getting telephone calls from bass fishermen as far away as New York wanting to book fishing trips on Lake Toho because of that catch, so it was getting far more attention than I realized.

As it turned out, I won the next Top 150 a month later at Toledo Bend, then finished third at Lake Wheeler, fourth at Lake Mead, and second at the Bassmaster MegaBucks tournament at Douglas Lake. The excitement of that one single day at Lake Toho carried me through those events, and it's still carrying me today, more than a dozen years later. During that tournament, I picked up an old duck decoy floating near my fishing area and put it into my rod locker for good luck. I named the decoy Buckshot, and I still carry it with me, so I have a constant reminder of that very special day.

★ ★ ★

Dean Rojas and his wife, Renee, and their two sons live in Lake Havasu City, Arizona, where he continues as an active professional bass tournament competitor and spokesman for the sport.

Chapter Forty-One

Billy Westmorland: "The Christmas Present I Lost"

In the years preceding and immediately following World War II, the smallmouth bass swam in relative obscurity, known and appreciated primarily by those fortunate enough to have fished for them in Canadian waters where the fish was common. Smallmouth bass were present and locally fished for in rivers across much of the northern half of the United States, of course, but even in those days the smallmouth never enjoyed the notoriety granted to its cousin, the largemouth.

One fisherman changed that. His name was Billy Millard Westmorland, and if ever a fisherman lived at the right place and right time in history to promote a single species of bass, it was Westmorland. Born June 3, 1937, in the small town of Celina, Tennessee, Westmorland grew up on the banks of the Obey River, which in 1943 was impounded to produce a smallmouth factory named Dale Hollow Reservoir. They grew up together, each feeding off the other; Dale Hollow became the most famous smallmouth bass lake in the world because of Westmorland, and Westmorland the most famous smallmouth fisherman in history because of Dale Hollow.

The lake had barely filled when Westmorland, along with his father and brother Bobby, began fishing there. Ironically, perhaps, they weren't after smallmouth, but rather, bluegills, many of which they caught right off the Celina Boat Dock. Westmorland's first smallmouth came from

No angler is more closely associated with the smallmouth bass than Billy Westmorland, who also enjoyed success as a tournament competitor on Ray Scott's Bassmaster Tournament Trail. Westmorland was a pioneer in the use of light lines and small lures for smallmouth, and often used those same techniques for largemouths. Photo courtesy of B.A.S.S.

that dock, as well, a two-pounder he caught on a minnow while fishing for bluegills.

The boat dock became his home away from home. By age 10 he was paddling other fishermen around the lake in the dock's rented wooden johnboats, and by 13 Westmorland was guiding those same fishermen, running a boat and outboard around the 27,700-acre lake by himself for $10 a trip. He and his clients used cane poles with bobbers, split shot, and minnows and dabbled them around the shallow stickups and brush in practically any cove on the lake. Westmorland himself often said in later years that guiding wasn't all that difficult, because there were so many smallmouth in the new lake, and so many places to find them.

Nevertheless, he became a student of the smallmouth, continually exploring new areas of the lake and trying to find answers to the questions of why the fish lived or acted the way they did. He donned scuba gear and swam underwater with the smallmouth themselves. He learned their preferred depths, the best months to catch them, and the most productive ways to retrieve his lures.

He'd skip school to go fishing, and even though he gained a reputation as a formidable football lineman, smallmouth fishing was always his first love. He played football at Middle Tennessee State University in Murfreesboro, but spent his non-football weekends back on Dale Hollow, locating smallmouth on Saturday and guiding clients on Sunday. After a knee injury ended his football career, he began concentrating even more on smallmouth.

His love for this singular fish seemed to know no bounds. In 1962, after graduating from the university, he became a high school teacher and football coach at Byrdstown, a small community just east of Dale Hollow, which still allowed him plenty of time on the water. One autumn Thursday afternoon, for example, as he prepared his team for their final game of the season the next day, Westmorland received a call from the opposing team's coach. He was canceling the game because too many of his players were either sick or injured. With their season then effectively over, several of Westmorland's players decided to skip school the next day and go fishing on Dale Hollow, and they talked him into joining them.

By then, Dale Hollow had begun to change, as all lakes do as they age. Although the water remained unusually clear, the stickups and brush where Westmorland had caught so many smallmouth in the past were disappearing. He'd already recognized the value of smaller lures, particularly hair jigs with a tiny pork rind attached, light lines, and spinning reels under such conditions, and so he inadvertently became one of the earliest and most influential proponents of using light tackle techniques for smallmouth.

With the shallow brush gone, Westmorland concentrated on fishing his jigs on Dale Hollow's deeper gravel/clay points, places he had not needed to fish before. With the $66 depth finder he'd purchased in 1964 to replace the spark plug he'd been casting to feel the bottom, he spent hours locating more and more of these bare points. His big-fish score increased quickly and dramatically, and rapidly added to the already growing Westmorland legend.

He caught a 10-pound smallmouth on March 17, 1972, a fish that weighed 10-1 on one set of certified scales and 10-0 on another. He caught it on a ⅛-ounce Hoss Fly jig and four-pound test line in 25 feet of water. To put this accomplishment into perspective, consider that less than ten smallmouth over 10 pounds have ever been officially recorded, even now more than three decades later. In Westmorland's case, the 10-pounder joined another smallmouth officially weighing 9-5, two more about 9-3, and perhaps as many as 75 others weighing 8 pounds or more over his career, numbers that no one else has ever come close to matching.

The year 1972 also marked Westmorland's entry into Ray Scott's professional B.A.S.S. tournaments, and while the tournaments were not conducted on true smallmouth lakes, Westmorland's mastery of the tough fishing conditions he was accustomed to on Dale Hollow served him well on Scott's largemouth waters. He won three national B.A.S.S. events and qualified for six consecutive Bassmaster Classic world championships. His heaviest three-day tournament catch came from stump-filled Toledo Bend Reservoir where, using his favorite spinning rod and ten-pound line, he weighed in just under 90 pounds of bass.

To many bass fishermen, Westmorland's tournament record is not nearly as notable as the bravery and concern he displayed on a single rough-water tournament afternoon in 1973 at the B.A.S.S. Arkansas Invitational on Beaver Lake, when, from a calm water cove, he happened to see a red six-gallon gas can floating in waves far offshore. Braving the rough water, Westmorland motored out to retrieve the can, as he said later, to keep someone from hitting it and possibly causing an explosion. As it turned out, two fellow tournament competitors were desperately clinging to the can, Robert Craddock and Johnny Morris, later to become famous as the founder of Bass Pro Shops. Westmorland pulled each of them to safety into his boat.

He developed several lures especially for smallmouth, including the famous Hoss Fly jig with its aspirin-shaped head that is still made today;

and in May, 1975, his own signature Billy Westmorland spinning rods were introduced. His weekly television program, *Billy Westmorland's Fishing Diary,* not only shared his personal smallmouth secrets with hundreds of thousands of viewers, but also certainly helped popularize the smallmouth bass as a gamefish. His 1976 book, *Them Ol' Brown Fish,* written with outdoor writer Larry Mayer, is still considered the definitive word on smallmouth bass behavior and fishing techniques. In 1998, he was inducted into the Fresh Water Fishing Hall of Fame, and in 2004 into the Bass Fishing Hall of Fame.

★ ★ ★

I think every bass fisherman, if he stays in the sport and fishes a lot, gradually evolves from simply wanting to catch any size bass to wanting to catch larger and larger fish. That's how it was with me with smallmouths, but it sure didn't come easy. I spent years fishing Dale Hollow and could

Successful smallmouth fisher Billy Westmorland. **Photo courtesy of B.A.S.S.**

hardly catch anything bigger than a four-pounder. During those years, I was really just fishing the shorelines like almost everybody else, because in those days we caught a lot of smallmouth that way. Now, I know I wasn't fishing the right places to catch larger smallmouth, because they don't spend much time in shallow water like that.

I wanted to start catching smallmouth on small jigs with pork rind, but when I'd try to bring the jig back through the brush where I was fishing, even in slightly deeper water like the creek channels and places, I'd get snagged and have to break it off. That just made me more frustrated, so I started looking for a cleaner bottom, and on Dale Hollow that meant some of the points, and that's where I started finding bigger smallmouths. I spent hours and hours, day and night, looking for more places with a clean bottom, and I fished places I'd been passing up for years, and I caught more and more big smallmouths.

On March 17, 1972, I caught a smallmouth that weighed 10 pounds on one certified scale and 10 pounds, 1 ounce on another certified scale. Needless to say, I was thrilled, because at that time only a couple of other fishermen had ever caught a smallmouth weighing 10 pounds or more, and one of them was the world record. A couple of years earlier, however, on Christmas Day, I lost a smallmouth I feel sure weighed between 12 and 14 pounds, which would have been a new world record.

I was fishing another of my favorite smallmouth lures, a Pedigo Spinrite, on different points where waves were really crashing in. The weather was pretty rough, but that day the smallmouths were biting. I had a seven-pounder and two more that weighed between five and six pounds. I had also lost two more fish between seven and eight pounds.

Over the years I'd caught a lot of nice smallmouths off the side of one particular point that had an old roadbed across it that dropped off into deeper water. When I threw out to the roadbed, this fish hit about 12 or 14 feet down as the Spinrite was still falling down that drop-off. It pulled hard and made a strong run so I knew it was a pretty good fish, and then when it came to the top and wallowed and I saw it, I thought it might go as heavy as ten pounds.

We didn't have powerful trolling motors in those days, so I had to follow the fish with my big engine. When it came to the surface again, the fish was only about 40 feet away and I saw it clearly, and that's when I started getting nervous. I'd never gotten nervous playing a big smallmouth before, but I'd never seen a fish that big before, either.

After another dive, the smallmouth came back up on top, this time only about ten feet away. I still couldn't believe how big that fish was. I could see my line but I couldn't see the Spinrite so I thought she was hooked really good. The fish went down a little and swam toward the back of the boat, and if someone else had been in the boat with me that day, they might have netted her then. I brought her to within just three or four feet, and if I'd had a net I could have gotten her.

The fish dived one more time, maybe 15 feet, but I knew she was getting tired and I felt the next time I brought her up I'd be able to grab her. Then the lure just came free and the fish was gone. I can't tell you how bad I felt. At that time I'd been smallmouth fishing for almost 30 years and this was the smallmouth I'd been dreaming about, a smallmouth bigger

Billy Westmorland. **Photo courtesy of B.A.S.S.**

than any other smallmouth anyone had ever caught.

For the next year and a half, that fish haunted me, and I mean haunted me. I couldn't get her out of my mind. I'd be at home asleep and wake up in the middle of the night thinking that smallmouth might be on that point just then, so I'd get up, launch the boat, and start fishing right then in the dark, regardless of the weather. I'd get up from the dinner table and go fishing, or leave right in the middle of watching television. I'd go after that fish at all hours, convinced she was on that point at that exact time.

I relived hooking, playing, and losing her over and over in my mind no matter where I was or what I was doing. I always dreamed about catching her again but I never hooked that smallmouth again, and I never heard anyone else talk about hooking her, either. I call that fish the Christmas present I lost.

★ ★ ★

Billy Westmorland died September 30, 2002. He is buried in Fitzgerald Cemetery in Celina, just a few long casts away from Dale Hollow Reservoir and the fish he loved so much.

Chapter Forty-Two

Manabu Kurita: "I Tried Not to Get Too Excited"

Manabu Kurita holds a mounted replica of his world record 22-pound, 5-ounce bass, caught July 2, 2009, in Lake Biwa, Japan. Officially, Kurita is tied with George Perry for the world record, since the IGFA requires fish to be 2 ounces heavier than the previous world record if the total weight is less than 25 pounds.

Manabu Kurita remembers catching his first fish when he was just three or four years old, but it was not a largemouth bass. It was a carp, but the species did not matter; Kurita, now 34, became hooked on fishing at that moment. The first bass did not come until age 12, after a 40-kilometer bicycle ride from his home to one of the few lakes in southern Japan that contained bass. That first fish measured 16 inches in length and hit a Carolina rig lizard, and from then on, he made the long bicycle ride to the lake two and three times a week, sometimes skipping school in the process.

"Even as a small child, Manabu was competitive, always trying to catch something larger than I did, even if it was just a beetle," laughs his close friend Jun Maeda, who made those bicycle trips with Kurita. "When he sets his mind to do something, he is very determined, so I was not that surprised when he called me that day on the lake to tell me he had caught a really big bass. More than being a fisherman, he is a hunter, and that day he was looking for just one fish."

George Perry's 22-pound, 4-ounce bass had stood as the world record for 77 years and 10 days when Manabu Kurita caught that one fish in Lake Biwa, Japan, on July 2, 2009. Technically, Kurita's bass weighed about one ounce heavier than Perry's, but did not meet the two-ounce minimum established by the International Game Fish Association (IGFA) for fish weighing less than 25 pounds, so Kurita and Perry are now listed as co-record holders.

Following the IGFA's ruling, Kurita was invited to the United States for two weeks by Yamaha Marine Group, now sponsoring him on his quest to catch an even larger bass. While in America—his second visit— Kurita attended the 2010 Bassmaster Classic in New Orleans, and later met George Perry's son during a visit to tiny Montgomery Lake, Georgia, where Perry had caught his record bass in 1932.

While in New Orleans, he was most impressed with the attention and excitement generated both by his fish as well as the Classic competition itself. In Japan, after catching his world record, he had received only one very brief mention by local television media. His work in an automobile inspection company near Kyoto allows him to fish Lake Biwa five to ten days a month, and he has already prepared an underwater cage to keep his next world record bass alive.

★ ★ ★

Even though I have been fishing almost exclusively for bass since I was 12 years old, my decision to only go after record-class fish evolved gradually, as my own experience increased and I learned more about the bass itself. I have always liked to catch "bigger things," so I guess this progression was natural, especially as my love for bass fishing grew.

On April 22, 2003, Kazuya Shimada caught a 19.15-pound bass from Lake Ikehara that became the Japanese national record, so breaking that record became my goal, practically an obsession. I thought about it every single day, and envisioned what that bass would feel like as I brought it to the boat. I would sharpen my hooks, then I would sharpen them again the next day, even though I had not gone fishing. I checked my line over and over.

I set the date I would try to break Shimada's record, and for several days prior all I did was concentrate mentally on catching that fish. Finally, late on April 6, 2008, almost exactly five years after Shimada caught his record, I caught the bass I'd been dreaming about, except it did not break his record. I was fishing Lake Biwa, and caught a bass weighing 18.7 pounds on a long, slender hand-carved wood lure. It was just six ounces under his record, but that day I saw even larger bass so for the very first time I knew breaking not only Shimada's record but also breaking the world record would truly be possible. From that moment on, that is what I began fishing for.

In late June the next year, I saw a school of six or seven big bass swimming close together at Lake Biwa, all of them over 20 pounds. I see schools like this two or three times a year so I was even more excited. It had rained hard the day before, and some friends and I had started fishing about 5:30 a.m. We were using different types of lures, including big swim baits, but weren't catching much at all, and no big bass.

After about an hour, we decided to fish for bluegills, instead, and during the next hour we probably caught 50 of them. Then we decided to try the bluegill as bait for a big bass. We went over to the highway bridge that crosses the lake. It's where the clear water of the northern part of Biwa meets the dingier water in the southern part, and there's always a lot of baitfish around. I'd seen some big bass there, too, and when we got there I saw what I believe was the same school of big bass I'd seen two weeks earlier.

I hooked a bluegill through the back and threw it out and pretty quick I had a strike and set the hook. I thought it was a big bass by the way it felt, but I didn't see it when it swam toward the back of the boat and splashed on the surface. My friends saw it, however, and started yelling, and just two or three minutes later they netted it for me. When we got it in the boat, it looked big, but I didn't think it was that big, not big enough to be a world record.

The very first thing I did was telephone my friend Jun Maeda, who is a guide on Lake Biwa and told him I had a big bass. I went straight to a marina where he met me and we measured and weighed the bass. We both tried not to get really excited because I remembered how disappointed we had been the year before when I'd come so close to breaking Shimada's Japanese record.

Manabu Kurita's world record-tying catch.

The bass measured 28.9 inches long and weighed 22.311 pounds on the marina scales, but died while we were photographing it because we had no place to put it. I had hoped I could release it after we did all the necessary certification. We began the certification immediately with the Japan Game Fish Association, who then sent all the documentation to the International Game Fish Association in America. It took nearly six months for approval, and all during that time I still tried not to get excited, but finally, on January 8, 2010, the record was approved. It was slightly heavier than the world record by George Perry, but not by the required two ounces, so I am listed as a co-record holder. I just never thought it was that big when I first got it in the boat.

I wish I had caught the bass on a lure instead of on live bait. I know there are bigger bass there now, however, because my fish was not the largest one in the school I saw. What I really want to do is catch one of those larger bass, and that goal is as strong as the goal I used to have for breaking Kazuya Shimada's record.

★ ★ ★

Manabu Kurita lives in Aichi, Japan, where he continues to fish Lake Biwa for an even larger bass whenever he can.

Index